A Precious Heritage

Praise from former congregants of Sidney Ballon

As a child in his congregation, I had a strong sense of the stability and the guidance Rabbi Ballon offered our community. Now, enjoying his sermons as an adult, I recognize in addition, his wisdom and brilliance, his insightful social commentary, and his deep Jewish knowledge. He framed the concerns of the day with faith and shared the wisdom of generations past to provide a path to the future. I feel blessed to renew my conversation with Sidney Ballon through the collection that Yesh has created as a tribute. **RABBI AMY B. EHRLICH, Congregation Emanu-El of the City of New York**

"Rabbi Ballon did more than serve the community and the temple; he was the temple and the rock of the community." **RICK EHRLICH**

"Rabbi Ballon was a leader, a scholar, a teacher who inspired and encouraged us all. We are blessed to have had him in our respective lives." **SUSAN & STANLEY KOLKER**

"When we die, there are many paths of immortality, some of which are rational and some of which are simply matters of faith. Rabbi Ballon taught me that we continue in life by the deeds we perform and the lessons that we teach. Whether it be in the *Yeshivah shel Maalah*, the heavenly academy, or through the words and deeds that impacted our lives, Rabbi Sidney Ballon continues to live. His memory alone is a blessing." **RABBI ROBERT LOEWY, Congregation Gates of Prayer, Metairie, Louisiana**

"It is a pleasure to remember his twinkling eyes and smile, and his sincere wishes for my benefit each time he lifted his arms and closed his eyes in benediction. I can clearly picture him now in my mind's eye." **JUDY FENER PERITZ**

"While I was always appreciative of what a wonderful man Rabbi Ballon was, it was only after I heard other rabbis that I began to truly realize what a great rabbi I had." **MARC JEFFREY SEIFER**

Rabbi Sidney Ballon, West Hempstead, New York, in the 1960s

Others say...

"This book is a beautiful testimony to a life well-lived and messages that are eternal. We rabbis have a sacred (and seemingly unrealizable) challenge—to help people struggle with faith, with depth, and divergence; to allow Jewish values to pervade every aspect of personal, communal, and global life; and to nurture faith—with all its nuances and permutations for each precious congregant. Rabbi Sidney Ballon's story and sermons achieve these goals in timeless ways. What a gift to the Jewish world—and a beautiful sharing of soul with family and friends." **RABBI NATHANIEL EZRAY, Congregation Beth Jacob, Redwood City, California**

> *An Elder is a person whose work it is to synthesize wisdom from long life experience and to formulate this into a legacy for future generations.*
> Debby & Barry Barkan

"Yesh Ballon's work is one of the most dedicated expressions of that statement. In respectfully editing his father's sermons, he not only brings honor to Rabbi Ballon's memory, he loves him into life such that together, they formulate their shared legacy and deed it to the future." **RABBI NADYA GROSS, Congregation Pardes Levavot, Boulder, Colorado; Director, The Sage-ing® Mentorship Program**

"Rabbi Ballon personified the great generation of reform rabbis. He was dignified; Judaically and secularly highly educated. Most of all, he stood for something and was not afraid to speak his mind to high and low alike. That generation will not come again." **RABBI EMERITUS JAMES L. MIREL, Temple B'nai Torah, Bellevue, Washington**

"A brilliantly conceived and carefully annotated retrospective on American and Jewish events through the stormiest years of the twentieth century. Before Internet (and, for a while, even TV), the sermons of great rabbis were our weekly window to the world, and Rabbi Sidney Ballon epitomized that greatness. Here, then, lovingly compiled by his son, is a set of enlightening reflections available nowhere else: lessons from World War I; the foreboding atmosphere of 1939; the birth of a Jewish state; the Civil Rights era; the spiritual significance of landing on the moon. The author's accompanying commentary looking back on the sermons from the perspective of today is itself extraordinary. And the sermons themselves are literary masterpieces—eloquent, passionate, even profound— and representative of the rabbinic best." **RABBI LAWRENCE A. HOFFMAN, PH.D., The Barbara and Stephen Friedman Professor of Liturgy, Worship and Ritual, Hebrew Union College - Jewish Institute of Religion**

"*A Precious Heritage* captures the essence of Rabbi Sidney Ballon's character, his relationship with his congregation, and his intellectual passions—including his engagement from the pulpit with the great religious and social justice issues of his time. This is also the story of a father and son. Yesh Ballon immersed himself in Sidney Ballon's life work. Yesh traveled a path that greatly deepened his relationship with his father and his Judaism. This is an excellent book. It demonstrates why all rabbis should archive their work, leaving to future generations the legacy of their wisdom." **RABBI DAVID SAPERSTEIN, Director Emeritus, Religious Action Center of Reform Judaism; Former U.S. Ambassador at Large for International Religious Freedom; Senior Fellow, Berkley Center for Religion, Peace and World Affairs; Senior Advisor for Strategy and Policy, Union for Reform Judaism**

A Precious Heritage

Rabbinical Reflections on God, Judaism, and the World in the Turbulent Twentieth Century

Rabbi Sidney Ballon

Selected Sermons, 1936–1974

EDITING, INTRODUCTIONS, AND NOTES
BY YESHAYA DOUGLAS BALLON

FOREWORD BY MURRAY E. SIMON

ezune press

Copyright © 2017 by Ezune Press

All rights reserved. No part of this publication may be reproduced, stored in a retrieval system, or transmitted in any form or by any means, electronic, mechanical, photocopying, recording, or otherwise, without the prior permission of the publisher.

Printed in the United States of America

EZUNE PRESS
3366 Ross Road, Palo Alto, California 94303

Library of Congress Cataloging-in-Publication Data
 Ballon, Sidney
A precious heritage: rabbinical reflections on god, judaism, and the world in the turbulent twentieth century; selected sermons, 1936-1974; editing, introductions, and notes by Yeshaya Douglas Ballon

ISBN 978-0-9995051-0-6
Religion/Sermons/Jewish

Editing: Emily Moberg Robinson, Woodshed Editors
Cover + Jacket Design: Frankie Winters
Cover Source Photography: Zachi Evenor (רונבא יחצ), used under Creative Commons 3.0 license.
Interior Design and Layout: Janine Winters
Text set in Alegreya, Alegreya Sans, and Raanana

Dedication

For Sidney Ballon's descendants, this book represents more than the words that he wrote down over the course of a career. It's his legacy of soul that moves down and touches them in very special ways. It becomes their legacy. It is in their cells. It's in their DNA. This is what they carry with them. It's so valuable for them to understand who they are. Ultimately, this is not a book about Sidney Ballon. It's a book about them, so they may know how they *are* Sidney Ballon. **IRA WIESNER, Rabbinical Student, ALEPH Ordination Program**

I dedicate this book to my family of origin: Dad, Mom, and Jeff—all three of blessed memory—whose guiding hands continue to help me find my way; and to my sister, Muff, who continues to be a loving presence, and who is uniquely positioned as a witness not only to Dad's life in the pulpit, but also to my sometimes turbulent, yet ever-growing relationship with him.

I dedicate this book to my beloved, Debbie, a remarkably resilient, patient, deeply kind, caring, and selfless partner, whose grounded-ness has been an essential element in keeping me from spinning off the planet. Her yin to my yang sometimes perplexes me, sometimes frustrates me, but always sustains me in ways I have increasingly come to appreciate and cherish.

I dedicate this book to my children, Jake, Alana, Becca, Josh, Shira, and Marty; to their children, Matan, Milly, Liav, and, God-willing, others in the future; and to their children's children, extending to all the generations that follow.

I dedicate this book to the entire family tree, in all directions. I look to past generations for inspiration. With this work, it is my intention to honor them and the precious heritage that they have handed down. And to the succeeding generations: it is to you most of all that I dedicate this book, that you may receive this heritage and find it precious as well.

Contents

Foreword 13
Preface 15
Introduction 31

1. Shall We Fight Again? – 1936 55
2. The Struggle of Jacob – 1936 61
3. A New Year and a New Venture – 1939 71
4. Three Ideals – 1939 77
5. In Search of a Home – 1939 83
6. The War and You – 1941 91
    D-Day Prayer 97
7. Thanksgiving – 1941 103
8. An Ethical Will – 1948 109
    Prayer for the New State of Israel 114
9. Israel: First Anniversary – 1949 117
10. Let My People Go – 1950 123
11. The Sabbath, A Reform Perspective – 1952 131
12. Holy, Holy, Holy – 1952 137
13. A Liberal Faith – 1955 143
14. Mid-East Crisis – 1956 151
15. Jewish Peoplehood in America – 1957 159
16. Mr. Sputnik – 1957 165
17. The Strange Call of the Shofar – 1958 171
18. The Complete Jew – 1958 177
19. Ignorance of Judaism – 1960 185
20. The Melody of Faith – 1960 191
21. Baal Shem Tov – 1960 197
22. The Wisdom of the Heart – 1961 205

23. Blowin' in the Wind – 1963 211
    John F. Kennedy Memorial Service 219
24. Joseph and the War on Poverty – 1964 221
25. Loneliness – 1965 229
26. Faith in God – 1966 237
27. The Aftermath of a Miracle – 1967 243
28. The Missing Al Chet – 1967 251
29. The Sins of a Nation – 1967 257
30. Remarks on the Death of Robert F. Kennedy – 1968 ... 265
31. Understanding Our Youth – 1968 271
32. The Sense of Prayer – 1968 279
33. Footsteps on the Moon – 1969 287
    Prayer for the *Apollo 13* Astronauts 294
    Prayer for Students Killed at Kent State 295
34. Is American Jewry Secure? – 1970 297
35. Mission of Israel – 1974 305
36. Chaim Weizmann – 1974 313

Afterword 323
Priestly Benediction 327
About the Editor 329

Foreword

Murray E. Simon

Cantor Emeritus, The Jewish Center, Princeton, New Jersey
Past President, American Conference of Cantors

The Hebrew words *"Ashreynu mah tov khelkeynu"*—"How fortunate are we and how good is our portion"—are taken from the *siddur* (prayer book) and are recited every morning by the pious Jew as s/he greets the new day. I express these sentiments when I think about the unexpected circumstances that led me to become the student-cantor of the Nassau Community Temple (NCT), West Hempstead, Long Island, in October 1964. I must state that I had never before served a congregation as a cantor, and I had never before been in a Reform temple. I had begun my studies only one month before at the Hebrew Union College-School of Sacred Music in New York City, as it was known back then, after graduating Temple University College of Music. Although they normally would not have sent a beginning student, the cantorial school administration asked me to interview at NCT to fill a sudden vacancy. I guess I must have done passably well, since I was offered the position and was invited to begin my tenure immediately. When I began my fifty-year career as a cantor the very next weekend, the term "novice" would be an understatement. But the words "patient and supportive" are *definitely* not understatements when used to describe how Rabbi Sidney Ballon and organist Florence Gode greeted their new "colleague."

I remember Rabbi Sidney Ballon as being a consummate spiritual leader—highly principled, deeply spiritual, wonderfully articulate, profoundly ethical, very grounded in his Jewish identity, possessing high professional standards. He always encouraged me as I began to spread my cantorial "wings." I could not have asked for a better mentor. To me, Sidney Ballon bore a remarkable physical resemblance to the actor Gregory Peck. He had a very calming manner in the pulpit, both in his soothing voice and his quiet but strong bearing. I couldn't say honestly that I remembered the contents of Sidney's sermons from fifty years ago. But reading some of the sermons in this book that were given during my time at NCT reconfirms my memory that they were always well prepared and concise and had a relevant message. Isn't that what sermons are supposed to accomplish?

I served as cantor of Nassau Community Temple for four years. I was living in New Jersey during my first year at NCT, so I was invited to stay at the Ballon residence every Friday evening after the Sabbath Evening service, in order to be able to officiate the next morning at the Sabbath Morning Service. Jean and Sidney Ballon took me into their home and into their hearts as one of their own adult children. Jean was the best cook ever. I relished her Shabbat dinners. Sidney was always soft-spoken at home—Jean was not! Sidney was conventional—Jean was not! *What a perfect couple*, I thought. They complemented each other so well.

Another benefit was that I got to know and love their children. Their eldest, Jeffrey, my contemporary, was in rabbinical school at HUC at the same time I was attending cantorial school there. Their middle child, Martha, whom we call Muff, and her husband, Alan, remain friends of my wife, Toby, and me to this day. Their youngest child, Doug, was a clone of his mother. Doug was the one who "colored outside the lines"—so to speak. Over the years, Doug became "Yesh" and now he has taken on so many of the wonderful traits of his beloved father as he has become much closer to his Jewish roots and religion. Rabbi Sidney Ballon would be so proud of his son Yesh, who is immortalizing his father's words, thoughts, and teachings in this precious volume.

Rabbi Sidney Ballon was taken from us too soon, passing just a few months after his retirement from NCT. I am grateful to Yesh Ballon for inviting me to write these words of introduction. To those of you who read the sermons of Rabbi Sidney Ballon contained herein, you will get to know something of the man and mentor I admired so much.

Preface

Yeshaya Douglas Ballon

PURPOSE

We have received a precious heritage. It is our duty to know it, enlarge upon it, and pass it on to the future. **RABBI SIDNEY BALLON**

In one sentence, taken from the last Yom Kippur sermon he would deliver (Chapter 35, *Mission of Israel*), Sidney Ballon sums up this book and, in many respects, his life. The archive of his sermons is testimony to his knowledge of his Jewish heritage, how he enlarged upon it by applying his interpretations of Jewish thought to life in the mid-twentieth century, and how he sought to pass this heritage on to the generations within his congregation and beyond. As a grateful recipient of my father's heritage, it is incumbent upon me, to the best of my ability, to likewise know it, enlarge upon it, and pass it on. My father sought to perpetuate our Jewish heritage in the broadest sense. It is my intention, with this book, to sustain the heritage that has been passed down through one specific individual—my father, Rabbi Sidney Ballon.

I was just twenty-seven years old when he died. I can't say that I fully grasped the preciousness of what I inherited at that age. I've since had more than four decades to mature as a person, to educate myself as a Jew, and, most fortuitously, to read, savor, and appreciate my father's words.

They say that each one of us has our own individual torah inscribed in our heart. This book, therefore, presents a glimpse of the torah of Sidney Ballon—and, candidly, through the editorial decisions and comments I have made, a bit of my own torah as well. Even before discovering the quote above,

I intuitively assigned myself the task of taking in, expounding upon, and sharing Sidney Ballon's torah.

From the beginning of this project, my primary goal has been for my children, and my children's children, and all of my father's descendants to know that a member of their family named Sidney Ballon was a good man, a rabbi who was smart, caring, and passionate about Judaism. Secondly, I want them to get a sense of my father's dedication to the history and values of the Jewish people. And finally, I want them to help my father fulfill his mission of passing on this heritage to future generations. To do this, they and each succeeding generation in turn must know it, enlarge upon it, and pass it on. I hope that the sermons I have selected and the words I have added as introductions, notes, and reflections help to fulfill all of these goals.

EVOLUTION

This book naturally originates with Sidney Ballon and his diligent labor of writing and delivering a sermon virtually every week of his rabbinate. That flow of words ceased on November 11, 1974, when he died during cardiac by-pass surgery. In the days that followed his interment and *shiva* (seven-day mourning period), his widow, Jean Hymson Ballon, my mother, was quick to rid herself of his sizable accumulation of professional books and papers. I assisted her in this endeavor. Upon opening his files, I came upon a massive and meticulously organized archive of his sermons, starting from his days as a student rabbi in 1936 and extending to the very last sermon preached days before his death. At that point in my life, I was mostly focused on my architectural studies; I was not particularly interested in Jewish thought or practice. Despite this, I intuitively knew I wanted to hold on to these sermons. As a callow 27-year-old, I was not able to articulate the reason; I just knew that I didn't want to see them destroyed. As everything else was being carted off to be incinerated in a rusty barrel in the St. Simons Island, Georgia dump, I exclaimed, "Not the sermons!" I had no idea what would eventually become of them. I simply boxed them up and brought them home with me, schlepping them from St. Simons to New Haven, from Connecticut to California, from one residence to the next, storing them in a dusty garage for nearly forty years until I was eventually called to open them.

Understanding the full context of how this book came about requires some knowledge of the evolution of my relationship with Judaism and my rabbi/father. Without getting too mired in my psychological profile, suffice it to say that as an adolescent, my normal rejection of parental authority took on an added dimension, given what for me was my uncomfortable status as a "rabbi's kid" (RK). I was a late bloomer in almost every respect—physically, emotionally, intellectually, and spiritually. Academically, I was a gross underachiever, and I masked my poor performance by acting out, not only in public school, but in temple religious school as well. I had little capacity for honest self-reflection or insight into the forces that influenced my behaviors. Therapy was offered to me and, for the most part, was rejected by me. My father must have been frustrated by his inability to guide me along a more productive path, as much as he tried.

While I resisted most of my Jewish education, I never rejected my identity as a Jew or divorced myself from participation in Jewish life altogether. I've long taken pride (perhaps to excess) in sounding shofar in synagogue on Rosh Hashanah virtually every year since my bar mitzvah. I attended and worked at Jewish summer camps. My wife and I met at a Hillel-sponsored event at UCLA where I wasn't even a student. We've consistently observed Shabbat and most festivals for the nearly five decades of our marriage, affiliating with synagogues most of those years, and educating our children in Judaism in the home as well as the synagogue.

That said, it was a long evolution that brought me from Rebel RK to lay spiritual leader. A significant milestone was the dramatic change in my filial attitude that occurred serendipitously in the spring of 1991, some 17 years after my father's death. A combination of some effective Jungian therapy and my discovery of Robert Bly's "Men's Movement" helped redirect my relationship with my father. I began a journey toward consciously seeking greater connection with him posthumously, in a way I had not done during his lifetime.

Another milestone was my decision to enroll in my synagogue's adult B'nai Mitzvah class in 2006. The class itself was educational, but the after-effects were no less than transformational. At the Shabbat morning service where my classmates and I celebrated this ritual, I explained to the congregation that since I had already "entered manhood" at my bar mitzvah at age thirteen, I must, in my sixtieth year, be entering something else that I could only describe as "elderhood." I confessed that I knew as little about being an elder in that moment as I had known about being a man at my first bar mitzvah in 1960.

This honest admission elicited an immediate response from two outstanding men in the congregation, men whom I am proud to call my friends—Chaplain Bruce Feldstein, M.D., Director of the Jewish Chaplaincy at Stanford Health Care, and Rabbi Paul Shleffar, now the Jewish Chaplain at San Quentin State Prison. Each approached me independently to recommend the book *From Age-ing to Sage-ing* by Rabbi Zalman Schachter-Shalomi, the founder of the Jewish Renewal movement. The book not only introduced me to fresh ways of looking at the aging process, it also introduced me to the world of ALEPH: Alliance for Jewish Renewal, which ever since has been my home for Jewish and spiritual growth. I have taken their courses in spiritual eldering and prayer and chanting leadership, and I recently completed their three-year certification in spiritual direction. The spiritual creativity and relevance of Jewish Renewal so fully captivated me that I gave serious consideration, even in my sixties, to engaging in their rabbinical ordination program.

I was heading in that direction until one day in 2011, when I saw one of my neighbors walking down the street pushing his granddaughter in a stroller. I knew how hard ALEPH rabbinical students worked; the program practically consumed all of their extracurricular lives, especially if they had jobs. At that point, I was still working full time as a corporate trainer. It occurred to me that if I chose to spend the next ten or so years studying my butt off to get a *smicha* (ordination), then, God willing, were I to be blessed with grandchildren in those years, I would have little time to enjoy them! I decided not to apply to ALEPH's ordination program. I rationalized that a rabbi is a teacher, and in that sense of the word I already was a "lower case" rabbi and would be content to remain so. Besides, as my father's colleague the esteemed Jewish scholar and educator Rabbi Eugene Borowitz once counseled me, "Judaism needs good laymen."

No sooner than I had made that decision—and God knows where this next inspiration came from—it spontaneously occurred to me that with all the time I had just freed up for myself, I could resurrect the sermons that had been languishing for decades in my garage. I had saved them from destruction in 1974, and I was soon to discover how great a gift to myself that had been!

Even the little I had observed of the sermons thus far made the project enticing. Scores of manila folders were inscribed with my father's familiar penciled handwriting. Most of the files were sermons sorted chronologically, but there were other topic headers as well. I was filled with anticipation of what I might learn about my father and myself, what lessons in Judaism or ethics or social action would unfold.

I started reading the sermons in the spring of 2011, a little more than a year before the centennial of my father's birth. Not recognizing the full magnitude of the project that lay ahead of me, I naively imagined that I might be able to peruse the archives and select significant sermons to publish in time for the centennial in 2012. (What I *did* manage to publish that year was a blog with some of my favorite sermons to that point. These may be found at http://harav-shimon.blogspot.com.)

People have asked me how much I remember from sitting in the pews while my father delivered these sermons decades ago. The short answer is, "Very little." There were probably only two titles that I could even recall, both from the High Holy Days of 1963. When he returned from that summer's historic March on Washington, my father captured everyone's imagination with *Blowin' in the Wind* (Chapter 24) and *I Have a Dream*. While I have scant recollection of the contents of specific sermons, my father's overall message still seems quite familiar. There were a few surprises, as well. Although I had never had much interest in history, I found myself fascinated watching the twentieth century unfold through my father's eyes. And even more surprising, I discovered that issues taking on new importance to me as an adult Jew had been addressed by my father when I was a child. For example, in his final sermon delivered from his first full-time pulpit at the Tree of Life Congregation in Columbia, South Carolina, my father described ethical wills to his congregation (*An Ethical Will*, Chapter 8). I had never heard that term until I studied spiritual eldering in 2007. Since then, I've written my ethical will and taught others to write theirs. I never knew my father had even discussed ethical wills, let alone written a sermon by that name. And yet, there it was. It was gratifying to discover something we had in common, even though we never talked about it during his lifetime.

My quest to connect to my father began in 1991 as a trickle of acceptance and a small portal to filial love. It became a gushing fountain as I pored through the archives of his sermons. Reading them represented more than a scholarly walk through time. They brought my father to life for me through the rich exposition of his most passionate concerns about Judaism and life itself.

As some RKs might testify, it is not easy sharing one's father with an entire community. It took me decades and the aforementioned Jungian therapy to be able to articulate just how troublesome I found that. By contrast, the sweet indulgence of grabbing a handful of sermons in quiet seclusion was an unanticipated delight. I came to realize that I was luxuriating so in reading these sermons because day after day, night after night, I would reach out for my father and he was there, palpably present in my hands—just the two of us alone in that moment. I would pick up the pages that he once held in his very hands. I would carefully release the corroded paper clips that he so casually adhered to these pages decades ago. I would sit back and read his words. I would quickly discover in each essay whether he was routinely responding to the duty of delivering his weekly message, or tapping into a deeper wellspring of fervor on a topic that emanated from his core beliefs. Either way, I would hear his voice. He may have been talking to a sparse gathering at his student pulpit in East Liverpool, Ohio in the 1930s, or to an assembly of soldiers at Keesler Army Airfield in Biloxi, Mississippi during the early years of World War II, or to his thriving congregation on Long Island in the 1950s and 60s. But regardless of the original audience, in these moments he was speaking solely to me, and we could engage in uninterrupted dialogue. Ironically, now that he and I have had this "alone time," I am more than eager to share his words, and him, for that matter.

SCOPE

When we disposed of most my father's papers, I made no attempt to save anything other than the sermons. However, he apparently had filed a variety of other writings of a similar nature with his sermons; these also escaped incineration. They included magazine articles, invocations and special prayers, and talks that he had given at various venues, including weddings, funerals, conversions, graduations, confirmation exercises, and interfaith lectures, as well as radio and television "sermonettes." I've included five of the special prayers that are particularly noteworthy, inserted chronologically among the sermons. My father was a saver. Also in the files were manuscripts from his days in seminary, including a 63-page award-winning paper on Passover and his 95-page graduation thesis, *The Procedure of Ordination and of the Appointment of Communal Judges from 70 C.E. to the End of the So-called Talmudic Period*.

It is very difficult to say exactly how many discrete documents there are in the Ballon collection. Some sermons were cannibalized, with parts of them used in other sermons. While my father typed out most of his talks in full, there are also innumerable 3x5 cards with speaker's notes. The best accounting I can offer is that I read close to 800 of his customary five- to seven-page, double-spaced, typed sermons. Taken from a thirty-five-year career, a few years for war, time for sabbaticals and summer vacation, and the occasional Boy Scout Sabbath or other special event, that seems like a pretty realistic number. A staggering way to look at it is that it amounts to about two million words!

I pondered how many of these sermons would be enough—or too many— to include in this book. I wanted to provide an overall sense of my father's voice, the scope of the topics he covered, and their place in history. I could have easily found one hundred sermons that impressed me for one reason or another, but that would have created quite the tome, and I hoped to make this as accessible as possible given the seriousness of the topics.

I sensed the number of sermons chosen should have practical as well as symbolic significance. Fifty-two sermons would correlate to one sermon for every week of the year, but this seemed somewhat arbitrary given that it appears my father did not actually give fifty-two sermons in any year. Moreover, many of my favorite sermons were from the High Holidays rather than from weekly Sabbath services, rendering tenuous the relationship to weeks. I considered rounding the number down to fifty, but given the introductory material and added notes, it would still have made this too weighty a volume. Forty had merit. We would be down to a manageable size, and it's a number that is often significant in a Jewish context—forty days and forty nights, forty years in the desert, etc.

Contracting the size of the book made it increasingly difficult to cut out some of my favorite sermons. Nonetheless, I finally reduced the number to thirty-six. Most Jewish readers will recognize the significance of this number. Every Hebrew letter has a numerical value. The Hebrew word *chai* means *life*. *Chai* is spelled with the letters *chet* and *yud*; these have the numerical values eight and ten respectively, totaling eighteen. Thus, the number eighteen has mystical significance as a symbol of life, as do multiples of eighteen. Thirty-six means *double life*, and that's what I hope to be giving my father and his sermons by resurrecting them here.[1]

When selecting sermons, I tried to provide some balance among the

Pulpit	Sermons
Temple B'nai Israel, East Liverpool, Ohio	2
Tree of Life Congregation, Columbia, South Carolina	5
Presumably North Africa	1
Temple Adath Israel, Lexington, Kentucky	2
Nassau Community Temple, West Hempstead, New York	24
Temple Beth Tefilloh, Brunswick, Georgia	2

Decade	Sermons
1930s	5
1940s	4
1950s	9
1960s	16
1970s	2

decades and the various pulpits.

---

1 Sometimes what is most obvious is most elusive. Literally hours before submitting this manuscript for publication, I noticed how I unwittingly selected thirty-six sermons from my father's rabbinate that began in 1938 and ended in 1974—a span of thirty-six years!

PROCESS

From the outset, I posited that throughout their lives in the pulpit, rabbis only truly deliver five sermons, and that they find multiple ways of preaching those same five ideas over and over. (I can't say for sure, but I may have even heard this from my father.) With that in mind, as I pored through his papers, I attempted to identify Sidney Ballon's "five sermons" and use them to create some balance among his favorite topics.

My process as I read and logged each sermon was to discern its fundamental message and then look for patterns among these messages. Patterns indeed emerged. To no surprise, the largest category was sermons dealing with a wide assortment of Jewish religious topics. A partial list includes Hassidism, faith, forgiveness, funeral practices, interfaith marriage, Kol Nidre, marriage, divorce, Passover, peoplehood, Reconstructionism, shofar, theology, *tzedakah* (charity or righteousness), and the controversial subject of women rabbis! Ultimately, I grouped these into two categories: *Faith in God* and *Jewish Practice*.

By contrast, I took two separate topics, anti-Semitism and external threats to Judaism on the one hand, and Jewish apathy and ignorance, or internal threats to Judaism, on the other, and combined them under a single header: *Jewish Survival*.

A fourth category was comprised of Sidney Ballon's dreams for and love of the *Jewish Homeland*. He expressed this in sermons he preached during the days of Palestine in the 1930s, the establishment of the State of Israel in 1948, and the development and defense of the land in subsequent decades.

The final category addressed in this book is a broad one. It explores *topical* issues, often taken from the day's headlines—local and global—and how they intersect with Jewish values.

The names that I assigned to each cluster of sermons evolved over time. Since so many sermons seemed like calls to action, I felt a need not only to identify each topic with appropriate nouns and adjectives, but also to extract key verbs—action words—to highlight in their subtitles. It is with full intent that each of these is punctuated with an exclamation mark, as shown in the table on the next page.

Admittedly, I had to cheat a bit in order to arrive at just five themes. There are numerous worthwhile sermons that I chose not to feature in this volume for a variety of reasons, and their inclusion might well have forced me to recognize additional subject areas such as history, biography, and book, theatre, and movie "reviews."

Theme	Action
Faith in God	Believe in God!
Jewish Practice	Do Jewish!
Jewish Homeland	Love Israel!
Jewish Survival	*Am Yisrael Chai!* (The People of Israel Live!)
Topical Sermons	"Seek justice, love mercy, and walk humbly with thy God!" Micah 6:8

I omitted most of the biographical sketches (and virtually all of the histories and reviews) even though they typically were educational and gave insight into the traits and behaviors of accomplished people whom my father admired. This is because these sermons tended to explore the thinking of the subject person (or work of art) rather than illuminate the thinking of Sidney Ballon himself. I did include the sermon-biography of Chaim Weizmann in this collection, not because of Weizmann's stature in Jewish history—which is significant—but because this just happened to be the last sermon my father delivered.

As I read the sermons, I also developed a rudimentary "rating system" to identify those that best represented both my father's views and his homiletic prowess. I was not out to prove a particular point. I found myself in agreement with many of my father's statements and less so with others. My selection criteria were highly subjective and maybe not entirely conscious. I tried to find essays that covered a variety of topics, spanned the years, and stood out for their prose or for their personal or historic importance. This was not an easy task because too many sermons met this standard. It is my intention to take some of my favorites that did not make the cut for this publication and, pending further editing, post them on my website www.yeshindeed.com/.

In laying out the structure of this book, and despite my quest to categorize the sermons as described above, I chose to present the sermons chronologically rather than by theme, partially to provide greater variety for those who choose to read the book from front to back. This also creates a closer simulation of the experience one might have had as a congregant, since frequent themes rarely were delivered back to back. Moreover, some sermons defy easy categorization because they encompass several themes. A chronological presentation sidesteps the dilemma of where to place multi-category sermons.

"BONUS FEATURES"

In addition to the thirty-six transcribed talks, I have provided three discrete additions to each chapter. First, I give a brief overview of the sermon, punctuated by a pithy quote extracted from the text. This is intended to set some context for readers, especially those who are not moving through the book consecutively, and to help them select topics of special interest. Think of these as movie trailers or appetizers.

Second, I've added footnotes to make it easier for future generations to understand references from an earlier era. Although I myself previously paid little attention to footnotes, I discovered from this process that even the references I already recognized were enhanced by the addition of background information that I either had forgotten or never known. All of this opened up history in a new way. Ergo, I implore the reader to read the footnotes. There are many relevant and intriguing details that may be found there!

After completing the process described above, I reflected on how Reform rabbis of my father's generation tended to be a fairly intellectual lot—and how my work with these sermons was likewise intellectually driven. At the same time, I have been a student of Jewish spirituality that at its core is less brain-centered and more heart-centered. I knew my father had a strong belief in God; yet I felt connected only to his intellectual arguments, as deeply held as they may have been. I thirsted for more of a heart connection with what he was saying. In seeking this, I relied on a model of study that our spiritual direction class used in a course offered by Rabbi Shawn Zevit. Instead of reading Torah with the usual intellectual approach to exegesis, we would meditate first and then read the text, paying attention to where the words moved us spiritually. I decided to adapt this approach to the selected sermons. I meditated briefly before and after rereading each one, and journaled what came from my heart in response to what I had just read. These reflections became the third addition to the chapters: the *Notes to Dad* that I am delighted to share after every sermon.

TACHLIS (NUTS & BOLTS)

What did it take to transcribe the text from the sheaves of yellowing paper on which Sidney Ballon dutifully typed his sermons? These pages could not be scanned using optical character recognition software, not only due to the variability of the ribbon on his manual typewriter, but also because of the handwritten corrections my father scrawled all over the manuscripts. Initially, Debbie and I both tried our hands at keying his words into our respective computers. Neither of us is a professional typist, although I readily admit that Debbie's touch-typing is far superior to my hunt-and-peck. Furthermore,

In our Torah reading this week we begin the second book of the Torah, Sefer Shmot, the Book of Exodus. Of all the five books of the Torah Exodus is most important for a proper understanding of our faith. We might get along without the others but could not at all without this one. In the course of reading Exodus we are told of the period of bondage in Egypt and the redemption from this bondage. We learn of the covenant at Sinai and the giving of the Law. And these thoughts are the foundations on which Judaism rest. Zecher Yetsat Mitrayim is a phrase which rings out again and again in the Bible. It is given us as an explanation for the keeping of the Sabbath. It is the justification for commanding the Jew to be generous and just in his dealings with his neighbors and with the underprivileged. The Jew who himself experienced the bitterness of and degradation of mistreatment in Egypt was was expected to be therefore all the more sensitive to the needs of those in distress and all the more sympathetic to those in danger of being robbed of thir human dingity. It was the story of the bondage and the release therefrom which planted the seeds of a liberalism which has been for the most part predomiant in Jewish thinking to this day.

The redemption from Egypt, however, implied more than something physical. In addition to the acquisition of physical freedom there was a spiritual aspect to it as well. The going out of Egypt was but a prelude to the covenant at Sinai which gave meaning to the history and to the Jewish people the life of each indivudal Jew. We tend to think of the redemption from Egypt merely in terms of the actual exodus, but Sinai is also an essential part of the redemption. The rabbis made this very clear to us in their Midrashic inte pre tation of this period of our history, hen they said that the Israelites could not really consider themselves fully free then but only until they had stood at Sinai and accepted their bodily freedom and had also achieved a Commandments and the covenant. Henceforth the purpose of Jewish existence was the commitment to live by the commandments

Faith in God (Chapter 27), manuscript, page 1

all of my father's cross-outs and insertions, coupled with his illegible handwriting crowding the margins and the spaces between the lines, made it very challenging to transcribe the sermons. The process was much improved when I started to use speech recognition software. I could dictate a sermon in less time than it took either of us to type it, and I probably spent no more time fixing dictation errors than I had spent on our typos.

Sometimes, the cross-outs and insertions were so indecipherable that I could not be completely certain of my father's intention. Although most pages were much clearer, the picture on the preceding page shows an example of what we were working with. In these cases, I tried my best to make educated guesses. When a word or phrase was particularly difficult to decipher, I bracketed the transcription to alert the reader. Occasionally, I may have guessed incorrectly. I hope I have not too greatly altered the meaning in such cases.

During the course of this endeavor, I heard a language expert make a distinction between spoken and written language. Grammar rules tend to be more tightly enforced in the latter medium. To that end, I did occasionally edit my father's usage, admittedly guided by the "wisdom" of Microsoft Word's Spelling and Grammar checker.

Having transcribed the sermons as faithfully as possible, and having made what I felt were reasonable edits, I nonetheless felt the collection deserved more scrutiny. I enlisted the support of a few friends and family to cross check the accuracy of the transcriptions. Moreover, I engaged the services of a professional editor. I'll say more about both of these contributions in the *Gratitude* section below.

For the most part, my father provided his own translations of Hebrew text. Where I have supplied a translation, typically in the footnotes, it most likely came from The Mamre Institute, http://www.mechon-mamre.org/.

There are many ways a Hebrew word may be transliterated into English spelling. Some Hebrew sounds have no English equivalents or multiple equivalents. For instance, some people spell *Hasid* (in its various forms, *Hasidic, Hasidim, Hasidism*) with a *Ch* to connote the guttural sound not found in English. Others spell it with a *double-s* in the middle. These are all correct. I picked the Wikipedia spelling—*Hasid*—and standardized it across the book, regardless of how my father spelled it, if for no other reason than that they will all be pronounced the same regardless of the transliteration.

Some transliterations vary because Ashkenazi was typically used prior to Israeli statehood, whereas Sfardic was popularized afterwards. In these cases, I remained faithful to my father's text to reflect how he would have pronounced the Hebrew at that given time.

ANACHRONISMS

These mid-twentieth-century sermons include many statements that stand the test of time, and other statements that clearly do not. Case in point: references to gender and race frequently do not reflect the sensitivities developed in recent decades.

In addition, my father tended to be somewhat chauvinistic about Judaism. He was thoughtful, but his words were direct and would not always meet today's standard of so-called political correctness, ecumenical tolerance, and acceptance. Were he still alive, no doubt my father would speak in more charitable terms about other religions than he did in those days.

With all of that said, I apologize to those who find some of Sidney Ballon's dated terminology offensive. Rather than sanitizing or modernizing this language, I have left these words and ideas intact, if for no other reason than to reveal the norms of another era. Often, the underlying message is acceptable once such flaws are removed. I leave that evaluation up to the reader.

One of the tenets inherent to Judaism is that Torah is a living document, and it is to be interpreted and reinterpreted to be relevant in every age. I propose that the reader apply this principle to Sidney Ballon's torah—the torah of his knowledge, the torah of his beliefs. They need to be constantly examined and turned over and over—sometimes remaining unedited, and other times reinterpreted to meet the situation of the current age. As this document gets passed on, God willing, from generation to generation, none of what my father has said ought to be stuck in time. I encourage you to think critically about what he wrote and about what I have written by way of introductions and responses to his sermons, and to formulate your own thoughts. Then, you can put these words into a context that is meaningful in your life, making them all the more relevant and accessible to future generations.

GRATITUDE

As mentioned above, transcribing the sermons to usable text files was a challenging process that Debbie cheerfully took on in the early going before I discovered the benefit of voice recognition software.

Debbie, had you helped me with the transcription alone—*Dayenu!*—that would've been sufficient. Of even greater significance, however, has been your ongoing intangible support: you have given me the space and encouragement to continue slogging my way through a much bigger project than I had ever envisioned. You were there when we spared the sermons from incineration. You were there when we lugged them from coast to coast and from house to house. You were there when I covered every horizontal surface of our dining room with piles of paper as I sorted and sifted through the sermons. You may or may not have been conscious every time I bounded out of bed in the middle of the night eager to read just a few more sermons before drifting back to sleep. You were often there when I told some fresh, unsuspecting person all about my exciting project; and you were *always* there to hear each of my latest "brilliant" flashes of insight about how I might pull this all together. I am grateful for all of this, for your enduring presence, and for our love.

Speaking of unsuspecting persons, there are countless among you, including about half of Congregation Beth Jacob in Redwood City, to whom I owe my gratitude (and perhaps an apology). It was you, over the last six years, who had to endure endless talk about how excited I was to be reading my father's sermons. Some of you demonstrated palpable enthusiasm as you noted the historical and personal significance of the work. Others smiled politely. Each of you, in your own way, supported whatever in me needed your ear. Notable among you are my *machatonim*—Steve and Cheryl Shapiro, Bruce and Barbara Kadden, and soon, Sharon and Marty Scigouski, Sr. Thank you all.

I am grateful for the local group of family and friends who helped scour this text for transcription errors. Remember those "spot the difference" puzzles back in the days of newspapers? Try that with 2500 words, hand-typed, with ex-ed out deletions and fuzzy pencil-scrawl edits squeezed between the lines—not an easy task. Yet you compared those original aging documents with my hardcopy proofs and caught so many of my transcription errors. (I take full responsibility for any that eluded you.) Not only did you provide this valuable service, but you also showed such joy and interest in the process that it further enlivened the project for me. I am grateful to Alana and Jacob Ballon, Debbie Ballon, Magdalena Cabrera, Mimi Ezray, Wendie Bernstein Lash, Jerry and Judith Lippe-Klein, Michael Nierenberg, Grace Rosenberg, Becca Shapiro, Doug and Susan Solomon, Elliot Stein, Janet Teman, Elia Van Tuyl, and David Winikoff for your time and attention to detail.

I have often seen authors render lavish praise to their editors. Now I know why. Emily Moberg Robinson of Woodshed Editors, you are a gift! We walked together through every page of this book, and the journey was not only productive and instructive, but most enjoyable as well. Where my father's spoken words may have occasionally lacked the precision demanded of the printed page, you demonstrated expertise and insight required to adapt them to this medium. You did so with a light hand, guiding me to never alter, but only enhance his message. For this I am deeply grateful.

The other professional support I was blessed to receive came from Winters Design. I know just enough about graphic design to be dangerous. Fortunately, Janine and Frankie, you know a whole lot more. With talent, a discerning eye, and a whole lot of patience you provided the excellent graphic design of this book inside and out. I thank you for the superb work and the pleasure of developing it with you.

In 2012, when I posted sermons on the blog in honor of the centennial of my father's birth, I requested that anyone who cared to share a memory or offer a comment do so on the Rabbi Sidney Ballon Facebook page that I had created. It is primarily from those postings that I gleaned the congregant quotations that appear in the opening pages of this book. I am grateful to Rabbi Amy Ehrlich, Rick Ehrlich, Susan and Stanley Kolker, Rabbi Robert Loewy, Judy Fener Peritz, and Marc Seifer. Your words provide a meaningful bridge to the halcyon days in West Hempstead.

Thanks also to a group of rabbis whose words and deeds have long been a source of learning and inspiration: Nat Ezray, Larry Hoffman, Nadya Gross, Jim Mirel, and David Saperstein. I am humbled by your generous comments. And to our dear friend Cantor Murray Simon, thank you for the gift of your voice, your friendship, and for your generous foreword.

I am grateful for Marc and David Saperstein. Although our communications regarding the creation of this book were brief, they were of profound importance. Our fathers were close friends and colleagues. Rabbi Harold I. Saperstein was the distinguished and dynamic leader of Temple Emanu-El of Lynbrook, Long Island, a mere four miles to the south of Nassau Community Temple. Marc and David, with distinguished rabbinical careers of their own, honored their father, much as I am attempting to do, by publishing a collection entitled *Witness from the Pulpit—Topical Sermons, 1933-1980, Harold I. Saperstein*. I unashamedly borrowed much of the structure of this volume from the model that their book provided. Marc made the valuable suggestion that I include introductions and footnotes for each sermon. In perusing *Witness*, it was of great interest to note the many times our fathers addressed similar topical issues. With no false modesty, comparisons between their book and mine end there. As a professor and academic scholar, Marc's commentary rises to a level of intellectual rigor to which I would not aspire. I am indebted to the Sapersteins for their guidance, support, and the lifelong friendship between our families.

I am also grateful for the support of my classmates and teachers in ALEPH: Alliance for Jewish Renewal. Whether we broached this subject or not, the spiritual path that I have been traveling underpins all I do, especially the works of my heart and soul, such as this. Among my classmates, I offer special thanks to my *chevruta* partners over the years who were a continual source of inspiration and reflection: Kenny Joseph, Judy Brown, Sarah Walsh, Linda Leah Greene, Betty Adler, Hannah Salander, Gavriel Strauss, and especially

Ira Wiesner, whose intellectual curiosity, generous heart, and expansive soul continue to be a true gift.

I am grateful for the ongoing spiritual support of my peer *hashpa'ah* (spiritual) group—Magdalena Cabrera, Bill Futornick, Karen Gould, and Elia Van Tuyl; and for the introspective, contemplative brotherhood of my men's group of over twenty-six years—especially Robert Badame and John Carlsen, who are still standing, and our brother Greg Kimura, whose beautiful presence was taken from us far too soon.

I am grateful for my rabbi of the last two decades, Nat Ezray, who has been a gentle and loving mentor, counselor, cheerleader, and friend.

Lastly, I am grateful for *every* member of my family—past, present and future—who exemplify love, bring abundant joy, and provide continual inspiration.

Introduction

A Brief Biography of Sidney Ballon

Sidney Ballon was born on May 25, 1912, in Pawtucket, Rhode Island, the son of Israel (1879–1932) and Sadie Needle Ballon (1890–1967).[1] Israel was a tailor; Sadie, a seamstress. (Our family has always been amused that a tailor married a Needle.) We believe that Israel and Sadie immigrated to the United States from Odessa, Ukraine, presumably just after the pogrom of 1905. Where and when they met is unknown, but given Sidney's birth date, it's safe to assume that they married in 1911. Two other children followed—Herbert Joseph (1917–2003), and Norma Dorothy (1927–2009). There is little information about the family's early life, other than that Sidney and Herbie excelled in mathematics and Latin at the renowned Classical High School in Providence, before distinguishing themselves in similar fashion at Brown University. Sidney was admitted to the Phi Beta Kappa national honor society as a member of the Brown class of 1932.

My father was raised in an observant Jewish home. He said that he decided to become a rabbi because he so admired his own rabbi, Morris Schussheim, who served as the spiritual leader of Temple Beth-Israel from 1922 to 1929. Despite his traditional upbringing, my father was persuaded by his mentor and lifelong friend Rabbi William G. Braude to pursue his studies at the Reform seminary, Hebrew Union College in Cincinnati, Ohio. We know from the sermons in his file that he served as a student rabbi at Temple B'nai Israel, East Liverpool, Ohio, now named Temple Beth Shalom, from 1936 to 1938. Braude, five years older than my father, helped him review and revise some of these early sermons.

---

[1] The family name was rumored to be something like "Baloytin" in the old country. We've been told it means "a muddy swamp." At Ellis Island, so the story goes, some became Bolotin and our branch became Ballon.

Sidney Ballon received his rabbinical ordination in 1938, and spent one year working for the Union of American Hebrew Congregations (now the Union for Reform Judaism). There are scant sermons in the files from that period, so it seems that he did not lead many services. He did preach in early 1939 in Huntington, West Virginia, and later in Columbia, South Carolina. The following excerpt from a history of the Tree of Life Congregation in Columbia describes how he came to his first full-time pulpit.

> *It was in [1939] that the Congregation, having decided to finance a rabbi themselves, were told that the young Rabbi Sidney Ballon, formerly of Providence, R.I. and at that time in the employ of the Union of American Hebrew Congregations, might be induced to accept the pulpit of the Tree of Life. In the previous year, Mrs. Julian Hennig had consulted the office of the Union regarding plans for a youth group which the Tree of Life Congregation was sponsoring. She was sent in to discuss the matter with a young regional rabbi, who so impressed her with his earnestness, courtesy, and consideration for this woman from a little unknown southern town, that she filed his name—Sidney Ballon—in her mental card index. At the time that she again heard that name recommended as rabbi for the Congregation, Mrs. Hennig was on her way to a National Sisterhood meeting in Cincinnati. The Board of Trustees asked her to interview Rabbi Ballon and find out as much about his record as possible. This she did, discovering that Rabbi Ballon had graduated with high honors from the Hebrew Union College and that the Union considered him one of the most promising young rabbis on its rolls. So exhaustive was Mrs. Hennig's inquiry, terminated by several interviews with Rabbi Ballon, that she felt competent to recommend to the Congregation that they employ this young man. Surely every question that she could think of had been asked of Rabbi Ballon. As the interview was about to come to an end, she was amused and a little embarrassed to hear this conversation.*
>
> *"Mrs. Hennig, are there any more questions you'd like to ask me?"*
>
> *"No, Rabbi Ballon, I think not."*
>
> *"Well then, may I ask you a question? Do you think I'll do?"*
>
> *The answer was an emphatic "yes," which was echoed enthusiastically by the Congregation after Rabbi Ballon had come to Columbia, in the spring of 1939, for the proverbial "trial sermon."* [2]

---

2 Helen Kohn Hennig, *The Tree of Life: Fifty Years of Congregational Life at the Tree of Life Synagogue*, Columbia SC, 1945.

Introduction

My mother (née Jean Hagar Hymson, 1917-2001) would tell the story of her introduction to my father something like this. When the new rabbi arrived in Columbia, the congregation held a welcoming reception. My mother was ladling punch when she looked up and saw the handsome young man who was to be their new spiritual leader. To put it in terms suitable for family reading, this elicited a certain prurient curiosity within her. They were married the following summer.

War broke out the next year, and my father enlisted as a chaplain in the Army Air Forces. He originally was deployed to Keesler Army Airfield, in Biloxi, Mississippi, where their first child, Jeffrey Lewis (1942–2011), was born. In 1945, Jean gave birth to Martha Elaine (Muff) in Columbia while Sidney was finishing his tour of duty in North Africa. In December 1947, I was born, also in Columbia.

In the spring of 1948, our family moved to Lexington, Kentucky, where my father assumed the pulpit of Temple Adath Israel. My mother's cousins in Lexington undoubtedly provided entrée. In 1951, we Ballons had our last major relocation as a family, moving to Metropolitan New York ostensibly to be closer to Sadie, Herbie, and Norma, who had all moved there from Providence. The post-war years were a time of tremendous growth in suburbia, and that was reflected in the growth of suburban synagogues as well. Hence, the Nassau Community Temple in West Hempstead, Long Island was flourishing, and my father spent virtually the remainder of his professional life in this pulpit.

It is hard to separate the man, Sidney Ballon, from the rabbi, partially because he devoted so much of his time to his professional life. More significantly, however, he wasn't the kind of person who turned on one personality when in the pulpit or in the community, and turned on another when among friends and family. He was a genuine, thoughtful, caring, and reverent person—and he was pretty much the same guy for everybody.

He was not particularly effusive. While sightseeing with my mother's family in the California redwoods, he was asked what he thought of the ancient trees towering above. He famously replied, "Not bad." As children, we used to tease him and call him *Stony* because when we were driving, he'd steer the car with a perpetual stone-like expression.[3] Mom was quite the opposite—a fiery, colorful, untamed free spirit, who scripted her own definition of the role of *rebetzin* (rabbi's wife). Theirs was definitely a case of opposites attracting.

---

[3] My sister's recollection is that Dad got the nickname based on his expression when faced with his children's unruly behavior at the Shabbat table. There is, no doubt, some truth to both versions.

When he did allow himself some downtime, my father had a few favorite pastimes and delights. He was an ardent solver of the Sunday *New York Times Magazine*'s double-crostic puzzle. He loved grabbing a nap while a baseball game droned softly on the bedside radio. The New York Giants were his favorite team, which set up a nice rivalry with Mom who grew up in Louisville, Kentucky, down the block from the one-day Hall of Famer Pee Wee Reese of the Brooklyn Dodgers. In 1962, a few years after both teams left New York for California, the whole family coalesced around the newly formed New York Mets. (Dad had a talent for finding sermon topics everywhere, and once spoke on the lessons to be learned from the 1969 Miracle Mets!)

My father had a taste for brandy and for Scotch. He also must have really liked apple pie, because one time when my mother made a peach pie he said, "This is really good. It would have made a great apple pie!" He liked his mother's cooking. She was an old world *balabusta*—making many Eastern European Jewish classics such as knishes, matzah ball soup, beet borscht, and p'tcha.[4] As for his favorite candy, that would have been the dark-chocolate-covered bar of sweetened coconut popularly known as a Mounds Bar.

Perhaps more than anything, my father liked to sit and read. He read two or three daily newspapers—*The New York Times*, *The New York Post* before it became a laughable tabloid, and *The Long Island Press* or the other local paper, *Newsday*. He was always reading a book.

For many summers, beginning in 1955, my father was a chaplain at the Ten Mile River Boy Scout Camp in Narrowsburg, New York. His congregation went on a hiatus of sorts, with lay-led services during the summer. That gave him two months in the serenity of the Catskill Mountains with relatively few responsibilities other than leading Shabbat services for the troops. He could be counted on to deliver sermons directed to young people in the form of an entertaining story illustrating a moral.

This summertime freedom gave my father the space to read widely and prepare extensively for his High Holy Day sermons. (Hence, over half of the sermons in this collection are taken from the High Holy Days.) His weekly sermons, on the other hand, were developed under much greater time constraints. He would have to squeeze them in amongst all of the other congregational responsibilities vying for his attention. Every Thursday night, like clockwork, my father would shut the door to his home office and we would hear the keys of his Royal Quiet DeLuxe Portable Manual Typewriter clacking out his weekly sermon. Almost half of the sermons in the book are from those

---

4 An aspic made out of jellied calves' feet and garlic. Grannie may have made a chicken foot version as well.

Friday night Shabbat services. The breakdown of all the sources is noted on the following table.

Event	Sermons
Shabbat evening	16
Rosh Hashanah evening	1
Rosh Hashanah day	6
Kol Nidre (Yom Kippur evening)	5
Yom Kippur day	7
Weekday (pre-Thanksgiving)	1

When I was a kid, my classmates would occasionally ask me, "What does your father do the rest of the week? Like, what's his real job?" They would see him for a few hours on Friday or Saturday, and could not imagine how he filled his time or what the scope of his responsibilities could be. It's important to note that beyond his weekly 20-minute sermon and the hour-and-a-quarter Shabbat evening service (both impeccably timed), he was a rabbi ministering to the needs of his congregation seven days a week. He took seriously his role as a pastor, as a tender of the flock. He was there for his people. He counseled them with great empathy. He taught them with great wisdom and enthusiasm. He rejoiced with them. He consoled them. He was a quiet, humble, and reverent man, not without enthusiasm and humor, but overall a very modest person. For this he was much beloved in his community.

He was there for the larger community as well. He was a civic leader in West Hempstead—a member of the West Hempstead Public Library Board of Trustees and the local Rotary International chapter, chaplain of the local volunteer fire department, a contributor to local radio and television stations' religious programming, and an active participant in many other social, professional, and philanthropic organizations.

In 1972, at the age of 60, my father had a heart attack. After his recovery, he felt a need to slow down. The idea of leaving the taxing New York pace and harsh climate appealed greatly to him. He discovered an opening for a semi-retirement pulpit at Temple Beth Tefilloh, a tiny congregation in Brunswick, Georgia. In August 1974, my parents returned very near to where they had started out thirty-five years earlier, moving south to St. Simons Island, at that time a sleepy resort village off the Brunswick coast. Unfortunately, Dad continued to experience cardiac problems. He sought relief from one of the country's most prominent cardiologists, a pioneer in cardiac bypass surgery,

Dr. Denton Cooley of Houston, Texas. An angiogram revealed significant heart disease requiring immediate surgery. On November 11, 1974, less than three months after retiring to Georgia, Sidney Ballon died on the operating table at the age of sixty-two.

My father simply liked being Jewish. It was his thing. I would like to tell you more about him, but I have many unanswered questions myself. There is a truism, one of those things that just happens: by the time a person comes up with certain questions—substantial as well as trivial—to ask their parents, the parents often are not there to provide the answers. Given how young my father and I were when he departed, I actually feel pretty lucky to find at least some of the answers in the treasured archive of his sermons.

Introduction

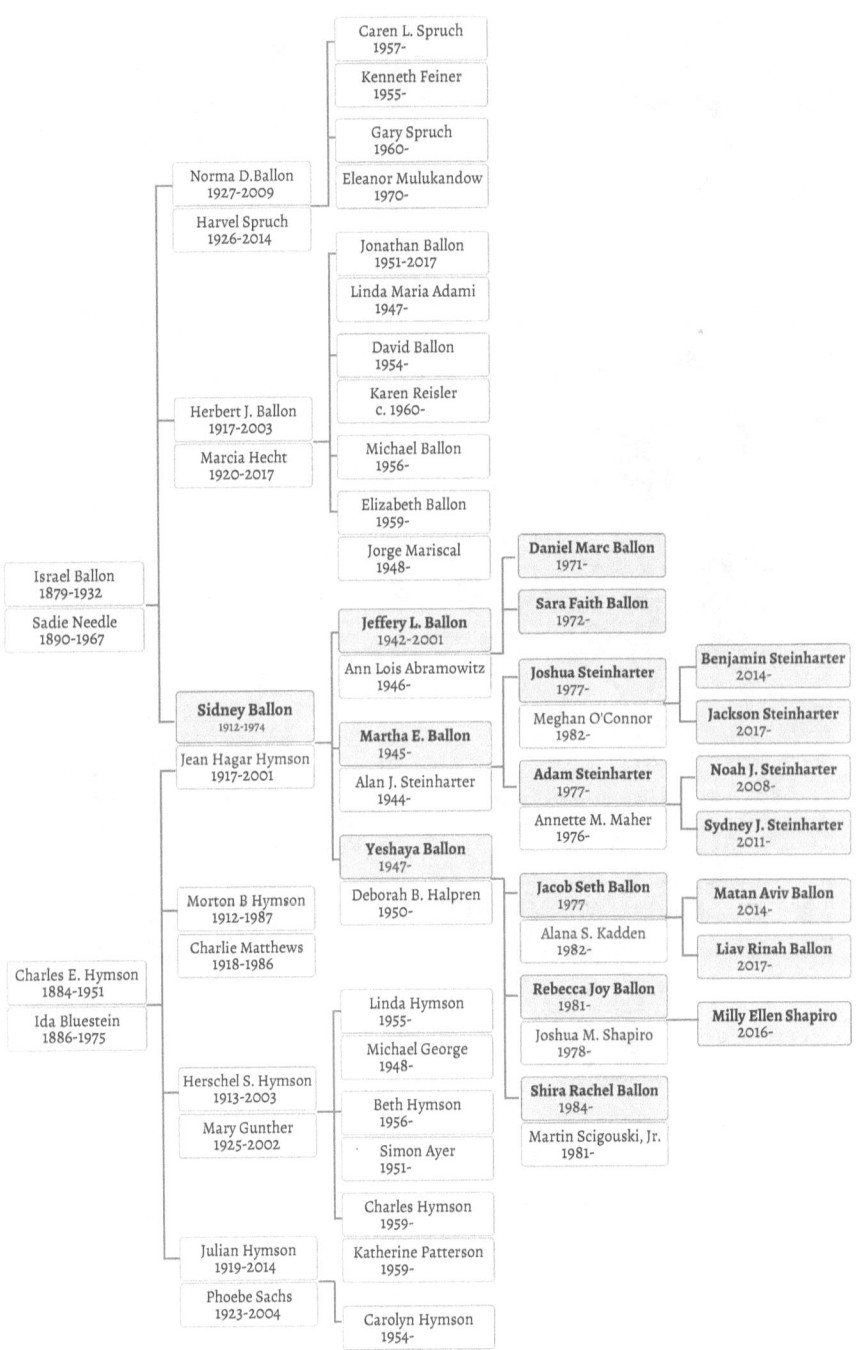

Sidney Ballon Family Tree

Israel and Sadie Needle Ballon, c. 1911

Standing, left to right: Israel, Sidney, Sadie, perhaps Sadie's father, Samuel Needle. Seated: Fannie Pickar Bolotin, Nachum Dov Bolotin (Israel's parents), Max Bolotin (Israel's brother). Kneeling: Harry Ballon (Israel's brother). Child in front unknown.

Sidney Ballon, c. 1912

Sidney Ballon, c. 1914

Sidney Ballon, c. 1915

Introduction

Sidney Ballon, c. 1924

Graduation, Classical High School, Providence, Rhode Island, 1928

Steps of Sayles Hall, Brown University, a favorite family portrait site

Five Themes

It may be a bit of an overstatement to assert, as I do in the Preface, that rabbis have only a few sermons that they rehash time and again over a lifetime. Nonetheless, establishing five themes for my father's sermons has been a useful organizing device. It revealed patterns in this vast accumulation of essays, and clarified the essential values by which he lived and about which he preached.

I realize that many sermons do not fall neatly into one category versus another. Some sermons encompass more than one category because the categories themselves are highly intertwined. *Faith in God* and *Jewish Practice* are inextricably connected. Each one, one might argue, may lead to the other. The history of *Jewish Homeland* and concern for *Jewish Survival* are similarly symbiotic. It's hard to imagine one without the other. Consequently, I invite the readers to play along at home and decide for themselves if the sermons I've designated in one category might just as well be placed in another, or in more than one!

My father was very consistent with his thoughts throughout his career. In fact, one of his techniques, not surprisingly, was to dip into his file from time to time and pull out a sermon from previous years, typically from a previous pulpit, and deliver it again. In most of these cases, he would do a little bit of updating. Every sermon had a date and a location scribbled on the last page, and more than a few had multiple dates and locations. Having said this, most of the sermons in this collection were uniquely crafted to a specific moment in time. The two exceptions are those delivered during his brief semi-retirement in Brunswick, Georgia, where, for the first time in twenty-three years, he had a new audience.

Certain of his favorite phrases, anecdotes, and parables show up in different contexts from time to time throughout the decades. He often repeated paragraphs rather than entire sermons; however, when editing the volume, I avoided including these redundancies.

I made an exception to this editorial decision, however, when it came to one of my father's favorite quotations.

> *When I behold Thy heavens, the work of Thy fingers,*
> *The moon and the stars, which Thou hast established;*
> *What is man, that Thou art mindful of him?*
> *Yet Thou hast made him but little lower than the angels,*
> *and hast crowned him with glory and honor.*

Thou hast made him have dominion over the works of Thy hands;
Thou hast put all things under his feet.[5]

These words from Psalm 8 appear in multiple sermons on different topics. After I reviewed the first draft of the manuscript, I noticed that this quotation appears in four of the thirty-six sermons I had selected. I could easily have found other worthy sermons to replace one or more of these and thereby eliminated the apparent redundancy. Instead, I decided to keep them all to underscore the importance these words held for Sidney Ballon—a reflection of both his humility and his longing for humanity to rise above its circumstances and achieve its full potential.

In *Holy, Holy, Holy* (1952), my father uses these verses to reflect the awe with which we contemplate the vastness of the universe (hence our humility in the face of it), while acknowledging the glory, honor, and power of our place as stewards of the earth. In *The Strange Call of the Shofar* (1958), he emphasizes the potential of mankind to rise above not only the animal kingdom but our own animal instincts. In *The Melody of Faith* (1960), he asserts that though mortal we may be, we are capable of great achievements in both the material and spiritual worlds. That is the plea that he again offers in *Footsteps on the Moon* (1969), when he reminds us that we have much more work to do here on earth, and that all of our achievements are in partnership with God.

It is not surprising that my father repeated certain themes throughout the decades. However, reading them in a concentrated period of time made me wonder to what degree he may have felt cumulative frustration not only with the state of modern Jewish life, but with society as a whole. Did he ever feel he was making any headway while fighting the same ethical, moral, and religious battles year after year? Perhaps this may be the lot of any preacher. In any case, here is a closer look at Sidney Ballon's "five sermons."

THEME NUMBER ONE: FAITH IN GOD—BELIEVE IN GOD!

I always knew my father believed in God. I just never really understood what that truly meant to him and what God he believed in. In our earliest conversations on the subject—this would've been during my ninth-grade religious school confirmation class—he was very clear. As he reiterated to every confirmation class before and after mine, just as a magnificent timepiece presupposes a watchmaker, the orderliness of the universe presupposes a creator. That really didn't take the conversation much further than the Little Golden Book image of God that we had in elementary school, one that many adults harbor throughout their lives—the old man with a white beard sitting on a throne dispensing rewards and punishment. Presupposing a world-maker

---
5 Psalm 8:4-7.

perpetuated the anthropomorphic metaphor that is the source of much discomfort for many. That concept is so hard to believe that it makes it easy to dismiss the idea of God altogether. As I (and other modern theologians) have often said to atheist friends and family members, "The God you don't believe in—I don't believe in that God either!" My father's god (and mine) is founded on an appreciation of the miracles and mysteries of the universe and an underlying moral code.

There are six sermons in this collection that I have categorized as dealing with faith in God. They are: *The Melody of Faith* (1960), *Baal Shem Tov* (1960), *The Wisdom of the Heart* (1961), *Loneliness* (1965), *Faith in God* (1966), and *The Sense of Prayer* (1968). Read as a whole, they offer a message that not only takes us beyond the personification of a creator, but also reaches out to grapple with the divine mystery.

These sermons provide a clear theology that is very useful in moving past any childish or adolescent concepts of God. My father makes statements that may resonate with many. His theology builds on a state of unknowing, sensing the mystery of life and the universe. He describes God as indescribable and indefinable, the mysterious source of the universe that precedes all scientific theories and is likely to be around after all the scientists are gone. He allows our mythology to support what we know about human behavior at its worst and at its best. He casts Sinai as a metaphor for the transformation of our people, suggesting that truly leaving Egyptian slavery and becoming God's people requires us to adopt a set of ethical standards.

The Melody of Faith and *The Wisdom of the Heart* both connect to the non-rational aspects of worship that may provide a sense of spiritual awareness separate from any specific image of God. Each sermon suggests that on Yom Kippur, whether because of our focus on fasting or prayer or listening to ancient melodies or reciting ancient words as a congregation, we often give ourselves permission to experience an undeniable spiritual connection. The challenge is to believe in the reality of that experience, and maintain it or return to it at other times. We are much more likely to cast that feeling aside and even deny its existence or importance in our rational day-to-day lives. My father urges us to do otherwise, to pay close attention to what has stirred us on Yom Kippur, to remember it well, to draw on it at other times when our rational minds might otherwise reject that such things are a part of our life. He argues that our non-rational experiences give meaning to otherwise superficial aspects of modern life, just as the melody of the *Kol Nidre* transcends its actual words.

The *Baal Shem Tov* sermon is one of two biographical sketches I've included in this collection because it provides insight into a way of looking at religion and connecting to God that is lost to many people. This essay reminds us that joy and enthusiasm are not only acceptable, but in some ways compulsory to the meaningful experience of Jewish life. By contrast, the sermon on *Loneliness* encourages us not to push away the pain of loneliness that we all feel at times. My father urges us not to try to escape loneliness, but rather move toward it, treasure it, exploit it, allow it to lead us to our inner creativity, and use it as a gateway to divine connection. This is ironic coming from my father, who often speaks of the importance of community.

The final sermon that I've included in this category, *The Sense of Prayer*, builds on our ethical obligations to God and suggests that one way to connect to these values is through prayer. My father maintains that we are not praying to an entity that is there to reward or punish us. The liturgy that has been handed to us over the generations reminds us of who we are and what our values are, and allows us to judge ourselves based on these standards through moments of self-reflection. For some people, this helps create a divine connection.

Even in these few sermons, we get a sense of the wonder and awe with which Sidney Ballon viewed the universe and its creator. He encourages a more abstract understanding of the presence of God in our lives, and offers multiple points of entry into such a spiritual life.

THEME NUMBER TWO: JEWISH PRACTICE—DO JEWISH!

The second category that I offer is *Jewish Practice*. The subtitle here is *Do Jewish*. I do not refer narrowly to the laws of ritual practice, but to the ways one comports oneself in the world at large when one is living according to the standards of Jewish conduct. My brother once told me a story about an outing he had with his fellow rabbinical students and some of their faculty. As they ran out to the field, a student facetiously asked their esteemed professor Harry M. Orlinsky if there were a Jewish way to play softball. In addition to joking "Thou shalt not steal," Orlinsky responded seriously, "There's a Jewish way to do everything!" By this, he clearly meant that all conduct must be influenced by Jewish law, ethics, and moral codes.

In a few of the sermons that fall under this category, namely *A New Year and a New Venture* (1939), *Three Ideals* (1939), *An Ethical Will* (1948), and *The Complete Jew* (1958), my father offers short checklists of behaviors that he feels are essential to leading a Jewish life. There is some redundancy—or, shall I say, commonality— in these lists, such as supporting the synagogue, identifying strongly with Jews of all places and throughout all times, and providing a Jewish education for oneself and one's children. (These themes crop up again in the sermons on Jewish survival.) *A New Year and a New Venture* and *An*

Ethical Will are bookends for my father's first pulpit, being his first and last sermons at Tree of Life Synagogue. It is telling that each covers the aforementioned tenets.

Other sermons in this category focus more narrowly on a single aspect of Jewish life. Adhering to my father's standard sermonic structure—thesis, three or four supporting elements, summation—these sermons delve more deeply and specifically into their respective topics. *The Sabbath, A Reform Perspective* (1952) reminds us that being a modern liberal Jew does not excuse us from the observance of Shabbat, and that there are real benefits to setting this day aside as sacred and different. *Holy, Holy, Holy* (1952) and *The Missing Al Chet* (1967) both connect the concept of holiness to ethical actions in daily life. *The Strange Call of the Shofar* (1959) suggests that each of us possesses a divine spark and that our job is to find it and use it.

THEME NUMBER THREE: JEWISH HOMELAND—LOVE ISRAEL!

Of the dozens of sermons Sidney Ballon delivered on the topic of the Jewish homeland, I've selected four that create an arc of the Palestine/Israel story. *In Search of a Home* (1939) gives us a foreboding glimpse of the plight of Jewish refugees during the early days of the war in Europe. The other three sermons share, at least in part, a common theme of military victory over Arab foes. My father describes the initial war of independence and the early challenges of the new state in *Israel: First Anniversary* (1949); this sermon is followed by *Mid-East Crisis* (1956), and then *The Aftermath of a Miracle* (1967), an account of the Six-Day War. Despite Israel's military triumphs, it's still hard to take much joy in this history. Little satisfaction is gained from recounting victories when, from our perspective of some fifty or more years later, we know that continual conflict is the antithesis of sustainable peace. All of these sermons, especially the one from 1956 where he compares Nasser to Hitler, could just as easily have been slotted among the ones dealing with Jewish survival.

THEME NUMBER FOUR: JEWISH SURVIVAL—*AM YISRAEL CHAI!* (THE PEOPLE OF ISRAEL LIVE!)

Concern for the survival of Judaism is a consistent theme in Sidney Ballon's sermons. He addresses it primarily in two ways. He expresses deep angst regarding those who have oppressed Jews throughout the ages: the anti-Semites, the Amaleks and Hamans and Hitlers who have sought to annihilate us. More often than that, however, he decries ignorance and apathy: the enemy from *within*. Concerns about both the external and internal threats are valid, especially for someone who lived through the Holocaust and who watched as the ranks of Reform Judaism grew numerically but without ostensibly deep knowledge and conviction.

I wonder how my father's congregants responded to his repeated lamentation that we can never feel assured that "it can't happen here." Did his words reflect their own post-Holocaust concerns, or did they seem like obsessive whining? Moreover, did they feel he was preaching to the choir when he railed against inadequate Jewish knowledge and observance, or did the truth of his message cause them to squirm a bit in the pews? My father would chide them, saying that it was insufficient to be defined by what practices one does *not* observe, such as *not* keeping kosher and *not* wearing *kippot*. How well could they articulate the significance of the practices that they *did* keep?

I've selected but one sample of each of these sermon types. In *Ignorance of Judaism* (1960), my father asserts that for a discerning liberal Jew, breaking from tradition might require even greater study and awareness than accepting all the doctrines as a fundamentalist. In *Is American Jewry Secure?* (1971), he looks over his shoulder, concerned that the long history of Jewish oppression, scapegoat-ism, and anti-Semitism has never been eradicated and that we must be vigilant in preserving democracy for all.

However, there is yet a third and more positive way that Sidney Ballon preaches on Jewish survival. He frequently makes the case for why Judaism is important to preserve. He takes pride in the differences that he sees between Judaism and other religions. Despite how much society at large has adopted Jewish values, he iterates time again in sermons like *A Liberal Faith* (1955), *Jewish Peoplehood in America* (1957), and *The Mission of Israel* (1968) that the world still needs us and our message is unique among the religions. I could have just as easily placed these three sermons in the "Do Jewish" category because they clearly lay out what actions need be taken in order for Judaism to survive.

THEME NUMBER FIVE: TOPICAL SERMONS—SEEK JUSTICE, LOVE MERCY, AND WALK HUMBLY WITH THY GOD!

This theme has by far the longest subtitle. Rather than be pithy, I chose to use one of my father's favorite quotes from the prophet Micah, one that reflects his vision of what God asks of us, and one that illustrates the way he sought to live his life. If I had decided to compose a book exclusively of my father's *topical* sermons, as did my friends the Sapersteins, I might have given it the title *Peace, Freedom, and the Great Beyond*. At least among the topical sermons included in this collection, the concerns he raises pretty much fall under that rubric.

Peace

Wherever conflict occurs, my father seeks *peace*. *Shall We Fight Again* (1936) demonstrates his early passion for peace as he contemplates the precarious position of the world. Living in the wake of one war and on the verge of another, he pleads for us to take the resources we would use to wage war and instead use them to wage peace.

As an aside, this sermon displays my father's very early ability to craft rich prose. He eloquently describes his memories of the original Armistice Day that ended the first world war in 1918:

> *Underneath this hysterical joy there may have been many a tear. The agony and suffering of the preceding months could not be so quickly be erased. For some, the Armistice meant the speedy return of dear ones, but for many also it brought the sad realization that there would be no return, that the happy homecoming planned from the very day of departure was never to be. But even those who suffered most, rejoiced. The sacrifice had been great, but the achievements were likewise great. Those who gave their lives and those who suffered did so for a holy cause.*

His pacifism pops up again in *Sins of a Nation* (1967), where he rails against the war in Vietnam, and again in his reflections on violence in America described in *Remarks on the Death of Robert F. Kennedy* (1968) and *Understanding Our Youth* (1968). He provides a different take on war and peace with his stirring and eloquent words in *The War and You* (1941), delivered just days after the Japanese attack on Pearl Harbor. Here, he bemoans the lost opportunity for peace since World War I, even as he calls his congregants to summon up courage and commitment to face the reality of the conflict at hand.

Freedom

Whether speaking on civil rights or poverty, my father seeks *freedom* from oppression, lack of opportunity, and other barriers to living a full, productive, and happy life. The theme of freedom is in evidence early on, as well as in more recent sermons. He speaks on civil rights in *Let My People Go* (1950) (as he did back in the 1940s in a Columbia, South Carolina sermon not included in this collection). It's not surprising, then, to hear his account of the historic March on Washington in *Blowin' in the Wind* (1963), delivered a few weeks after the event. In *Joseph and the War on Poverty* (1964), he links civil rights and poverty, and holds us accountable for failing to meet our religious obligation to feed the poor. He notes that with all our sophisticated aerospace technology, we should be able to solve problems on earth, a theme he hammers home in *Footsteps on the Moon* (1969).

The Great Beyond

As regards the *great beyond*, Sidney Ballon quite literally looks at our achievements in the "great beyond" of outer space and despairs that our spiritual lives do not have us soar even higher. He moves beyond the boundaries of the material world as he decries the materialism and greed that disconnects us from spirit. He reminds us of our place in the order of things, that we may feel part of an unfathomable oneness and at the same time maintain our humility. These themes are explored in *The Struggle of Jacob* (1936), as well as in the two aerospace sermons, *Mr. Sputnik* (1957) and *Footsteps on the Moon* (1969).

His aspirational and inspirational values include a genuine patriotism. As a member of the "greatest generation," he prized the precious heritage of American democracy almost as much as his Jewish heritage, for he saw them as inextricably linked. This is evidenced in his wartime *Thanksgiving* talk (1944), and his 1968 sermon *Understanding Our Youth*.

All of his comments on and criticisms of society's ills take us full circle to my father's theology and fervor for Jewish values. Our family often joked that my father was able to find the Jewish message in everything—politics, pop culture, any and all current events.

The topical sermons are a rich tapestry with common threads woven among the different shapes and hues. They add up to a man whose faith formed his vision for his community, his country, and the world.

Carry On!

This collection concerns itself with three stories. Foremost is the story of Sidney Ballon, writing and delivering words that reflected his passion about Judaism—its past, present, and future. I have written much about this, and had I not, the sermons would very well speak for themselves. A second story is that of my discovery of my father's voice and what it has meant to me—not only the content of the words, but the powerful link that it reestablished between the two of us, even posthumously. This, too, should be fairly well elucidated by the Preface to the collection as well as in my *Notes to Dad* that follow each sermon. The third story is the passing down of this precious heritage—the creation, facilitation, and amplification of a legacy and the emerging value that this legacy has among its readers as it is passed on *l'dor vador*—from generation to generation. This, the most important of the three stories, is yet to be written. It will unfold only as these words and the hopes and prayers behind them are passed on. If you are reading this now, the fate of Sidney Ballon's dream is in your hands. In his *Ethical Will* sermon, his final words from his first pulpit, my father beseeches his congregation to build on all that they had accomplished together: "Carry on, I say to you as my parting wish. Carry on!"

1. Shall We Fight Again?

November 13, 1936

Among the very earliest sermons from Sidney Ballon's days as a student rabbi is the following passionate plea for peace in the face of the impending war in Europe. My father looks back at how deceitful governments and industries profited from the first world war, and argues that we should not allow ourselves to be duped into engaging in future wars. He takes a strong stance for pacifism.[6]

The common voice today must take a stand not against war in general, but against one specific war—and that one is the next one.

AMONG THE VAGUE MEMORIES OF CHILDHOOD, there are very few things that can be recalled with any great degree of clarity and certainty. Only the most unusual and impressive circumstances so fix themselves upon the mind that in later years their picture may be vividly recaptured. Such an occasion was Armistice Day 1918.

Young though I was at that time, there still remains with me a vivid recollection of the day.[7] I can still hear the shrill sound of factory whistles in the morning, announcing to the anxious populace that at last the peace had come, the war was over, the boys would soon be back. I can still recall being taken to the center of the city where the mad celebration of victory took place in the evening.[8] What a frenzied throng was there, shouting jubilantly and rejoicing. Everyone was drunk with excitement and reckless with joy. Flags were waving,

---

[6] It is likely that my father was influenced by Rabbi Abraham Cronbach, an outspoken pacifist and professor of Social Studies at Hebrew Union College in Cincinnati, Ohio, where Sidney Ballon attended rabbinical school.

[7] Sidney Ballon, born May 25, 1912, was 6½ years old on November 11, 1918.

[8] Providence, Rhode Island, in all likelihood.

streamers flowing, as through the streets swept the happy citizenry, singing their war songs and shouting their cheers, pausing only now and then in their wild march to hang the Kaiser in effigy and burn his supposed corpse in the street.[9] Underneath this hysterical joy there may have been many a tear. The agony and suffering of the preceding months could not so quickly be erased. For some, the Armistice meant the speedy return of dear ones; but for many, it also brought the sad realization that there would be no return, that the happy homecoming planned from the very day of departure was never to be. But even those who suffered most, rejoiced. The sacrifice had been great, but the achievements were likewise great. Those who gave their lives and those who suffered did so for a holy cause. Liberty and freedom had been saved from the trampling feet of the barbarous Hun, and the world made safe for democracy. The war to end war had been fought and won, and in the dying flames that consumed the effigy of the luckless Kaiser perished also the last vestiges of injustice and intolerance. Here we were at last, at the dawn of a new era of peace and liberty such as the world had never known before.

Armistice Day 1936 provides a shocking contrast. Eighteen years after the war to end war, all Europe waits merely for the gong to start all over again. The machinery of peace, so optimistically hailed upon its inception, is completely broken down. The World Court has failed.[10] The League is impotent.[11] One false move on the continent of Europe and the smoldering sparks of its suspicions and hatreds will again burst into a flaming fire, and we wonder whether there is anything that can be done. Must we sit idly by and watch once more as the world takes a running jump over the precipice? This time, the fall will be a longer and a deeper one, and perhaps it will be impossible

---

9 "Friedrich Wilhelm Viktor Albrecht of Prussia (1859–1941) was the last German Emperor (Kaiser) and King of Prussia, ruling the German Empire and the Kingdom of Prussia from 1888 to 1918... An ineffective war leader, he lost the support of the army, abdicated, and fled to exile in the Netherlands." Wikipedia contributors. "Wilhelm II, German Emperor." *Wikipedia, The Free Encyclopedia*. Wikipedia, The Free Encyclopedia, 18 Sep. 2017. Web. 19 Sep. 2017.

10 "The Permanent Court of International Justice, often called the World Court, existed from 1922 to 1946. It was an international court attached to the League of Nations, initially well-received; many cases were submitted to it during its first decade of operation. With the heightened international tension of the 1930s, the Court became less used. By a resolution by the League of Nations on April 18, 1946, the Court ceased to exist and was replaced by the International Court of Justice." Wikipedia contributors. "Permanent Court of International Justice." *Wikipedia, The Free Encyclopedia*. Wikipedia, The Free Encyclopedia, 25 Aug. 2017. Web. 19 Sep. 2017.

11 "The League of Nations was an intergovernmental organization founded in 1920 whose principal mission was to maintain world peace... The League ultimately proved incapable of preventing aggression by the Axis powers in the 1930s. Germany withdrew from the League, as did Japan, Italy, Spain, and others... The United Nations replaced it after the end of the Second World War." Sinrod, Eric. "The Failure of International Organizations to Prevent War." *Duane Morris TechLaw*, blogs.duanemorris.com/techlaw/2014/10/15/the-failure-of-international-organizations-to-prevent-war/. Accessed 19 Sep. 2017.

to clamber back again up the side. Are we then doomed to silence, helplessly waiting for the inevitable collapse?

It is strange that we should find ourselves in such a predicament, for we know now more than ever before what the last war really meant. The illusion of 1918 did not last very long. Time passed and the hysteria wore off. Like a drunkard who arouses himself from his stupor and surveys his stupidity with disgust and self-reproach, so we finally came to our senses and realized the cost of the war. It has been pointed out that with the sum that was spent on death, we could have built beautiful homes, furnished them with costly furniture, placed them on spacious estates, and given one to each and every family in every country that participated in the war. We could have given each city of more than 20,000 inhabitants in every one of these countries a $5 million library and a $10 million university. And with the remainder, we could have established a fund providing an adequate, steady salary for an army of 250,000 teachers and nurses.

And the cost in lives! If on some Armistice Day, instead of watching the healthy, vigorous steps of youths in trim uniform with shiny buttons as they march to the blaring of military music, we could review a parade of those who died in the trenches! Four months the procession would last, marching ten abreast, all through the day and all through the nights without a stop—two months and a half for the dead of the allies and over six weeks for those of their enemies. But even so, we might have said, "Why count the cost when the fruits of victory were so great? A tremendous price, but are not liberty and democracy worth it?"

But we learned still more, and we realized that liberty and democracy were merely blinds. We thought we were fighting for principles. The only purpose, we now know, was profits, and these were not for the men who fought.[12] We had been completely taken in by an avalanche of propaganda. We had been sacrificed as a burnt offering upon the altar of greed. Our American financiers had gambled on the defeat of Germany. One company had made a loan of $500 million to England and France. Other bankers and even the government followed suit. Unfortunately, Germany began to gain the upper hand. And so, out came the news of atrocities committed upon poor defenseless children. Out came the slogan that the world must be made safe for democracy. And in we went to save the bankers' millions. Our munitions makers,

---

12 During World War I, "some companies and corporations increased their earnings and profits by up to 1,700 percent, and many companies willingly sold equipment and supplies to the U.S. that had no relevant use in the war effort." It has been estimated that the war cost the U.S. $52 billion. Of this sum, $39 billion was expended in the actual war period, yielding $16 billion in profits. Wikipedia contributors. "War profiteering." *Wikipedia, The Free Encyclopedia*. Wikipedia, The Free Encyclopedia, 18 Sep. 2017. Web. 19 Sep. 2017.

too, had to earn their daily bread, and so while bullets poured into the bodies of our soldiers, dollars poured into the treasuries of our corporations. For every three Americans killed in battle, an American millionaire was made. The profits realized from the sale of munitions sent DuPont stock up 5000% in value, and United States Steel and Bethlehem Steel watched their incomes soar to astronomical figures. The price of the war was great to be sure, but it was worth it—to the merchants of death and the bankers.

In the face of such disillusionment, we might think the lesson would have been learned. We might think the realization of these facts would do more to end the war than was expected even of the war itself. But again, we would be wrong, for the world today is ready to repeat.

Facing things realistically, one must admit that the chances of averting the war in Europe as matters stand now are very slim indeed. No one likes to be pessimistic about such things. We like to hope to the last moment that a way to peace will be found. But the greatest optimist today, if he be realistic at all about the question, can hope only to postpone but not avert another conflagration in Europe. Everywhere, people want peace; yet the economic and political forces brush aside all resistance and draw the masses after them. Europe appears to be doomed. The question is only one of time.

We in this country, however, are in a situation quite different from that of Europe. We have plenty of land for our people, plenty of resources to fall back upon. We are not beset by the troubles of difficult neighbors. If we but set ourselves to the task, we can definitely escape the clutches of another war, and thus preparing ourselves for peace, who knows but that perhaps Europe, too, will learn to follow.

Back in the 1790s, President Dwight of Yale University said: "It is probable that whenever mankind shall cease to make war, this most desirable event will arise from the general opposition to war by the common voice."[13]

We in America today must raise this common voice. You may say that if this is all that is required, then we are already prepared for peace, for truthfully no one in America today wants war. We all want peace. But the same was true in 1916. Then, as now, the entire nation was opposed to sending our men to fight on foreign soil. Wilson was re-elected that year on the strength of his promise to keep us out of the war.[14] And yet, when the showdown came, we

---

13 "Timothy Dwight (1752–1817) was an American academic and educator, a Congregationalist minister, theologian, author, and the eighth president of Yale College (1795–1817)." Wikipedia contributors. "Timothy Dwight IV." *Wikipedia, The Free Encyclopedia*. Wikipedia, The Free Encyclopedia, 7 Sep. 2017. Web. 19 Sep. 2017.

14 In the United States presidential election of 1916, incumbent Woodrow Wilson, the Democratic candidate, defeated Supreme Court Justice Charles Evans Hughes, the Republican candidate. The election took place while Mexico was going through the Mexican Revolution and Europe was embroiled in World

went in, we clamored for battle, and unpopular was the man who in the face of overwhelming opposition dared to take a stand for peace. Then, as now, we were certainly opposed to war; yet the trouble was then, as it also is now, that what we were against was war in general. Wars in general, we admitted, were wrong, and even when we entered the fight this principle still prevailed. However, the particular battle upon which we were entering was excusable. Most war was needless, but this particular one was righteous, waged for a holy cause.

The common voice today must take a stand not against war in general, but against one specific war—and that one is the next one. Braced firmly by the conviction that the next war is the one that is wrong, we will not be swept off our feet by any future flood of propaganda as we were in 1917. We will not be led into the false distinction between good wars and bad ones. It was easy to deceive us in those days. We were unprepared. But now we know what sort of propaganda to expect. We know who will reap the benefits of the conflict. Should the occasion again arise, we ought not to be tricked, for whatever they tell us, we must be convinced that it is this very next battle that we must not join.

The militarists tell us that the best defense is an offense. Well and good! Let us turn their own strategy against them and wage an offensive for peace. It is too late to talk peace when the crisis is already at hand. The foundations of peace must be laid long in advance. If the common voice would make it clearly and explicitly known that the masses of this country would absolutely refuse to participate by any manner of service in any future war, there would be no future war. The churches could stop war if their members would insist upon following the commandment, "Thou shalt not kill." Labor could stop war if it refused to provide the instruments of death. No nation will venture to fight unless its people are in a suitable frame of mind. When there are large groups of citizens, however, who refuse to yield to a war psychology, whose reason is strong enough not to permit them to give in to artificial hysteria, war cannot be waged. The people cannot be used to fight against their will; and without the bodies of drafted men to feed its hungry mouth, the monster of war must starve and die.

The road to peace is a hard one. The obstacles that stand in its path are many; the sacrifices to be made in its behalf are great. Yet we must not give way to a paralyzing sense of futility. Our name must be on the record of every

---

War I. "Wilson's campaign used the popular slogan "He kept us out of war" to appeal to those voters who wanted to avoid a war in Europe or with Mexico." Wikipedia contributors. "United States presidential election, 1916." *Wikipedia, The Free Encyclopedia*. Wikipedia, The Free Encyclopedia, 17 Sep. 2017. Web. 19 Sep. 2017.

organization working toward peace. Our voice must lend its strength to that common voice which must shout for peace. Progress to be sure is slow, but man in his drive for perfection moves steadily onward. For the present, we pray only that we may be endowed with the courage and strength to face the crisis with intelligence. We pray that we may learn and understand how to direct our energies and our spirits to the improvement of humanity rather than to its destruction. Let us but think and live in terms of peace and in terms of justice to mankind, and ultimately the day must come when "Nation shall not lift up sword against nation; neither shall they learn war anymore."[15]

Amen.

Note: Attached to this sermon was a benediction that my father undoubtedly offered at the conclusion of the service. It was taken from *The Jewish Peace Book* by Rabbi Abraham Cronbach.

> O God of love, Father of men, from Whom alone desires of peace and fellowship come, and in Whom alone can such desires bear fruit, pour out Thy blessing that it may bring peace, abolishing war among the nations, and hasten in Thy love, the time when all men will have been gathered to Thee in perfect unity.
>
> *Adonai Oz L'Amo Yiten; Adonai Yivarekh Et Amo Ba-Shalom.*
> May God grant strength unto His people;
> May God bless His people with peace.

Dad—

Delivering this sermon as a 24-year-old rabbinical student, your youthful energy, passion, and eloquence abound. To some degree, your naïveté does as well, but I have the benefit of hindsight on world events upon which you could only speculate. I am also writing this in my late sixties, an age, sadly, you did not achieve. When I was in my early twenties, I marched against the War in Vietnam, though less passionately than you, and with about the same results.

The feelings of betrayal, anger, fear, and frustration that you espouse could easily be voiced today. How sad that is. That's pretty much a message I derive throughout your archive of sermons—"The more things change, the more they stay the same." Does that make the preaching in vain or make it all the more necessary? Perhaps my need to pass your words on to the succeeding generations answers that question. Perhaps your final note of hope, that peace may prevail, answers that question as well. The only other choice is to remain silent in the face of injustice, and that's not really an option.

Blessings.
Yesh

---

[15] Isaiah 2:4.

2. The Struggle of Jacob

November 27, 1936

This sermon, ostensibly about the story of Jacob, actually takes on materialism from a unique post-Depression, pre-World War II perspective. It's hard to believe that this deep and passionate essay is from the hand of such a young rabbinical student.

Most men do not discover their spiritual natures... They fail to acquire the social sympathies which make their hearts beat for the oppressed, their souls cry out against the unjust, and their hands ready to give in proper measure to those who need their help.

THE TORAH PORTION OF THIS WEEK presents us with a dramatic picture.[16] After long and patient exile, the patriarch Jacob was finally returning to the land of his birth. Blessed with wives and children, and enriched by flocks and herds, with countless camels bearing his servants and his goods, he journeyed in a long-stretched caravan toward home. He was flushed with success and filled with pride at his great achievements. For many long years he had struggled, but now, as he plodded slowly onward and dreamed of the future, what happiness and prosperity he could foresee for himself and his family.

But all at once, his dreams were rudely shattered, and Jacob "was greatly afraid and distressed."[17] He had not reckoned with his brother, Esau, but his advance guard came running back with the news that Esau was on the way toward him with four hundred men. All at once, [Jacob's] self-assurance failed him. For the first time in his struggle for success, Jacob lost his nerve. He himself could not understand why he should feel as he did. Until now, he had faced and overcome every obstacle without fear. He had deceived his father and tricked his brother out of his birthright. To him instead of to Esau had been promised the mastery over all peoples. He had gone to live with his uncle, and there, too, he had prospered. He had managed the affairs of Laban

---
16 Parashat Vayishlach, Genesis 32:4-36:43.
17 Genesis 32:8.

so cunningly as to win most of Laban's wealth for his own. Never had he been outwitted, never had he failed to gain the upper hand.[18] But suddenly, as he heard of Esau marching toward him with his men, he was overcome with misgiving. His wealth and strength seemed on the verge of annihilation. His smug self-confidence was shaken. Of what avail had been his labor! And he wrestled with the forces of doubt in his questioning soul. The spiritual struggle within him raged on through sleepless hours of the night. As he tossed upon his couch, it appeared to him as though the struggle were a real one. He seemed to be wrestling with an actual though unknown adversary, an angel of God. The exhaustion that he felt was real. The cold sweat upon his brow was there, and in his determination to win the fight, he murmured to his imaginary antagonist, "I will not let thee go, except thou bless me."[19]

And suddenly, Jacob realized why he was afraid. All his life, he had lived by deceit and worshiped force. All his life, he had pressed hard for material advantages whatever the cost to others. His whole existence had been selfish and self-centered, and now there came to him the realization that he was trapped by the very forces upon which he had pinned his faith, that he who strives constantly after power must eventually be brought up against a power stronger than his own to which he must submit and yield supremacy.

But the angel was not to leave without a blessing. In the realization of the futility of his past came his salvation for the future. A brother was not one with whom to struggle. Material gain was not the ultimate goal of life. There came to him an understanding of the things of the spirit, and Jacob's self-confidence returned. He exclaimed in his exultation, "I have seen God—my life is preserved."[20] And physically exhausted but spiritually renewed, he went forth to meet Esau in the morning with open hands and bearing gifts.

The survival of the Jew through long centuries of difficulty and hardship can be traced back to this very same spiritual struggle. Rolling back the pages of history, we find that the beginnings of the Hebrew people were no different than that of the other Bedouin tribes of the Arabian Desert. The early life of Israel, no less than that of other Semites, was dominated by the struggle for existence, by the attempt to gain a blessing from the land and mastery over the peoples. Eventually, the constant search for more fertile places led Israel into the land of Canaan. Forcing their way in by the sword, they dispossessed its peoples who already lived there, and in the course of time made themselves supreme throughout the land. Philistines, Edomites, Moabites, and all the rest

---

18 One could reasonably argue that Laban outwitted Jacob by substituting Leah for Rachel and forcing Jacob to work an additional seven years to win Rachel's hand in marriage (Genesis 29:18-20).

19 Genesis 32:26.

20 Genesis 32:21.

were likewise dominated by the same motives. Each fought the other with varying success in the attempt to keep their hold upon life. Each looked with envy at the fertile bits of land that the other possessed and wanted to wrest them forcibly away. And one by one, they who lived by the sword perished by the sword. Their every trace was removed from the earth so that only their memory remains. The little Hebrew kingdom of Judah was among the last survivors, but eventually it, too, found itself trapped by the material struggles in which it was enmeshed. Newer and mightier forces were arising in the East. Assyria and Babylon were casting their long shadows over the land, and the inevitable came.

According to all the rules of the game of history, the Babylonian destruction should have been the end. No neighbor of this peculiar people had survived the might of Babylonian power. The books of history had been closed to all of them—and yet Israel was only beginning to write upon its pages. There was good reason for this. Side by side with the external struggle for supremacy which the Hebrew nation carried on with the others, there waged within its midst an internal struggle such as other peoples could neither understand nor appreciate. Like Jacob, their forefather, confronted by his brother Esau, so this people, too, at the height of their success wrestled with forces of doubt. Out of the mouths of the prophets of Israel came forth the message of justice and love, the universal Fatherhood of God. From Amos came the cry, "Seek ye the Lord and live," and ultimately, they listened.[21] In the darkness of the Babylonian exile, Israel dedicated itself to those goods of life that are of eternal value. They became the "People of the Book," inspired with the word of God. Thus, they were enabled to outlive their conquerors and exclaim in exultation, "I have seen God—my life is preserved."[22]

The whole of Jewish history from that time on is a record of miraculous survival. When the legions of Rome battered at the gates of Jerusalem to destroy for a second time the capital of Israel and the Temple in its midst, Rabbi Johanan ben Zakkai stole stealthily from the city, and in the obscure town of Yavneh[23] founded a school that the study of the Torah might be

---

21 "Seek the Lord, and live—lest He break out like fire in the house of Joseph, and it devour, and there be none to quench it in Bethel" (Amos 5:6).

22 Genesis 32:30.

23 "Yavneh is considered to be the most significant site for post-biblical Jewish history after Jerusalem, since it was here that modern Judaism was born after the destruction of Jerusalem in the year 70 CE... The process, begun here, of developing laws, calendar, and liturgy, was essential for adapting Judaism to a new situation where there was no central Temple. This became the base for Jewish religious practice throughout the world until modern times." Wikipedia contributors. "Yavne." *Wikipedia, The Free Encyclopedia*. Wikipedia, The Free Encyclopedia, 16 Aug. 2017. Web. 21 Sep. 2017.

perpetuated.²⁴ Again, Jerusalem fell but Judaism lived. Israel has faced a thousand similar deaths through the years, but clinging desperately to its spiritual vision and struggling to preserve the ideals of Torah, it has survived the materialistic blows of injustice, hatred, and intolerance. If, in the future, we continue to live, this, too, will be only because the strength of our religious ideal has been maintained.

The world today, however, places no confidence in spiritual goals. The civilization in which we live has been fully conscious of the religious heritage that the great teachers of all times have bequeathed to it. It has continually mouthed its truths and sworn its allegiance to them, yet never has it actually lived them. And today, more than ever, it presses them deeper and deeper into the background. It is an age that has set all its goals toward the continually greater accumulation of all manner of material wealth and power. We have taken advantage of all our natural resources so that the earth yields us bounties the extent of which were heretofore undreamed of. We have all kinds of mechanical inventions that have made distance meaningless and have relieved us from the necessity of many of our manual labors. We have vast reservoirs of wealth dammed up in vaults by which all of our population might well be cared for. We have everything that makes for prosperity and self-satisfaction; yet in spite of it all, the specter of Esau marching with his men confronts us and terrifies us. Everywhere poverty and want stalk the steps of workmen. Justice and equality have lost their meaning. The state is glorified as God, the dictator becomes its prophet, and the ritual appurtenances of its worship are the military machines preparing for the time when each national group may wrest away its brother's birthright and assert its mastery over him. And, in the face of all this, civilization hovers on the brink of destruction as the spiritual blessing that alone can save it goes unasked for and unwanted.

As individuals, too, our lives are marked by endless grasping. Before the Depression, we had become obsessed with the idea that the only worthwhile way of life was to be prosperous.²⁵ Our only purpose was the continual building up of our personal bank accounts. In those days, it had suddenly become easy to make money. Everyone had his own private get-rich-quick scheme and

---

24 "Johanan ben Zakkai (30 BCE–90 CE) was one of the *tannaim*, important Jewish sages in the era of the Second Temple. A primary contributor to the core text of Rabbinical Judaism, the *Mishnah*, [Zakkai] was widely regarded as one of the most important Jewish figures of his time." Wikipedia contributors. "Yavne." *Wikipedia, The Free Encyclopedia*. Wikipedia, The Free Encyclopedia, 16 Aug. 2017. Web. 19 Sep. 2017.

25 The Great Depression was a severe worldwide economic depression that took place during the 1930s. The timing of the Great Depression varied across nations; however, in most countries it started in 1929 and lasted until the late 1930s. It was the longest, deepest, and most widespread depression of the twentieth century.

to this his energies were devoted. And what was the result! The thin bubble of prosperity was blown larger and larger until inevitably, it had to burst. The crash came. It was no new phenomenon. It had happened over and over in the past under similar conditions. It was but one more bit of evidence in a long chain that man can never work out the problem of his life in terms of materialistic indulgence. He has tried with a persistence worthier of better things, but always has encountered the same failure that we experienced once again. It would seem as though we might have benefited from the experience, but as once more the business cycle rises slowly upward from the depths of depression, the stock markets are again besieged by the dollars of those who would get rich quick, and we have already seen days on which the volume of business has exceeded the heyday of 1929. We have not learned that there is neither permanency nor happiness in material things. Only those who have everything can be satisfied, but then there is nothing further for which to live. Most men do not discover their spiritual natures. They do not realize they are more than animals living for the selfish ends of sustenance and pleasure. They fail to learn the art of human living that takes men and women, neighbors and friends, and molds them into relations of dignity, reverence, and goodwill. They fail to acquire the social sympathies which make their hearts beat for the oppressed, their souls cry out against the unjust, and their hands ready to give in proper measure to those who need their help. They live unto themselves, and unless they themselves receive a blow, they cannot understand the pain it may bring to others.

We need in these times a renewal of our moral and spiritual insight. Too many of man's noblest visions have lost their luster. In Amsterdam, the Dutch treasure, a masterpiece of Rembrandt incorrectly called *The Night Watch*—three centuries ago, this picture was placed in a large hall and in time came to be covered with smoke and soot. The colors grew so dark that those who looked upon the canvas thought it portrayed the night guard marching out to meet the enemy. Then, the canvas was cleaned and restored to its original color, and behold: it was a picture not of night but of day filled with glorious hues and flooded with sunlight. Too many of our great ideals are similarly covered with the smoke and soot of this age of steel. We mistake them for pictures of darkness and despair, when in reality they are brilliant with light. Today, as man wrestles with the invisible forces that attempt to beat him down, let him not cease the struggle except he gain a blessing. And let this blessing be a vision of the values that are eternal, so that like Jacob of old, he may exclaim in exultation, "I have seen God—my life is preserved." Without fear or despair, he will be able to go forth into the world and face his fellow man with open hands and bearing gifts.

Dad—

What can I say? The power of your words leaves me close to speechless. I think, rather than to put my own coda on your symphony, I'll just allow for a space of silence in which to deeply take in what you have offered.

Blessings.
Yesh

Rabbi Sidney Ballon, Columbia, South Carolina, c. 1939

3. A New Year and a New Venture —1939

Jean and Sidney, Columbia, South Carolina, c. 1940

Honeymoon, Lake Placid, New York, 1940

2. The Struggle of Jacob—1936

Honeymoon, Lake Placid, New York, 1940

Tree of Life Synagogue, Columbia South Carolina. c. 1940

3. A New Year and a New Venture

September 13, 1939

Erev Rosh Hashanah

It should not be surprising that this early sermon, by all accounts the first he delivered in his first fulltime pulpit, captures themes that dominated my father's thinking throughout his career—themes such as the importance of Judaism to the world and of the synagogue to Judaism.

The feeling that Judaism represents a certain ideal which is vivid and real and which is needed in the world and which we as Jews must have the courage and understanding to proclaim, is lost to almost all of us.

IT IS AN OLD CUSTOM IN JEWISH LIFE that when we celebrate either the hopeful beginning or the successful conclusion of some worthwhile undertaking, we recite the benediction *Shehechiyanu*, which praises God and renders thanks to Him for having preserved us and permitted us to witness the joyful occasion in question. Tonight, therefore, as we enter the turn of the Jewish century and greet the new year 5700, we, in common with our fellow Jews the world over, lift our voices in gratitude for having been spared to celebrate the New Year and recite together with them the traditional blessing of our faith. But we in this congregation on this Rosh Hashanah evening have yet an additional reason for reciting these ancient words, because for us this evening marks not only the beginning of a new year, but also the beginning of a new venture for this community. You and I stand on the threshold of new activity together, at the beginning of what we hope will be a happy and fruitful experience for both of us. And so, because of this, I can think of no better way of greeting you at this time than with the ancient benediction: *Baruch atah Adonai, Eloheinu Melech haolam, shehechiyanu, v'kiy'manu, v'higianu laz'man hazeh.* Blessed art Thou, O Lord our God, who hast preserved us and established us and granted us this opportunity of working together. Blessed art Thou, O Lord our God, who hast preserved and established this congregation and hast permitted it to attain this significant occasion when it looks forward so hopefully to the future.[26]

On setting out upon any new undertaking, there are several things that are well to consider. We must first of all think of and be fully convinced of the significance and importance of the task we have set before us. All too often in these days, we find the synagogue and the church relegated to a position of secondary importance. Lack of interest in the synagogue, we will be told, makes no difference to one's standing as a Jew. Religion, we will be told, is a matter of individual action. When one does what he thinks is good and what is right, he has fulfilled his religious obligations, and even should he wish to pray, the space of his own room is sufficient and the synagogue is superfluous.

But man does not and cannot live by abstract ideals alone. In order that any ideal be rendered meaningful in the life of an individual or in the life of a people, the idea that it expresses must be symbolized in concrete form. Loyalty to country is aroused by a waving flag. The British Empire is held together by the Crown of England. Religious ideals, too, must have symbolic expression, and this expression is afforded by the synagogue. The rabbis of old made the observation that before Israel accepted the Law at Sinai, God did not ask them to build a sanctuary; but immediately after the acceptance of the Torah, God commanded the building of the tabernacle. They point out that once Israel had attained the religious heights it reached at Sinai, immediately the tabernacle was necessary for the preservation and transmission of its ideals. The religious consciousness of man is not so acute that he can rely upon the intuitions of his own heart for inspiration. A Jeremiah could feel the word of God burning within him, but who of us is so bold as to declare himself gifted with the religious insight of the prophets? We are in need of stimuli. We are in need of something that can lift us out of the prosaic drabness of our everyday life. The synagogue as a symbol of the sanctity of life, as the embodiment of all that is holy and worthwhile, as our one avenue of contact with the classic traditions of our faith is that source of moral energy which is so necessary to every one of us in lifting us toward the ideals of our faith.

---

26 More literal translation: *Our praise to You, Eternal our God, Sovereign of all: for giving us life, sustaining us, and enabling us to reach this season.*

The man who cuts himself off from the synagogue all too often also cuts himself off from his people. The synagogue is not only the symbol of the Law of God, it is also the symbol of the people of Israel. The very prayers we utter are chiefly not prayers on behalf of the individual or the congregation, but prayers for the whole community of Israel. A quick glance at the prayer book will show that the language of prayer is only rarely *I and me*, but almost always *we and us*. The God to whom we pray is not merely the God of the individual, but, in the words of the prayer book, the God of Abraham, Isaac, and Jacob, the Holy One who dwells amidst the praises of Israel. We pray not alone and for ourselves, but together with our people. It is impossible to overrate the value of these historic bonds. As we stand here in the synagogue on this Rosh Hashanah in the midst of our own congregation, there is something thrilling in the thought that by the mystic bond of worship we are linked to the whole house of Israel, past and present, that we are united to living Jews the world over, and that we are bound by a mighty bond to the dead. We are Israel, the heirs to a spiritual tradition of inspiring grandeur. In the synagogue, the past of our people stretches out its hand to us, and, with the assurance of its support, we are enabled courageously to face the future.

Secondly, in setting out upon a new undertaking we must consider how our task is to be approached. So many of our people in these days come to their Judaism through the back door, so to speak. Their connection with their people is maintained not because of any urge from within themselves, but rather because they feel compelled to do so as a result of the often-unfriendly forces of the environment. To many, it has become a matter of a certain social allegiance. To others, the expression of Judaism has developed into merely a question of self-defense. Neither the positive values inherent in the teaching of our past nor any hope for achievement in the future bind them to their people. The feeling that Judaism represents a certain ideal which is vivid and real and which is needed in the world and which we as Jews must have the courage and understanding to proclaim is lost to almost all of us. It is most praiseworthy to be concerned with the fate of our fellow Jews throughout the world. It is praiseworthy to spring to the defense of the Jewish name wherever and whenever it is attacked. But anti-Semitism cannot be made the essence of Judaism or the sole reason and purpose for Jewish survival. A people who permits the psychology of fear to dominate its actions and control its thoughts is not in a very healthy state of mind. There must be a positive faith in the value of Judaism for its own sake and a will to survive as Jews regardless of the outside. There must be an awareness of the joyous aspects of Jewish life and the advantages to be derived therefrom. And the goal of all congregational activity must be to maintain such a positive attitude: to make ourselves more familiar with Jewish teaching and to give expression to its truths. In the process of so doing, we become not only better persons, Jewishly speaking, but better citizens of the land in which we live and more sympathetic to the cries of all humanity.

Here in Columbia, I feel confident that we do fully appreciate the importance and significance of whatever we do to strengthen the synagogue, and that the approach to our task will be a proper one. For this congregation is particularly blessed. It is the bearer of a fine tradition built up by the love and devotion of workers both past and present. What has been lacking perhaps in numbers has been more than made up in strength of purpose and will to survive. For over two decades, the congregation has been without professional leadership; yet throughout this time, the succession of Sabbath services has remained unbroken.[27] For over two decades, the congregation has been without professional leadership; yet during all this time, it has maintained without interruption its position as custodian of religious education for the entire community. Zealous and capable leadership has maintained a school whose high standard of curriculum and spirit of those associated with it might well be the envy of many another community with the benefit of a professional staff.

And now, the fact that a rabbi has finally been called to this pulpit and asked to remain with you I interpret as an indication of hearts that are sensitive to Jewish life and the evidence of a sense of kinship with the remainder of our people. It indicates further an awareness of responsibility toward the younger generation, and is an expression of the desire to face the confusion and chaos of these times guided by the inspiration and direction of religious teaching. These are rich resources with which to begin our work together, and for all of this, the congregation is to be highly commended. Traditions such as this congregation has built up are not lightly to be esteemed. I am afraid that perhaps not everybody who lives amongst them is always fully aware or appreciative of all that they mean, but one who comes in from the outside and who has seen all too often the lack of such traditions in other communities can appreciate them fully. This spirit must be maintained and guarded zealously in the future, and our task will be therefore not so much to create anew but to develop and build upon the old.

It is precisely when a community is so richly endowed, however, that the responsibility of the rabbi who comes to it is greatest. All the traditions that have been built up in the past become standards to live up to. They serve as the foundation upon which he is to build, and unless the structure that he builds is a sturdy one, the foundation also is apt to suffer. When a rabbi

---

27 Rabbi Harry Abrams Merfield served as spiritual leader of Tree of Life Congregation from 1914 to 1916.

comes to serve a barren community, come what may, if there be nothing gained, yet neither can anything be lost; but when a man is entrusted with an accumulation of spiritual treasures previously acquired, his responsibility is great, for though these treasures are not easily accumulated, they can very easily be dissipated. This responsibility with which you have entrusted me, I fully realize. I pray only that I shall measure up to it.

As we take stock, therefore, at the beginning of this new year and the beginning of this new venture, let us resolve to take full advantage of the abundant resources that are ours. Let us remember constantly that the cause for which we labor is vital and living, and the manner in which we approach it must consequently be proud and courageous. We come together in a most difficult time. The darkness that hovers over the world on this Rosh Hashanah is frightful to behold. All spiritual values seem to be hopelessly crushed. It is easy to lapse into cynicism and despair as decency, honor, and reverence seem to be fighting a losing battle. And yet it is only these spiritual qualities that are capable of a lasting triumph, and we must not lose faith in the possibility of their ultimate attainment. As long as the power remains with us, we must continue to be their standard bearers and their protagonists on this earth. May God strengthen us in this resolution. May He bless this congregation and vouchsafe unto all of us a *Ksee va vachaseema tovah*—a favorable inscription in the book of life, health, and happiness—and may He speedily bring His blessing of peace to all mankind.

Amen.

Dad—

Baruch atah Adonai, Eloheinu Melech haolam, shehechiyanu, v'kiy'manu, v'higianu laz'man hazeh.

Mazel tov on your first Rosh Hashanah service, in your first full-time pulpit! *Yasher koach!* How fortunate was the community that had you as a leader. You were so gentle, so thoughtful, so deeply imbued with a love of Judaism.

You preached what you knew. And you knew that the synagogue is the necessary hub of Jewish life, that Jews have an obligation to stay connected to all Jews of all times and places, because Judaism has a unique message that must be preserved—not just for the sake of the Jewish people, but for all people.

Blessings.
Yesh

4. Three Ideals

September 14, 1939

Rosh Hashanah

In this second sermon delivered to Tree of Life Congregation, my father lays out three additional guiding principles that are woven throughout his sermons for the next thirty-five years.

God, Israel, and Torah! These have been the three Jewish ideals of the past, and these are the ideals of which we are reminded today.

THERE IS AN OLD TALMUDIC TRADITION that the great mothers in Israel, who for many years were childless, gave birth to sons on Rosh Hashanah. Sarah, Rachel, and Hannah, who are all mentioned in the traditional scriptural readings of the two days of Rosh Hashanah, at last found an answer to their pious prayers that they be blessed with children when Isaac, Joseph, and Samuel were ushered into the world. It is not without reason that the rabbis of old thought to group these three women together in such fashion. If we review carefully the lives of their sons, we can readily see that each one of them typifies in himself a certain ideal toward which we must strive in promoting the well-being of ourselves and all Israel.

The story of Isaac, which we read from the Torah today, clearly portrays the classic example of loyalty to God and religious ideals.[28] Obediently, the son accompanies his father up the mountain. Willingly, he permits himself to be bound upon the altar and makes ready to offer up his life to the God whom he reveres. This willingness of Isaac to die for his faith was to our forefathers no mere Sunday school tale. It gripped their hearts and was a

---
28 Genesis 22:1-24.

source of inspiration to them in their own moments of trial. It symbolized to them the peak of faith and devotion of the perfect man, a perfection that the blast of the shofar, blown on the day of Rosh Hashanah in memory of this very incident, challenged them to attain. And when in the course of their own lives the story of Isaac was all too often reenacted without the happy ending, they gained comfort from its words of hope and consolation from the blessing given to Abraham: "In thy seed shall all the nations of the earth be blessed."[29]

Today, we are in need not only of Jews but also of people of all groups who are saturated with this faith in and loyalty to the highest. This is a time when the greater part of the world has abandoned ideals. Men do not worship God, but the idols of their own selfish desires. They are not ready to sacrifice themselves for ideals, but are all too ready to sacrifice ideals and other men for themselves. It is only a short time ago that we dared to hope that all injustice had been brought to an end, that oppression and bloodshed had ceased forever—but continued hatred and strife have now brought us to the point where the flames have already been kindled and threaten to sweep the whole world once again. Extremists of the left and right have set themselves up as the saviors of mankind, but both are alike in that the will of their particular state is the only justice they know, and to conform or perish the only measure of human freedom they allow. And even in democracies such as our country, where liberty and equality are still the rule, we have the all too ugly exceptions that challenge it. We have our industrial disputes and strikes where violence and bloodshed are resorted to instead of peaceful methods of arbitration. We have our sharecroppers whose every ounce of energy is exploited for the benefit of those who own the land they live on. We have our hundreds of organizations dedicated to the oppression of minorities. And we have numerous more subtle and less striking forms of material greed and intolerance, of which even we may be guilty in our daily life.

It is easy, then, to lose sight of all spiritual goals. It is easy to fall prey to the materialistic influences that surround us. To be ever on the side of right, to seek justice and love truth, to cherish and actively strive after social ideals, demands strength of character and heroism of soul such as we have seen exemplified in the patriarch Isaac. It demands sacrifice, if not *of* life then *in* life, but sacrifice nevertheless of ourselves and of our comforts, of our energies and of our treasures as an offering to God.

And just as Isaac is the classic example of loyalty to God, so is Joseph the example of loyalty to Israel. Never for a moment did this prince of Egypt forget his love for the people of Israel and the land of Israel. Proudly he proclaimed upon his arrival in Egypt, "I have been stolen from the land of

---
29 Genesis 22:18.

the Hebrews."[30] And although he had attained the rank of second to none but Pharaoh and was surrounded by all the luxuries of the Egyptian court, he nevertheless did not forget before his death to charge his brothers that when God redeemed them at last out of the land of Egypt, they should remove his remains with them and bring them to the land of Israel.[31]

And today, we need Jews with the loyalty of a Joseph. Today in this twentieth century, the total amount of suffering endured by Israel throughout the world is at least equal to if not greater than the darkest days of the middle ages. The story of German Jewry during the past few years has been one of dramatic brutality, while three million Jews in Poland, in less spectacular fashion, face daily the threat of starvation.[32] But what will happen in Central Europe now that war has come? We must shudder to think. These Jews look to us for assistance, which unfortunately even at its best can only slightly alleviate their ills. We dare not turn deaf ears to their pleas nor listen with stony hearts. We who live in comparative luxury in this free land dare not plead that we cannot afford to help. In Poland, Jews would banquet on black bread and potatoes. Jewish business was ruined by government interference. But we, the poorest of whom is so prosperous by comparison, we who throw away better food than Polish Jews eat, we who do not deny our own most frivolous fancies, all too often have to be hounded and shamed into giving in proper proportion to our means.

But it is not only Jewish relief that needs our support. There are fortunately more constructive aspects to Jewish life today. There is a Jewish land in the process of rebuilding. Elsewhere, misery and sorrow may be the keynote of Jewish existence; but here, not sorrow but joy and determination has been written on the face of the Jew, and wounded pride is healed by the glory of constructive achievement.

It has been no easy task to convert the wasteland into a fruitful field and the swamp into a blooming garden. It is a task now sorely threatened by the state of affairs in Europe. But it is a task which must go on as long as it is humanly possible for us to continue, and demands great loyalty on our part. And today, more than ever, we need Jews such as Joseph, Jews with self-respect and self-esteem, Jews with the interests of their people at heart; Jews who realize that what we have given to the land of Israel in monies or in labor

---

30 Genesis 40:15.

31 "And Joseph said unto his brethren: 'I die; but God will surely remember you, and bring you up out of this land unto the land which He swore to Abraham, to Isaac, and to Jacob.' And Joseph took an oath of the children of Israel, saying: 'God will surely remember you, and ye shall carry up my bones from hence'" (Genesis 50:24-25).

32 My father wrote this sermon less than a year after *Kristallnacht* or *The Night of Broken Glass*, a massive, coordinated attack on Jews throughout the German Reich on the night of November 9, 1938.

is not to be placed in the rank of relief or charity, that we, too, have reaped the benefits of the enrichment of Jewish life and likewise shared in the note of joy which has come forth to the corners of the world and brought courage and pride in its wake.

In the third great biblical figure whom we remember today, Samuel, we find the quality of loyalty to Torah. It was Samuel who was the last and best of the judges of Israel. In the days when the life of the Hebrew tribes in Canaan was still rather unsettled, before there was a king in the land or the Temple in Jerusalem, Samuel realized the need of the people for proper guidance and instruction, and he spent the years of his life traveling in a circuit to satisfy that need. From Shiloh to Bethel, from Gilgal to Mizpah he journeyed, and in each of these places he set up his tent and gave the people of his knowledge.

Today, we are also in need of this type of Jew who is eager for Jewish knowledge. Of all three loyalties of which we have just made mention this is perhaps the most important, for it is only upon the foundation of knowledge that we can build solidly a true love of God in Israel. But a strange phenomenon has come to pass in American Jewish life. We who have been called the *People of the Book*, we who enumerated all the virtues of life and then said *Talmud Torah k'neged kulam*—the study of Torah is greater than all of them[33]— we have forsaken Torah until Jewish knowledge among American-born Jews is now almost exclusively the privilege of a professional group. If this knowledge is found occasionally outside of that group, it is an exception to be wondered at. The problems that are before us at this time are too complex to be met with ignorance. How sad is the spectacle of those Jews who suffer the indignities of intolerance and cannot understand why. How completely bewildered are those Jews who have tried to dethrone Torah as the ideal of life and have bowed before the false Messiah of their environment. Loyalty to Torah might not always have protected their bodies, but at least their spirits would not have been crushed, their heads would not have been bowed.

There is an old story told of the famous Rabbi Akiba.[34] During the time of Roman persecution, when every Jewish school was forbidden to teach and when study of the Torah was made a crime punishable by death, Rabbi Akiba persisted in his studies and teaching and refused to obey the imperial

---

33 *Talmud, Kiddushin* 40b: Is study greater, or practice? R. Tarfon answered, saying, "Practice is greater." R. Akiba answered, saying, "Study is greater, for it leads to practice." Then they all answered and said, "Study is greater, for it leads to action."

34 "Akiva ben Joseph (c. 40–c. 137 CE), widely known as Rabbi Akiva, was a *tanna* (a Rabbinic sage recorded in the *Mishnah*) of the latter part of the first century and the beginning of the second century. Rabbi Akiva was a leading contributor to the *Mishnah* and *Midrash Halakha*. He is referred to in the *Talmud* as *Rosh la-Chachamim* (Head of all the Sages)." Wikipedia contributors. "Rabbi Akiva." *Wikipedia, The Free Encyclopedia*. Wikipedia, The Free Encyclopedia, 8 Sep. 2017. Web. 19 Sep. 2017.

command. He was repeatedly warned by his friends of the danger to which he subjected himself, but he did not heed them. To all their warnings, he had one reply. He told them of the parable of the fish and the fox:

> *A fish was swimming in the river, but many nets had been placed in the waters by fishermen and the fish was having a hard time trying to keep out of them. A fox happened to be running along the riverbank, and, seeing the struggles of the fish, called to it and said, "Come up with me on the riverbank. Here there are no nets and you can dwell with me in peace." Whereupon the fish exclaimed, "You foolish fox! If I am not safe here in the element in which I live, how much greater will be my peril out of it?*

"Our element, likewise," said Rabbi Akiba, "is Torah. If we forsake it we destroy ourselves."

This statement still holds true. We need men and women who can wear with dignity the crown of the Torah, men and women who are imbued with the desire to know and to study the story of their past, who are familiar with the beauties of their language and the grandeur of their literature, who understand the principles of their faith and the hopes and aspirations of their people. Torah must again become the standard about which the spiritual forces of Israel rally if Jewish life is to be healthy and sound.

God, Israel, and Torah! These have been the three Jewish ideals of the past, and these are the ideals of which we are reminded today. But we must also remember this: if Isaac became the model of faithfulness to religious ideals, it was because his mother was the pious Sarah. If Joseph became the classic example of loyalty to one's people, it was because his mother was the inspiring Rachel. If Samuel became the pattern for love of learning, it was because his mother, Hannah, carried him as a babe into the sanctuary. And if we are to have our modern Isaacs, Josephs, and Samuels, then we must have our modern Sarahs, Rachels, and Hannahs to raise them. Too often do we cast the burden of raising a generation of good Jews upon the limited efforts of the Sunday schools, while home influences work in a contrary direction. Too often, the few hours of synagogue training are forced to contend with the handicap of indifferent parents. And when there is a tug-of-war between the school and the home, there is no question as to which will emerge the victor. It is the home that wins every time. When your children are taught a few precepts of Judaism, it is the home that has the power to either lock them out of the child's heart or seal them in.

On this day of Rosh Hashanah, then, when we remember these three venerable heroes of our past, let us be reborn in spirit with a measure of the ideals that they represent. May the mothers in Israel resolve to follow the noble examples of the matriarchs who bore them, and may God give us the strength to create a generation of Jews which shall be worthy of the heritage of its past and shall never cease to cherish and respect it, which shall live in accordance with its spirit and bring honor and glory to all Israel.

Amen.

Dad—

Like the prophets and patriarchs of old, you have clear ideals that you espouse and you never waver in the thirty-five years of your spiritual leadership. Here, you are a young twenty-seven-year old in your first High Holy Days in your first full-time pulpit. Where did you get such idealism in the face of a very flawed society? How did you maintain it?

God, Israel, and Torah are the first precepts you declare, and, in one way or another, they permeate every sermon thereafter. It's both enriching and depressing to note, once again, how your sermon is as apt today as it was in the 1930s.

Blessings.
Yesh

5. In Search of a Home

October 20, 1939

Even as he expresses certain fears, my father remains optimistic about the fate of European Jewish refugees. He admires President Roosevelt's humanitarian stance, although some historians would argue that Roosevelt's actions did not support that conclusion. Remarkably, my father makes about as strong a case for a new Jewish homeland in Alaska as he does for one in Palestine. Perhaps the most chilling aspect of this sermon is that in 1939, without the historical perspective we have today, my father needed to consider how refugees might be handled should Germany prevail.

...and even if Hitler is victorious, there still will have to be some settlement of the problem....

THIS WEEK IN WASHINGTON, PRESIDENT ROOSEVELT has furnished us with additional evidence, if such be necessary, of his broad humanitarian spirit. For at the call of the President, there is now in session at the nation's capital the meeting of the intergovernmental committee on refugees. This meeting had been planned for some time, and is, indeed, the outgrowth of another such gathering, also initiated by the president, at Évian, France about fifteen months ago. Due to the war conditions now prevailing, it was considered possible that the great powers, in their preoccupation with the tasks of war, would abandon their attempts to deal with the problems of the refugee and concentrate their energies solely on fighting the enemy. However, Roosevelt persisted in his original purpose of holding such a meeting. As a result, the committee, which is representative of thirty-two nations, is now in session and is searching for new homes for Europe's afflicted wanderers.[35]

---

[35] The Évian Conference was convened at the initiative of President Franklin D. Roosevelt in July 1938 to "discuss the increasing numbers of Jewish refugees fleeing Nazi persecution." Representatives from 32

The thought of such a gathering fills us at the same time both with hope and with despair. When we think of thirty-two nations consulting together at the call of the President of the United States, we feel that at last the conscience of the world is at work and something will be done. Out of such deliberations surely some plan will be evolved which will bring relief. But on the other hand, when we think of the problem itself, when we think of how much more acute the situation becomes day by day and how little the last conference accomplished, we begin to fear that the task is an impossible one. It is no longer a problem of caring for a few political refugees who must be transported from one place of danger to another of safety; it is rather the problem of a whole world in upheaval, and it can no longer be dealt with as if it were an isolated matter.

Just a few months ago, the task was the comparatively simple one of resettling from two to three hundred thousand unfortunate people, who were for the most part young and healthy and who could go out to a new land and work, reestablish themselves, and make a contribution to the welfare of the country which adopted them. But since the outbreak of the war, the number of the afflicted has been increased to millions, and the question of emigration has become a secondary aspect of the refugee problem. The situation is further complicated by the necessity of providing hundreds of thousands—old and young, strong and weak—with their daily bread.

Ironically enough, in a certain sense the cruelties of the war have lessened rather than increased the immediate difficulties of this particular refugee committee. Previously, the major problem was emigration from German territories—how to evacuate as quickly as possible the thousands who found life under Nazi domination intolerable. As German aggression advanced, the problem naturally became ever greater and the number to be helped increased. But now, for the present at least, most of the committee will find it impossible even to try to help most of those who are suffering under German rule as well as those Jews who are now in any other part of what was formerly Polish territory. For Hitler, now that the war is on, is unwilling to let Jews leave, while of course Stalin never has permitted anyone, Jew or non-Jew, to leave Russian soil. Hitler must conserve his manpower for the struggle that is coming, and Jewish labor, formerly despised, is now a welcome addition to his ranks. And so in Germany today, in the manner of Egypt of old, Jews are enslaved by the government, the able-bodied condemned to work in the war

---

countries met at Évian-les-Bains, France. Since both the United States and Britain refused to take in substantial numbers of Jewish refugees, the conference was ultimately seen as a failure by Jews and their sympathizers; and in fact, thousands of Europeans Jews were denied escape and ultimately became victims of Hitler's genocide. Wikipedia contributors. "Évian Conference." *Wikipedia, The Free Encyclopedia.* Wikipedia, The Free Encyclopedia, 19 Sep. 2017. Web. 19 Sep. 2017.

industries plants, while the remainder given all manner of other shameful tasks to perform. Stalin will, of course, now subject his new people to the process of Communist enlightenment, and God help those who fail to enlighten quickly enough in accordance with Communist principles. And so, much of the committee's problem is solved. At present, there is no need for new homes for Polish and German Jews who are still in their native lands, because it is now impossible for them to leave their old ones.

But in spite of these hundreds of thousands who are hopelessly trapped for the time being and for whom nothing can be done, there are nevertheless many thousands who have escaped to Romania, Hungary, and the Baltic regions. There are still many thousands who are wandering about in western countries, both war countries and neutral ones, who have only temporary visas and have not yet found a permanent home. These people are in need of immediate relief, and for them, the governments of the world must act quickly.

But what can they do and to what lands can they look for help? Throughout the civilized world, in spite of expressions of sympathy, governments have, because of their own internal problems, raised higher and higher the restrictions on immigration, and as the problem grows greater, the world seems to grow smaller, and the prospects for immigration diminish. It is for this reason that so many wild and undeveloped lands have been suggested as cities of refuge. We have been hearing Ceylon, and Tanganyika, and Rhodesia, and Madagascar, and other such places suggested as the solution to the problem, but before any large-scale immigration to these places could be hoped for, millions of dollars would have to be spent and years of labor put in, until these wastelands were sufficiently developed. Unfortunately, most of those who need these places cannot wait so long. By the time all the necessary experiments were made and surveys conducted, the problem would solve itself in quite another way. There would not be many left to immigrate.

The situation, however, is not altogether hopeless, and there are at least two places to which the committee should give maximum attention. The first and more important of these is Palestine. Before the last conference at Évian, it was agreed that Palestine was by no means to be considered; it was not in any way to enter into the discussion. However, a conference on refugees that refuses to take Palestine into consideration is a vain conference, because at the present time, the only land that seems to be ready and willing to absorb refugees in any great number is Palestine. The population of that land today is slightly over a million, but the possibility of Palestine supporting several millions of people has long ago been shown by experts.³⁶ The only bar to immigration in Palestine has been the perfidious policy of the British and the supposedly insuperable difficulties with the Arabs. Today, however, the war, unfortunate in so many respects, at least has the silver lining that the British need manpower in Palestine and are now in a mood to make concessions with regard to immigration. Only a short time ago, the British White Paper limited drastically all further Jewish immigration; and then because of the great amount of illegal immigration which resulted, it stopped immigration altogether for a period of six months from the first of this month to next March.³⁷ Although the British attitude officially remains unchanged, unofficially, illegal immigration now is being ignored, boats are allowed to land their passengers in spite of their illegal status, and the British consul in Trieste is reported even to have granted visas to over three thousand people. If the intergovernmental committee can persuade Great Britain to change its policy openly and officially so that full advantage may be taken of the possibilities that Palestine offers, it will have rendered a great service to the cause.

As for the trouble between the Arabs and the Jews, that, too, seems now to have completely disappeared. The past month has been one of almost complete peace. There are [?] Arabs willing to sell land to Jews again [?] considerable proportions [?]. It would seem that with Great Britain distracted by the war, the Arabs could seize the opportunity to stir up a lot of trouble and win many concessions from Great Britain to keep them quiet. Strangely enough, they have not done so, and the reason may well be that since all German diplomats have had to leave English territory and all other German citizens have been interned, there no longer has been any one around to spread German propaganda inciting the Arabs. And similarly, the Italians, due to their uncertain position in the war, have had to temper their propaganda activities. The present peaceful attitude may be due to these facts, and if so, they point to the possibility of lasting Arab/Jewish peace to follow—a peace of which advantage must be taken.

---

36 Various sources provide differing data on the population of Israel in 1939. According to www.populstat.info, the population of Palestine in 1939 was 1.46 million. Regardless, history has borne out the hypothesis that the land could support multiple millions of people, inasmuch as the 2010 census has the population of Israel greater than 7.5 million, according to the Israeli Central Bureau of Statistics.

37 "*The White Paper of 1939* was a policy paper issued by the British government under Prime Minister Neville Chamberlain." It proposed creating an independent Palestine governed by Palestinian Arabs and Jews in proportion to their numbers in the 1939 population. A limit of 75,000 Jewish immigrants was set for the five-year period of 1940–1944, consisting of a regular yearly quota of 10,000 and a supplementary quota of 25,000, spread out over the same period, to cover refugee emergencies. After this cut-off date, further immigration would depend on the permission of the Arab majority. Restrictions were also placed on the rights of Jews to buy land from Arabs. Wikipedia contributors. "White Paper of 1939." *Wikipedia, The Free Encyclopedia*. Wikipedia, The Free Encyclopedia, 10 Aug. 2017. Web. 19 Sep. 2017.

The second great opportunity for the committee to be of service is in Alaska.[38] This country is not immediately prepared to do as much as Palestine, but its development could be carried on much more quickly and it is a much more certain project than any of the other distant places that have been mentioned. Secretary of the Interior Ickes has already mentioned the possibilities of Alaska as a refuge for the oppressed, but as yet no action has been taken to open its doors.[39] The territory is equal to about one fifth of the United States in area, and yet its total population is only sixty thousand. The popular impression of Alaska is that it is a land of ice and snow, and that especially in the wintertime its climate is rigorous and unfavorable for large-scale settlement. But, according to reports, this conception of the country does it a grave injustice. The southern parts of the land, we are told, are actually warmer than New York and Chicago, and only three percent of the country, in the extreme north, is perpetually covered with ice. Its mineral resources and agricultural and industrial possibilities have been estimated to be sufficient to maintain not a population of thousands, such as is found there now, but rather a total of five million, if the country were to be properly developed and all its resources put to good use.[40] The only difficulty in colonizing the country thus far has been its lack of transportation facilities. An insufficient number of railroads and highways has kept prices high and made shipment of goods difficult, but while such a handicap would be too difficult for individual settlers to surmount, if the government would launch a huge settlement project, properly financed, this small handicap would be quickly overcome, and America would not only have lived up to its good name as a home for the oppressed, but would have provided itself with a new outpost for defense and a market for its goods.

In his welcoming message to the committee at a White House luncheon, President Roosevelt stated that because some of the nations are at war, at the present time, they can be asked to do little more than lend their sympathy in dealing with this problem. "Upon the neutral nations," he said, "there lies an obligation to humanity to carry on the work." It is to be hoped that Congress will take these words to heart, and at its first opportunity will, as a neutral power, fulfill this obligation to humanity by making the vast areas of the

---

38 Then a U.S. territory, admitted as the 49th state on January 3, 1959.

39 "In November 1938, two weeks after *Kristallnacht*, U.S. Secretary of the Interior Harold L. Ickes proposed the use of Alaska as a 'haven for Jewish refugees from Germany and other areas in Europe where the Jews are subjected to oppressive restrictions.'" Wikipedia contributors. "Slattery Report." *Wikipedia, The Free Encyclopedia*. Wikipedia, The Free Encyclopedia, 17 Jun. 2017. Web. 19 Sep. 2017.

40 The population of Alaska was 72,524 according to the October 1, 1939 census. In 2017, the population of Alaska is just over 741,000.

north available. If such a project were contemplated, American Jewry would be certain to cooperate, and the necessary funds would not be lacking.[41]

There is one more great service that the intergovernmental committee can render, and this not with the immediate present in mind but looking forward to the future. This is the time that must come when the war will be ended and the problem of the refugee will have to be taken up in earnest. President Roosevelt warned the committee that when the war is over, there may be

> ...not one million, but ten million or twenty million men, women, and children belonging to many races and many religions living in many countries and possibly on several continents who will enter into the wide picture of the problem of the human refugee.[42]

And this conference can now pave the way for that future. It must prepare itself to deal with whichever side is victorious and to insist that the problem of the refugee not be pushed aside in the eagerness to conclude a peace. If the Allies win, and it seems likely at least, the committee can exert a great influence and play a great role, if it is prepared with the proper suggestions. If Hitler should be victorious, there still will have to be some settlement of the problem, and the committee must be prepared to intervene and mitigate the severity of his actions.

The refugee situation is a dark one, but there is much good that the committee can do. One hope is that it will act and not merely talk. To quote the president once more,

> It is not enough to indulge in horrified humanitarianism, empty resolution, golden rhetoric and pious words. We must face it actively if the democratic principle based on respect and human dignity is to survive—if world order, which rests on the security of the individual, is to be restored.

---

[41] Although thousands of Jews had been admitted into the United States under the combined German-Austrian quota from 1938 to 1941, the U.S. did not pursue an organized and specific rescue policy for Jewish victims of Nazi Germany until early 1944. "Once the United States entered World War II, the State Department practiced stricter immigration policies out of fear that refugees could be blackmailed into working as agents for Germany." It was not until January 1944 that President Franklin D. Roosevelt, under pressure from officials in his own government and an American Jewish community then fully aware of the extent of mass murder, took action to rescue European Jews. Fariborz Ghadar, *Becoming American: Why Immigration is Good for Our Nation's Future* (New York: Rowman & Littlefield, 2014), 118.

[42] The United Nations Relief and Rehabilitation Administration was set up in 1943 to provide humanitarian relief to the huge numbers of existing and potential refugees in areas facing Allied liberation. "UNRRA provided billions of U.S. dollars of rehabilitation aid, and helped about 8 million refugees." This followed years of expulsions and exterminations affecting millions more. Wikipedia contributors. "Marshall Plan." *Wikipedia, The Free Encyclopedia*. Wikipedia, The Free Encyclopedia, 19 Sep. 2017. Web. 19 Sep. 2017.

May God grant these men the wisdom and the will to act in accord with these words spoken to them by the president, that they may truly bring a measure of comfort to a bereaved humanity.

Amen.

Dad—

This is a very dark moment in history of which you speak. I sit writing this in a time that has similar earmarks—a world in crisis and confusion, governments in turmoil, countless refugees fleeing oppression, demagogues finding their strident voices. God forbid the next few years in any way resemble what lay ahead for you.

I hear the anguish, the yearning, and yes, even the optimism in your voice as you beseech the world leaders to deal humanely with the refugees of your time. There is bitter irony in your anticipation that even in the event of a Nazi victory the fate of refugees would have to be handled—not recognizing the unimaginable horror that Hitler would perpetrate upon the Jews and all humanity even in defeat.

You also linger on the false hope that a temporary cessation of hostilities between Arab and Jew could lead to a lasting peace. Reading these hopeful musings, I get a sense of how sharp your pain must have been when these hopes were so severely dashed. We no longer live with such false optimism. We may still harbor some hope for peace and freedom in all lands, but with so little evidence today, this hope is truly tempered.

I'd like to capture your hope and optimism, and pray that the days ahead are filled with more blessings than were the years of war and horror in which you lived.

Blessings.
Yesh

6. The War and You

December 12, 1941

This sermon was delivered at an historic moment—the first Shabbat evening service after Japan's brutal attack on Pearl Harbor and the declarations of war. When confronted by the harsh reality of defending the world from totalitarianism, my father could easily have dismissed all of his youthful idealism and the pacifism he had espoused from his student pulpit in the 1930s. (See Chapter 1, *Shall We Fight Again?*) Instead, he carefully wove a multifaceted message, railing against those whose political and economic policies after the First World War had led to this conflagration, while rallying his congregants, in an hour of confusion and despair, to face the challenges ahead.

It remains for us but to keep our morale high, to keep our faith in our way of life, to keep our nerve in the face of the blustering mad men who already see the handwriting on the wall.

SINCE LAST WE MET FOR SABBATH WORSHIP, a great shock has come to our nation. As a result of a sudden and treacherous attack by the navy of Japan, and as a result of the declaration of war upon us by Germany and Italy, our government has been left with no choice but to declare war in return and to throw itself fully and actively into the world struggle which began a little over two years ago. We had felt for a long time that at some future date we, too, might find ourselves in the war. We had been preparing for such an emergency. We had already been accustomed to the sight of large numbers of men in uniform, and yet the blow, when it did come, came at such an unexpected moment and was delivered with such fury and effectiveness that Americans, in spite of all preparation, were left stunned and unbelieving.

The involvement at last of the United States brings a few troubled thoughts to our mind. We cannot help but think of the vain labor of all the peace organizations that were active in the twenties and the early thirties. We cannot help but remember the peace pledges that many of us signed as idealistic students in those days. We think of the ministers such as Stephen Wise[43] and John Haynes Holmes[44] who rose in their pulpits and condemned themselves for supporting the last war and who promised never to lend their pulpits to the support of another. We remember the idealistic propaganda that claimed laboring people all over could easily stop war by refusing to produce the materials of war. We remember the statements that war could be brought to an end easily by the simple refusal of men to bear arms. We think also of how religious institutions were condemned because they gave their blessing to those who fought. We think of these things of the past and sigh in the face of the realities of the present. We who are faced with the responsibility of leading men from the pulpit, and who have so frequently spoken of the ugliness of war, we especially are disturbed by these thoughts. What will those men say who promised never to support another war? What will happen to the pledges of yesterday? What choice do we have today? The jingoists and those who cried preparedness and opposed disarmaments will now cry, "I told you so." Are they right and all the others wrong? Are idealists all fools?

In spite of these troublesome thoughts, the fact remains that no one can withdraw from the struggle. The war is upon us and it must be supported to the full, regardless of our dreams of peace in the past. It is idle to think back over our futile efforts to have peace, but this does not mean that the jingoists who cried for more armaments were right. Not at all. The roots of this war go back to our economic and political actions after the last, and those who opposed disarmament and international cooperation are among those responsible. Regardless, however, of our lack of foresight in the past, we must face the realities of the present. We know that when a patient does not follow the proper diet, he is subject to disease; but when the disease comes, if we are interested in the life of the patient we must fight it at once, and if a major bloodletting operation is necessary, we have no choice. We can only hope that when the patient recovers, the lesson will not have been lost upon him and that he will not be so careless with himself in the future. We know now that

---

43 "Stephen Samuel Wise (born Weisz, 1874–1949) was an Austro-Hungarian-born American Reform rabbi and Zionist leader." Wikipedia contributors. "Stephen Samuel Wise." Wikipedia, *The Free Encyclopedia*. Wikipedia, The Free Encyclopedia, 15 Sep. 2017. Web. 19 Sep. 2017.

44 "John Haynes Holmes (1879–1964) was a prominent Unitarian minister, pacifist, and co-founder of the NAACP and the ACLU. He is noted for his anti-war activism." Wikipedia contributors. "John Haynes Holmes." *Wikipedia, The Free Encyclopedia*. Wikipedia, The Free Encyclopedia, 24 Jun. 2017. Web. 19 Sep. 2017.

the wrong political diet brought on the present calamity. It could have been prevented in the beginning, but because the situation is what it is, regretfully but full-heartedly we must proceed with the operation which alone can save the patient. We can only hope that the patient will not listen to the "I told you so's" of those who helped mislead him in the first place.

When the news of the war first came to us, it was quite natural for us to become quite emotional and upset. We would scarcely have been human if it had been otherwise. But now that we have had time to absorb the shock, there are several things that we should tell ourselves. First, we must realize that we cannot continue in the same confused state of mind as we found ourselves in at the beginning. In times of emergency, there is no place for hysterical emotion. The most elementary course in first aid will teach us that when an emergency occurs, the person who gives way to weeping and wailing is of no use whatsoever and is in the way. Cool deliberate thinking is required. This does not mean we are to be indifferent to what goes on, but it does mean that our senses are to be organized for effective response to the demands of the situation. Insofar as possible and consistent with the emergency, our personal and community life must continue in a normal manner. For example, we in Columbia, like any other community, have our organizations and we make plans for their activities.[45] We should not permit ourselves to become so upset emotionally as to hinder or suspend the normal functioning of these organizations or to drop all plans for the future because of fear due to the war. To refuse to carry on is to play into the hands of the enemy. It means we are frightened and confused. It means we are filled with a spirit of defeatism, and this to the enemy is worth more than his planes and his bombs. Above all, we must not become demoralized and panicky.

The description of Congress that came over the radio during the broadcasts dealing with the various declarations of war was impressive. On Monday, when Roosevelt spoke, Congress was excited.[46] A constant hum of noise could be heard throughout the gathering until the president actually began speaking, and when he finished there was an almost hysterical applause. On Thursday, however, Congress was calm. The first flush of excitement had passed. Congress was down to business in a serious, calm manner. We must take our cue from the national legislature. Our outbursts of emotion must yield to quiet reason.

To continue to function in a normal manner, however, does not mean to overlook that we are actually in a state of emergency. We cannot hope to

---

45 This sermon was delivered at Tree of Life Congregation in Columbia, SC.
46 On Monday, December 8, 1941, President Franklin D. Roosevelt delivered an address to a Joint Session of Congress in which he famously described the previous day as "a date which will live in infamy."

remain completely unaffected by the situation. The need for defense will cause the government to call upon us all in one way or another. And even if we do not find ourselves actually in the armed forces, there will be things for us to do. War in these days is not for armies and navies alone. Total war involves the whole population, and there will no doubt be something for all of us to do. As the organization of defense proceeds, there will undoubtedly be more and more calls for service. Thus far, the radio constantly reminds us to buy defense bonds.[47] Calls have been sent out for women to report to the filter centers.[48] The Red Cross, the Volunteer Bureau of the Defense Recreation Committee, and the U.S.O. centers all need civilian help in carrying on their important task of boosting morale.[49] It is time to think of what we are going to do with ourselves. It is time to cut out the extravagances and indulgences to which we have been accustomed. We have to learn to do with less and not complain. We have to learn to conserve our energies and to stop wasting time. Idle pleasures must give way to more purposeful activity. There is a death struggle before us, and everyone must lend a hand.

In this task, we shall be strengthened by the knowledge that what we are struggling to protect is a precious heritage and is worth the effort. On December 15th, next Monday, we celebrate in this country the 150th anniversary of the Bill of Rights. For a century and a half this Bill of Rights has been the foundation and guarantee of American democracy. It has secured for every American freedom of conscience and religion. It has secured freedom of speech and of the press and of assembly. It has secured the citizens of this country against unreasonable demands by the government. It has guaranteed

---

47 "By the summer of 1940, Nazi Germany's victories over Poland, Denmark, Norway, Belgium, the Netherlands, and France brought urgency to the government discreetly preparing for possible United States involvement in World War II. Of principal concern were issues surrounding war financing. Rather than increasing taxes, Secretary of the Treasury Henry Morgenthau, Jr. preferred a voluntary loan system and began planning a national defense bond program in the fall of 1940." Series E bonds were introduced as "defense bonds," later called "war bonds" after the Japanese invasion of Pearl Harbor. Wikipedia contributors. "War bond." *Wikipedia, The Free Encyclopedia*. Wikipedia, The Free Encyclopedia, 18 Sep. 2017. Web. 19 Sep. 2017.

48 Filter centers were part of the "World War II Civil Defense program of the United States Army Air Forces to protect against air attack. 1.5 million civilian observers at 14,000 coastal observation posts used the naked eye and binoculars to search for German and Japanese aircraft. Observations were telephoned to filter centers, which forwarded authenticated reports to the Aircraft Warning Service." Wikipedia contributors. "Ground Observer Corps." *Wikipedia, The Free Encyclopedia*. Wikipedia, The Free Encyclopedia, 14 Sep. 2017. Web. 19 Sep. 2017.

49 "The United Service Organizations Inc. is a nonprofit organization that provides programs, services, and live entertainment to United States service members and their families. Since 1941, it has worked in partnership with the Department of Defense... During World War II, the USO became the G.I.s' 'home away from home' and began a tradition of entertaining the troops that continues today. The USO operates 160 centers worldwide." Wikipedia contributors. "United Service Organizations." *Wikipedia, The Free Encyclopedia*. Wikipedia, The Free Encyclopedia, 17 Sep. 2017. Web. 19 Sep. 2017.

to all fair treatment before the law. It was proclaimed to guard the dignity of every human being and to recognize his value. It was the official proclamation that government exists for the sake of the people, to protect their well-being and their interests.

To the governments of our enemies, such a bill of rights is meaningless. To them, human life is valueless. People exist only to do the bidding of the state. The whim of the state is law, and against [it], the people have no recourse. They hate freedom. And their ambition is only to enslave the world and make themselves its master. Hitler, in speaking to the Reichstag this week when he made his declaration of war against the United States, said that this struggle will determine history for centuries to come.[50] This is perhaps the only truth he has ever spoken. History *will* be determined for centuries to come. This struggle will determine whether man will have a chance to continue to develop his democratic institutions and continue the type of government that cherishes a Bill of Rights, or submit as a slave to a master state and the rule of brute force. Lincoln once said the Union could not exist half free and half slave. The same is true of the world today. It is either Hitler's way or ours. There is no compromise. And if it is his way that wins out, the law of the jungle will be the only law and everything that gives life dignity and beauty will be destroyed.

Fortunately, though the situation is serious, it is not hopeless. We have the resources to win. We may accept the word of our president that the outcome is not in doubt. The blow against us is but the desperate struggle of a cornered rat, and though it may take time to kill the rat, his fate is sealed. It remains for us but to keep our morale high, to keep our faith in our way of life, to keep our nerve in the face of the blustering mad men who already see the handwriting on the wall.

The prayer of the chaplain in Congress yesterday was a beautiful thing. It was stirring, inspiring and full of faith. In it, he quoted the psalmist who said, "Though weeping may tarry for the night, joy cometh in the morning."[51] Let us gird ourselves to endure the weeping of the night, but let us look forward hopefully, optimistically, and with faith to the joy that will come with the morning.

Amen.

---

50 *Reichstag* is a German word which in political terms means "Parliament."
51 Psalm 30:5.

Dad—

What you saw in your lifetime! From a recollection of the first Armistice Day, the fervent desire for a peaceful world, to the bombing of Pearl Harbor and the abrupt awakening from that dream. You entered World War II with sadness, yet you were calm and resolute. You framed it as a worthy struggle to protect "a precious heritage," much as you describe our obligation as Jews. You must have truly been seen as the pastor of your flock, even as a man not yet 30 years old. You exhibited strength and clarity and the kind of courage that I'm sure you drew on even more deeply when you tended your flock of soldiers in North Africa during your tour of duty.

Now, of course, much too late, I wish we had spoken more of these times and what they meant to you. I suspect, given your quiet humility, you would have significantly understated your contribution to the effort and the honor you brought to your Army Air Force uniform.

Blessings.
Yesh

6. The War and You—1941

D-DAY PRAYER
KEESLER ARMY AIRFIELD BILOXI, MISSISSIPPI. JUNE 6, 1944

Let us bow our heads in prayer.

Our Heavenly Father, in Whose Hand lies the destiny of all nations! We stand before Thee at this moment, thankful that we have survived through hours of darkness, and now look hopefully toward a new day; that we have been preserved through hours of weakness, and now march unflinchingly with increasing strength. On this Day of Decision, we pray to Thee for the spiritual power with which to face the uncertainties of the future. We pray Thee to endow us with the courage to go forward bravely and the determination to press on relentlessly on whatever path our duties call us. Be with our forces who are actively engaged at this moment in overpowering the enemy. Strengthen their hand and crown them with achievement. Their task is difficult. Their peril is great. O Lord, grant them endurance and make light their afflictions.

Be with our leaders. Grant them wisdom in their decisions, and make them an inspiration to all who follow. Be with their parents and friends, who anxiously await the outcome. May their hearts be gladdened by good tidings. And those for whom there are no good tidings, may they be strengthened to accept the will of the Almighty; and may they be consoled by the unselfish devotion and heroism of their loved ones. Be with our nation and keep the will to victory strong within us. Be with our Allies and keep strong the bond between us.

Above all, our Father, we pray that all our sorrow and all our trial not be in vain. Willing we sacrifice; yet we pray that out of the fires of destruction a new and beautiful world shall emerge—a world which through its bitter experience shall have acquired a more sensitive conscience; a world to which has come a new reverence for God and a deeper love for humanity; a world which shall have wiped away the false barriers that divide men from men; a world free from oppression and tyranny and filled with justice and freedom.

Make us each conscious, O Lord, of our individual responsibility in this moment of crisis, and let us each rededicate ourselves wholeheartedly to the completion of our task. May we stand united with our fellow Americans of all backgrounds and our fellow Allies of all nations, pledged with mutual respect and trust to carry on together toward a triumphant victory and a righteous peace. O Lord, may the justice of our cause be vindicated, and may Thy blessings be upon us. May the Lord grant strength unto His people; may He bless all humanity with a speedy renewal of peace.

Amen.

United States Air Forces Chaplain, 1942-1945

6. The War and You—1941

The "1944" on the I.D. card may reflect when Ballon was deployed to North Africa.

Keesler Army Airfield, Biloxi, Mississippi, 1943

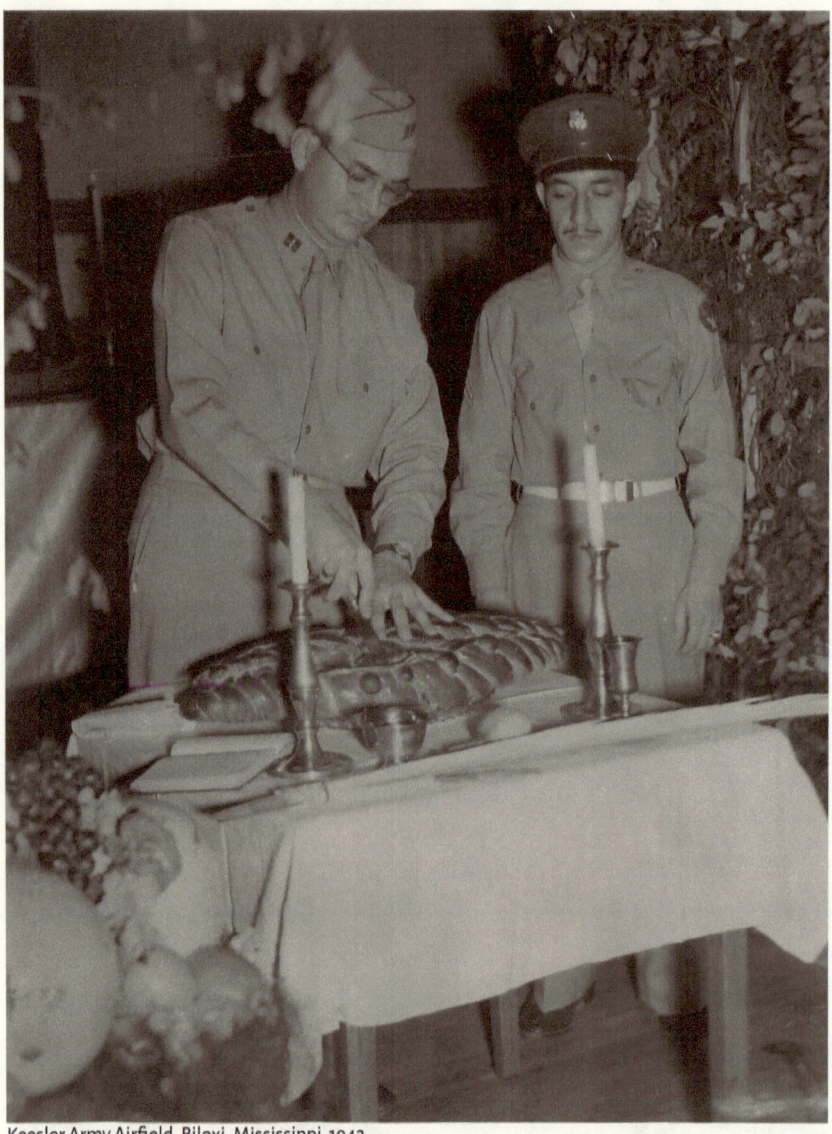

Keesler Army Airfield, Biloxi, Mississippi, 1943

6. The War and You — 1941

Deployment in North Africa, 1944-45

A Precious Heritage

7. Thanksgiving

November 22, 1944

This pre-Thanksgiving talk, probably delivered somewhere in North Africa, extols the virtues and accomplishments of the United States. It is from an era before it had come to our national consciousness that conquering the indigenous people and the natural environment of this vast continent was anything but a good thing. Twenty-first-century hindsight gives us the perspective to recognize that the liberties that Sidney Ballon cherished were denied to the Native Americans, who, unlike their conquerors, found their spiritual sustenance in the very earth, water, and skies that the settlers and pioneers sullied with their exploitation. Furthermore, although my father says, "Our families have not been forced to evacuate their homes," we now know, sadly, that that was not true for all Americans: more than 100,000 Japanese Americans were interned during the war. Nonetheless, given the time in which he spoke, these are words filled with gratitude, idealism, and hope for better times ahead.

There is then so much for which we can be truly grateful at this time. There are so many blessings that are ours. But... blessings also imply responsibilities.

DURING THE COMING WEEK, WE AMERICANS WILL celebrate a festival that is uniquely our own, the festival of Thanksgiving.[52] The festivals of a people give clues to its national character, and the fact that there exists such a one as Thanksgiving is, I believe, a credit to our nation. The spirit of humility that it reflects is in striking contrast to the arrogance of our enemies, who set

---

[52] I suspect Dad was speaking to a multi-religious gathering. Had he been addressing a Jewish group, it's hard to imagine that he would have failed to mention that the pilgrims modeled the first Thanksgiving after the Jewish festival of Sukkot, a celebration of the fall harvest. Hence, it cannot be said that Thanksgiving is a uniquely American event.

themselves up as the master race and hold the rest of the world in contempt. The sense of dependence on the Divine that it expresses is indicative of a people with soundness of character and goodness of heart.

The keynote of this Day of Thanksgiving is perhaps best expressed by the opening verse of the Psalm that was read just a few minutes ago. "It is good to give thanks unto the Lord," says the psalmist, "and to sing praises unto Thy name! O Most High!"[53] That was the feeling of the Pilgrim Fathers when they proclaimed the very first Day of Thanksgiving over three centuries ago, and that also was the feeling of the various presidents of our country when they were moved to declare a similar celebration annually.[54] It is, indeed, good to give thanks unto the Lord, because in so doing we come to take notice of blessings previously taken for granted or overlooked completely. It is good to give thanks unto the Lord, because in counting our blessings, we are led also to consider the responsibilities they bring us.

The peculiar circumstances in which we find ourselves at this time might tend to make us a bit cynical. Well may we be tempted to ask, "What have we to be thankful for so far away from home? What has anybody to be thankful for in a world fighting a war which moves so slowly?" Therefore *it is good* for us to pause a moment and think, to see why there is so much for which we, particularly as Americans, can be so truly grateful.

We must render our thanks for the great material resources that have been at the disposal of our nation. When the Pilgrim Fathers first came to those shores, they were confronted with a hostile wilderness and unknown terrors. They were compelled to exert their mightiest effort to wrest from their environment merely the bare necessities of life. But the courage and ingenuity of our pioneers pushed back the frontiers from the Atlantic to the Pacific. The continent was spanned by railroads and pathways created in the air. The rivers, forests, and plains have yielded their wealth. The hidden treasures of the earth have been uncovered and great industries established. And these great resources of our nation are proving to be the salvation of the world and the guarantors of our victory.

Not only do we have great material wealth for which to be thankful, but a great spiritual heritage as well. Great ideals have been envisioned in our land. Great principles have been proclaimed. Great traditions established. The Pilgrim Fathers came in quest for freedom. The Revolutionary Fathers wrote

---

53 Psalm 92:2.

54 In 1789, President George Washington "issued a proclamation naming Thursday, November 26, 1789 as a 'Day of Publick Thanksgivin [sic].' Subsequent presidents issued Thanksgiving Proclamations, but the dates and even months of the celebrations varied. It wasn't until 1941 that Congress passed a joint resolution declaring the fourth Thursday in November to be the Federal Thanksgiving Day." https://www.archives.gov/legislative/features/thanksgiving. Accessed 19 Sep. 2017.

7. Thanksgiving —1941

this freedom into the very foundation of our government. They proclaimed to the world the self-evidence of the truth that: "...all men are created equal and endowed by their Creator with certain unalienable rights, that among these are life, liberty, and the pursuit of happiness." This has been a cherished fundamental of Americanism ever since, and has been the cornerstone of a political heritage which is the finest the world has ever seen.

And we can, furthermore, be thankful that even though we are a nation at war, compared to others, we have suffered so little. We have been spared the brutal bombing of our own cities. Our families have not been forced to evacuate their homes. We have not had to fight an enemy beating at our very gates. We have been spared hunger and devastation. We may not be home for Thanksgiving, but we can be thankful that this is because there is no fighting to be done at home. In a world of distress, we may be thankful that our nation is so fortunate as to be able to help others rather than be dependent on help itself.

There is then so much for which we can be truly grateful at this time. There are so many blessings that are ours. But as was indicated earlier, blessings also imply responsibilities. First among these is the obligation upon all of us to continue strong in the defense of our nation and to give our best to the task of bringing the war to a successful conclusion. Not all of us are called upon to give alike in this effort, but to each one of us there falls some task, and though we may become restive at times, each one of us is duty-bound to perform devotedly whatever falls to his lot.

Our second obligation is to preserve our heritage of freedom, not only by defending it with arms against our external enemies, but also by defending it against the less obvious dangers from within. Winning the war will not in itself guarantee the preservation of our freedoms, for unfortunately there are some among our own people who for selfish reasons are not averse to stirring up prejudices and fomenting hatreds—religious, racial, or industrial in nature. Especially when the war is over, they may take advantage of the relaxed vigilance of our people to spread their perverse teaching. We must always be on the alert against such doctrine, now and when we return, always on guard against those who act contrary to the spirit of our democracy, and always zealous to continue and extend its blessings.

And a final responsibility that will be ours as Americans, will be to lead the world in building and maintaining a sensible, just and enduring peace. Some time ago, in a speech entitled *Why God Made America*, Vice-president Wallace said:

> And if America is a chosen land, it is not for her sake that she is chosen of the Lord at a certain stage of world history, but for the sake of all the world.

> *We appreciate all that has come to us out of the past, but we insist that it be transformed into a greater hope for the future, into something which Europe and Africa and Asia will welcome as their brightest hope to come.*[55]

It will be to America that the harassed nations of the world will look for intelligent leadership when this war is over. We failed the world last time, but this time, profiting by our experience, we must put aside the spirit of selfishness and do what we did not do before: strive to create a world that is economically, politically, and spiritually sound. In this same speech, Mr. Wallace goes on to quote the prophet Malachi:

> *For behold the day cometh that shall burn as an oven, and all the proud, yea, and all that do wickedly shall be stubble: and the day that cometh shall burn them up, saith the Lord of hosts, that it shall leave neither root nor branch. But unto you that feareth my name shall the sun of righteousness arise with healing in its wings.*[56]

And he continues:

> *America, without pride of race, but with complete tolerance and great power, can be that sun of righteousness with healing in its wings. America can establish the time of truly great peace based on justice to all the peoples.*

This is, indeed, the expression of a great spiritual challenge that we must be prepared to accept.

At this time of Thanksgiving, we all join in worship and give thanks to the God who is the Father of all men, and as we do so, we must likewise resolve that we shall not falter in the service of our nation and in fulfilling the responsibilities which history has placed upon her, that in harmony and unity with all our fellow Americans we shall bend our efforts to the maintenance of that great hope that the sun of our America will always be the sun of righteousness and that the sun will always rise with healing on its wing.

Amen.

---

55 "Henry Agard Wallace (1888–1965) was the 33rd Vice President of the United States (1941–1945)." Wikipedia contributors. "Henry A. Wallace." *Wikipedia, The Free Encyclopedia*. Wikipedia, The Free Encyclopedia, 17 Sep. 2017. Web. 19 Sep. 2017.

56 Malachi 3:19-20.

7. Thanksgiving —1941

Dad—

You were a true patriot, before patriotism became partisanized and fell out of favor among certain segments of the population. I admire your love of country and the principles upon which it was founded, and the clarity you have fighting to preserve it. At the same time, you were not blinded to the challenges our democracy faces internally as well—from those who polarize and exploit fears of our differences. Once again, these are concerns that sadly we still face today.

Thank you for your vision of and your prayers for a better America.

Blessings.
Yesh

8. An Ethical Will
March 26, 1948

My heart skipped a beat when I read the opening lines of this 1948 sermon—my father's farewell remarks to Tree of Life Congregation of Columbia, South Carolina, given as he departed to his next pulpit in Lexington, Kentucky. I had written my ethical will and shared it with my family and friends only a short time before reading this sermon. The concept of an ethical will had never been discussed when I was young, so I was delighted to learn that my father shared my enthusiasm for providing one, and had written this sermon to be his own ethical will. While I consider this book and, for that matter, the entire archives of his sermons as his ethical, spiritual and intellectual legacy, this sermon stands out in this regard.

The thesis herein is what it takes to be a "good Jew." There is something about my father's use of the terms "good Jew," "real Jew," and "loyal Jew" which may seem a bit jarring in an age of ecumenism and political correctness. Nonetheless, the gist of the message is cogent and enduring.

He closes with what he refers to as "a word of caution." This stirring conclusion in many ways could have been his epitaph, his ethical will condensed into two words: "Carry on!"

Build your new temple and fill it with your prayers and with your love. And carry on for your sake and for your children's sake and for the sake of all Israel.

MY DEAR FRIENDS: DURING THE MIDDLE AGES IT WAS THE CUSTOM for dying fathers to leave their children not only a will disposing of the physical assets of the parent, but also something called an ethical will, in which the parent offered to his offspring some advice with regard to their future behavior and some thoughts about life in general. There have been preserved for us a number of such documents with very fine and profound material dealing with ethical and moral questions. A departing rabbi, I believe, is likewise expected to leave some profound last words, an ethical will, to his congregation. I do not expect to be very profound. The mood of last night's delightful get-together with its pleasant and light touch is still with me, and it would be difficult to get profound even if I were able. But if they will not be profound last words, they unfortunately must at least be last words, and they should be somewhat serious words because the task in which we have been cooperating these past few years is a serious task and the situation that confronts Jewish life today is a serious one.

I thought back over the few years since I first came here, and thought of what I had to say that first time that I spoke to you. I found that my message then was on how to draw comfort and how to face the world in the midst of the serious problems confronting the Jew in that time. It was 1939, just before the war in Europe, and the crescendo of hate and fury against our people was mounting. Today, my friends, after fighting a war, a second war to preserve the world and save human decency, it is saddening to note that Jewish troubles are not over, that war has served only to put six million Jews out of their misery, and it has taken from us the sanguine pre-war hopes for redemption and salvation. The struggle is on, and although there was a faint gleam in the sky, the dawn has not yet come. These critical times make it all the more difficult for a rabbi to prescribe for his people, for even the rabbi of today is troubled and faced with uncertainties before the difficulties of the moment.

But there are one or two traits of Jewish character that I would call to your attention on such an occasion as this. These traits, I believe, mark the good Jew today without regard to the particular brand of Judaism he espouses or the particular solution he may have in mind for Jewish problems and [these should not be controversial in nature]. And so I say to you that to be a good Jew in these days, our first consideration must be to have a love of fellow Jews. I came across a new poem recently written by Rabbi Louis Newman of New York that I think expresses this perfectly, and I will read it to you.[57] It is entitled, "When I Shall Die," and he says:

When I shall die, may I win praise or blame
As one who little prized an honored name

---

57 Louis Israel Newman (1893–1972) was the rabbi of Temple Rodef Shalom in New York City from 1930 until retirement. Newman was also a poet and a playwright, composing numerous plays and cantatas.

8. An Ethical Will—1948

For deeds he wrought within the market place
Which pleased the fancies of the populace.

But I demand that men shall give me due
As one who loved his anguished fellow-Jew
Who tilled a plot of scorned forsaken earth
And helped it give eternal harvest birth.

As one who loved his anguished fellow-Jew—this is one of the prime requisites today of the real Jew. No man today can call himself a loyal Jew unless he feels and feels deeply the plight of his co-religionists abroad, unless he has been shaken and quivers within himself at the fate of world Jewry these past few years and at the gigantic hoax and betrayal that have been perpetrated upon Israel at present. He who does not respond to the plea of the hour, whether it be through the United Jewish Appeal or some other way of indicating one's sympathy and indignation, has ice water in his veins and not Jewish blood.

A second trait of Jewish character that comes to my mind is this—and I hope that I can make it understood because I am afraid that it is more of an emotional feeling rather than a clearly defined trait of character. The good Jew and the loyal Jew should have a sense of identification with the sweep of Jewish history as it has traversed the centuries. The good Jew does not conceive of himself as an isolated individual living in the twentieth century and confining his interests to this particular period of world history. The good Jew feels strongly his roots in dim antiquity. He cherishes deeply his ancestry going back to the days of Abraham, and there is pictured vividly in his mind the story of his people as they came into and departed from Egypt, as they went into the land of Canaan and gave birth to the ideals of the western world, and as they studied and taught and suffered and hoped through the many centuries in many lands down to this very day. He feels this as a part of his personal experience. He is entranced by the destiny of Israel and feels himself as a part of that destiny. And he looks not only at the past but ahead into the dim future, and although darkness prevails at the moment, he is confident and he is essentially an optimist as to the outcome. With all his heart and soul, he believes that "they that sow in tears shall reap in joy,"[58] that sorrow shall be turned into gladness and mourning into a good day as the Book of Esther has it.[59]

Thirdly, we here in this country, if we are good and loyal Jews, need a sense of obligation for American Jewry as a whole. We need an appreciation of the destiny of the Jews in this country. If we are aware of Jewish history, we

---

58 Psalm 126:5.

59 Esther 9:22.

know that there has been one center after another in the lands of dispersion that have nourished and maintained the Jewish faith. We have had Babylon and North Africa, and Spain and Poland, and others, and each in its turn on the stage of history has played a heroic role in the life of our people and been the center of culture and faith. It is now American Jewry that must carry the torch and accept the responsibility. We are now numerically the strongest and financially the soundest and have a great role to play in the history of the Jew, even with a Jewish center in Palestine, and the loyal American Jew senses the challenge. He supports those institutions of learning which nurture Judaism, he sustains the synagogue which is the dynamo of Jewish life. There is a tendency today amongst American Jews to give their devotion and their dollars chiefly to those causes which deal with relief and defense, and to disregard to a large degree those causes which speak of the more intangible values of culture and religion. We dare not forsake these, however, for if we have a Jewish heart we must surely know that without the preservation of our culture and our faith, we shall soon lose the incentive to do other things as well. It is not only physical life that must be our interest, but our spiritual life as well, and American Jewry carries the greatest responsibility in this regard.

These are some of the chief qualities of the good Jew, things that we feel intuitively, things that are difficult to describe but which must be carefully nurtured and developed within our hearts if Jewish life is to be meaningful and strong. And as I leave these thoughts with you, I should like to add a word of caution of a more personal nature. I should like to refer to a number of remarks I have heard from good people who are my friends and who think they pay me a great compliment, but who actually leave me somewhat saddened. On several occasions, I have heard them say that now that I am leaving they will not have such great responsibilities to the synagogue, because they really had either joined or contributed or were active out of a personal sense of friendship for the rabbi. With a new rabbi, they would have no reason to continue to the same extent, or to any extent, their association with the synagogue.

My friends, I appreciate the friendship and I cherish it. But if all that I have been able to leave with you is a sense of personal friendship, then I have failed. My ministry has sought to instill in you and in all this community the qualities and feelings that I have already described to you. And if I had succeeded in this, then it would make no difference who stood in this pulpit. You would know that such a great work is above any one personality, and that such a great work must be carried on regardless of personalities. And if there is any one word which I would make my last, it is the prayer that you would not let that which we have so carefully built up together slide back. Maintain your ground here and go on further. A new man will give you new insights. You will have fresh incentive and fresh inspiration. Build your new temple and fill it with your prayers and with your love. And carry on for your sake and for your children's sake and for the sake of all Israel. I would hate to think that I have given to you these years of activity only to have these efforts go to waste. And you will be paying me much more of a tribute by carrying on your efforts than by informing me that after all, it was only for me. Carry on, I say to you as my parting wish. Carry on. Remembering always that—

> *It is a tree of life to them that lay hold of it. And all the supporters thereof are happy. And may God bless you in your endeavors.*

Amen.

Dad—

You mention your disappointment in some who approached you, saying that with your departure, they would no longer be as interested in Temple life. You demonstrate your humility by calling that a failure on your part. You ask them to make Judaism not about a particular rabbi, but about the entire Jewish people.

I pray that others read these words and take them to heart, that our people find the relevance of staying connected to the vast Jewish history, to Jews in Israel, the United States, and all lands, even as we reach out with ever greater appreciation and respect to people of all faiths.

Blessings.
Yesh

PRAYER FOR THE NEW STATE OF ISRAEL
MAY 14, 1948

Our Heavenly Father, at this historic moment when the State of Israel has been born, we pray for its success. On this day, when for the first time in many centuries the flag of Zion flies proudly in independence, we pray that it may stand. Extend Thy help and guidance onto our fellow Jews, in whose hands lie the destiny of this nation reborn. Strengthen them that they may defend themselves against those who would destroy them. Endow their leaders with wisdom that they may lead them victoriously.

Not for conquest, nor for glory has Israel entered the struggle that prevails; and not for vengeance, but only that justice may come to a suffering people, that a haven may be found for those who are beaten, that a nation may be built on the foundations of decency and the dignity of man.

Bring light, we pray Thee, to those whose minds are filled with darkness, who, in their greed, care neither for people nor for ideals, but delight only in blood and in spoils. Fill the nations of the earth with wisdom that they may aid in bringing peace to the troubled Holy Land and to all its inhabitants. And with peace with victory may the State of Israel take up its tasks in a spirit of reconciliation and with devotion to the cause of all humanity.

May the land of Israel be a source of inspiration in these times, even as it has so often been in the past. May it be the salvation of our people, and a bearer of light unto its neighbors and unto all mankind. Give us reason, O Lord, to be proud of our brethren, and may we be moved to do all within our power to grant them comfort and aid in their trial. Cause a new light to shine upon Zion and cause our eyes to behold Thy return unto Zion in mercy and in peace.

Amen.

8. An Ethical Will — 1948

Temple Adath Israel, Lexington, Kentucky, c. 1948

201 Woodspoint Road, Lexington, Kentucky. Left to right: Sidney, Martha (Muff), Doug (Yesh), Jean, Jeff, c. 1949

Vacationing on Pawleys Island, South Carolina, 1950

9. Israel: First Anniversary

May 13, 1949

It's fascinating and sad to look at the early days of Israeli statehood and recognize the seeds of decades of discontent and violence. The first footnote describes the work of the American Council for Judaism, which advocated for a joint Jewish-Arab state rather than dispossessing the Arabs. One can only wonder whether much strife might have been avoided had that approach been taken.

The problem of the Arab refugees is also a pressing one for Israel... Israel did not create the problem, yet it must concern itself with the problem... since it is a question of relieving the distress of thousands of Arabs, whose co-religionists care little about them.

JEWRY THROUGHOUT THE WORLD HAS BEEN CELEBRATING these past few days. Jewry throughout the world has joined with Israeli Jewry in celebrating the first anniversary of the State of Israel. The Congress of the United States halted for two hours of speeches. Even the American Council for Judaism saw fit to publish greetings to the new State of Israel in Cincinnati's *The American Israelite*, and to wish life, liberty, and happiness to the Israelis.[60] This anniversary has indeed been an occasion for rejoicing. A year ago, when Israel was first proclaimed, there was also great joy—but it was joy tempered with uncertainty. Arab armies were on the march. The confidence and determination of Israel were strong, but the outcome had not been fully determined. Though we did not let ourselves think of it, there was nevertheless the possibility of disaster. Suppose the vast Arab hordes would prove to be

---

60 "*The American Israelite* is a Jewish weekly newspaper published in Cincinnati, Ohio. It was founded in 1854 as *The Israelite* and assumed its present name in 1874. It is the longest-running English-language Jewish newspaper still published in the United States." Wikipedia contributors. "The American Israelite." *Wikipedia, The Free Encyclopedia*. Wikipedia, The Free Encyclopedia, 13 Feb. 2017. Web. 19 Sep. 2017.

too strong for the small, new nation. Suppose the British with some new bit of treachery would choke the life out of the new state. United Nations action was uncertain. There was confidence that all difficulties would be overcome, but there was danger. And today, Israel is on a firm foundation. The danger has been removed. How weak were the vast Arab hordes, and how little could they cope with the faith and determination of the Israelis. During the year, the United States granted Israel a loan. And to climax the matter this week, we have at last learned that Israel is recognized as a member of the United Nations. Its stability is no longer questionable. Its ability to handle itself in a mature manner and its readiness to join the charter organization whose objective is to unite the nations of the world in peace is unchallenged. This first anniversary has been a most gratifying one. One can look back over the preceding year and note that a number of significant goals have been attained.

One must not think, however, that all the problems of Israel have been solved. Israel is off to a good start, but much remains for it to wrestle with. There still remains the question of what will happen with regard to Jerusalem. There still remains the unfinished business of the Arab refugees. There still remains the problem of Jewish immigration into Israel. One reason for the delay in admitting Israel into the UN was the question of what to do with Jerusalem. Many nations did not vote for Israeli admission because they hoped to use it to gain concessions from Israel with regard to the disposal of Jerusalem. Although Jerusalem was not included in the Israeli territory in the original partition plan, the Jewish sections of Jerusalem fell into Israeli hands by virtue of military conquest. And the Israeli government, for sentimental and practical reasons, has maintained that the vast numbers of Jews who live in Jerusalem should remain under their sovereignty. When we speak of Zion, we mean [the Jerusalem Partition with, according to the pope, its] 100,000 Jews. The Catholic Church has been in the forefront of the attempt to keep Jerusalem out of the State of Israel and has openly declared its support of the [five] proposals for internationalization of the entire city. Its concern is readily understandable, since from a religious standpoint Jerusalem is equally sacred to the Christians and to Jews and, for that matter, to Moslems. The Israeli government itself is not insensitive to the religious sensibilities of other groups, and it offers a compromise that seems to be fair and should satisfy all concerned. The Israeli government wants Jerusalem to be a part of Israel, but at the same time, the Israeli government is willing to turn over to international supervision all holy places throughout Jerusalem, whether in the old city or the new. And it is willing to turn over the supervision of each holy place to the particular denomination involved, and to guarantee the security of all religious institutions.

France and the Scandinavian countries also were in favor of the internationalization of Jerusalem. The Scandinavian countries, it is reported, favored it for religious reasons, but France more for political considerations. The French are smarting under the success of British political maneuvers that have eliminated them from the political scene in the Near East. The French had held mandates over Syria and Lebanon and had a foothold in the Levant; but they were eased out, and now they feel that an international regime in Jerusalem would provide them an opportunity to return to that section of the world and restore their influence.[61] This plan of the French, however, not only is contrary to Israeli interests, but also to the political desires of the Turks. The Turks also want influence in Jerusalem. They want to provide the balance of power between Israel and the Arab states. Thus, they want to assume the leadership of the Arab nations which Egypt has now lost in her defeat. Consequently, the French have little hope of being successful. The fact that Israel has been admitted to the UN and that such admission can no longer be used as a bargaining item seems to foretell that a compromise will be effected and that there will be no general attempt to withhold Jerusalem as a whole from being included in the State of Israel.

The problem of the Arab refugees is also a pressing one for Israel. It is a problem for which Israel cannot be blamed. Israel did not create the problem. Yet, it must concern itself with the problem since from a practical standpoint, it involves its relationships with the Arabs, and since it is a question of relieving the distress of thousands of Arabs whose co-religionists care little about them. Weizmann feels that only a comparatively few can be repatriated into Israel, and that these few must be carefully screened.[62] He fears the renewal of old strife and new group problems. It is estimated that over 400,000 Arabs fled while about 80,000 remained. Those who remain have been absorbed into the State of Israel with full citizenship and have three representatives in the Israeli parliament. Those who fled had been urged to remain, but were incited by Arab leaders and British officers to flee. In only a few weeks, they

---

[61] "The Levant is an approximate historical geographical term referring to a large area in the eastern Mediterranean... In its widest historical sense, the Levant included all of the eastern Mediterranean with its islands; that is, it included all of the countries along the eastern Mediterranean shores, extending from Greece to the eastern coastal region of Libya once known as Cyrenaica... The term Levant derives from the Italian *levante*, meaning "rising," implying the rising of the sun in the east." Wikipedia contributors. "Levant." *Wikipedia, The Free Encyclopedia*. Wikipedia, The Free Encyclopedia, 27 Aug. 2017. Web. 19 Sep. 2017.

[62] Chaim Azriel Weizmann (1874–1952) served as the first President of Israel from 1949 until his death. He "convinced the United States government to recognize the newly formed state of Israel." Wikipedia contributors. "Chaim Weizmann." *Wikipedia, The Free Encyclopedia*. Wikipedia, The Free Encyclopedia, 18 Sep. 2017. Web. 19 Sep. 2017.

were led to believe, they would be able to return to reclaim their property and to divide Jewish property as their spoil.

Suggestions have been made—we do not know how seriously— that they be exchanged for Jews in Arab countries who at present cannot emigrate, or that many of these Arabs be resettled in Iraq in the Tigris Euphrates Valley, the traditional site of the Garden of Eden. Others feel it depends on general boundary solutions.

The reabsorption of Arab refugees is further aggravated by the needs of absorbing so many thousands of Jewish immigrants who are pouring into Israel now at the rate of 25,000 a month. The rate of Jewish immigration into Israel would be comparable to 40 million immigrants coming into the United States within one year, so great an increase in percentage of the population does the present immigration represent. This is perhaps the greatest problem that Israel faces now on its first anniversary: the task of sheltering and rehabilitating the vast numbers who have been suddenly released from the camps of Germany, who come from Arab countries when they can get away, and who have fled the Soviet-dominated nations, whose policy on Jewish emigration is vacillating (soon, they may be forbidden altogether to leave these countries).

The threat has been uttered that Israel may have to close its doors to further immigration for awhile. This might seem like a breach of faith on the part of the Israelis, who have heretofore maintained that all Jews have a right to enter Israel. But we can be certain from their previous record and from what is happening now that it would not be a breach of faith if this were done. It would simply indicate how tremendous is their problem. They need not have fought the war if they did not want this immigration. They need not have let themselves in for the very strict rationing that has just been instituted there if they did not want this immigration. They need not be paying the tremendous income taxes that exceed ours by far if they did not want this immigration. And if immigration is ever shut off, you may be sure it is because the magnitude of the problem of housing and providing food and employment is overwhelming them and threatening the State of Israel with bankruptcy. Immigrants today, we have heard, are arriving so fast that they must remain on their ships for a number of days prior to being debarked to camps of tents. A DP camp in Israel is much better, it is true, than those in Germany or Cyprus, but the fact remains these unfortunates remain in camps for long periods of time.[63]

---

63 "A displaced persons (DP) camp is a temporary facility for displaced persons. The term is mainly used for post-World War II camps established in Germany, Austria, and Italy, primarily for refugees from Eastern Europe and for the former inmates of the Nazi German concentration camps." Wikipedia contributors. "Displaced Persons camp." *Wikipedia, The Free Encyclopedia*. Wikipedia, The Free Encyclopedia, 15 Sep. 2017. Web. 19 Sep. 2017.

9. Israel: First Anniversary—1949

The solution to this problem lies with the American Jew more than with the Israeli. We have been tired of the large quotas asked for in the past by the UJA, but the UJA is the only means of a quick solution to the new problems of the DPs.[64] Some of us thought that now that Israel is free and open, we would be free of these urgent pleas and requests for funds. The creation of Israel did hasten the end and the urgency of these pleas, but though the end is in sight, it has not yet quite come.

[Here there is a notation to suggest that he inserted a story from the war, which is not recorded on this page.]

Thus, the first anniversary of Israel is a joyous occasion. It points the way to a bright future. But there are problems that remain, and together with our joy in this moment, let us also pour forth our prayer that the second anniversary will see the problems of this year considerably improved. Just as this year is a vast improvement over the period of life and death struggle of last year, so may we during the coming year continue to make progress and further strengthen the redemption of our people.

Amen.

---

64 "The United Jewish Appeal (UJA) was a Jewish philanthropic umbrella organization established in 1939 to support Jews in Europe and Palestine. In 1999, it was folded into the United Jewish Communities, a merger of UJA, the Council of Jewish Federations and the United Israel Appeal, Inc." Wikipedia contributors. "United Jewish Appeal." *Wikipedia, The Free Encyclopedia*. Wikipedia, The Free Encyclopedia, 17 Sep. 2017. Web. 19 Sep. 2017.

Dad—

I share your happiness. It meant so much to you that Israel, as an infant nation, survived to reach its first anniversary. How pleased you would be to know that as of this writing, Israel is on the verge of celebrating its 70th anniversary (an easy calculation since I was born only a few months before Israeli statehood).

Even in your celebration, you note that though the initial danger had been nullified, problems persist—as they do today. You hold the Jewish state blameless in the mass departure of Arabs. Many would dispute that claim. Even if we were able to wind back the clock to 1948, the truth of your assertion could not be fully substantiated to the satisfaction of all. Somehow, we need to move beyond blame. Sadly, there are still those whose power is derived from fear and blame. It is such a different world than the one you knew in 1949, and in too many ways very much the same.

> Oseh shalom bimromav, hu ya'aseh shalom aleynu,
> v'al kol Yisrael, v'al kol yosh'vei teiveil. V'imru: Amein!

> *May the one who makes peace in the heavens, make peace upon us, for all of Israel, and for all who inhabit the earth. And let us say: Amen!*

In recent years some have added to the traditional prayer for peace the clause "and for all who inhabit the earth". I'm sure that you would have readily accepted the notion that praying for Israel alone is no longer a generous or sustainable position.

Blessings.
Yesh

10. Let My People Go

January 27, 1950

The following is a strong message on civil rights offered in Lexington, Kentucky in the early days of the mid-twentieth century Civil Rights movement, a time when Kentucky, like the nation, was just tiptoeing into expanding rights for African Americans. My father uses Jewish text and Jewish principles to underpin his arguments. One can only wonder how much resistance to this message there may have been among his border state congregation in that era.

And is it not hypocrisy for men to think of themselves as being devoted to Christian and Jewish principles, and then so pointedly ignore the Golden Rule and refuse to heed the prophetic challenge, "Why do we deal treacherously every man against his brother?"

OUR TORAH PORTION FOR THIS SABBATH TELLS US of the perverseness of Pharaoh in his dealings with Moses.[65] Again and again, Moses appears before Pharaoh with the cry, "Let my people go!" Again and again, we read that Pharaoh gives promises, only to have the Bible tell us each time that Pharaoh's heart was hardened and he did not let the Children of Israel go. And each time Pharaoh changes his mind about letting the people go, he is smitten by a plague; only after ten of these horrible plagues do the Israelites finally manage to make their exodus from Egypt.

"Let my people go!" is a cry not confined to biblical times alone. "Let my people go!" is a cry that has been repeated throughout the ages by many peoples in many places, and in this very day in our own land dedicated to freedom and democracy, that cry is still heard. Most of us are aware of the

---

[65] Parashat Bo constitutes Exodus 10:1–13:16, and describes the first Passover. Wikipedia contributors. "Bo (parsha)." Wikipedia, The Free Encyclopedia. Wikipedia, The Free Encyclopedia, 23 Jul. 2017. Web. 19 Sep. 2017.

cry today, but what we so often fail to realize is that our hardness of heart in refusing to heed that cry brings with it its plagues as well. Today, we do not escape the inevitable punishment that is inflicted because of the refusal to emancipate the enslaved, any more than Pharaoh did in ancient times.

Large segments of our people are denied elementary educational opportunities, find it difficult to enter our professional schools, are discriminated against in the matters of housing and employment, are denied the basic privileges of citizenship. And so we are visited by the plagues of poverty and slums and juvenile delinquency and crime. While we need more and more research into the causes of major diseases, we're deprived of the talents of so many who want to become students of medicine. While we are so disturbed by the dangers that threaten our American way of life today, we render large numbers of our people restless and dissatisfied and make them the prey of the "isms" which are a threat to democracy. Our modern hardness of heart is no different in spirit from that of Pharaoh of old, and we suffer the same consequences. We are paying the price today, if not literally in plagues, then in dollars and cents, in human life, and in the loss of potentially productive human energy which is being permitted to go down the drain.

The stubbornness of our people is being highlighted at this very moment by the actions of Congress, which has sidetracked the legislation so sorely needed to mitigate these plagues in our midst. One of the most forward-looking steps ever taken in this country was the work of the President's Committee on Civil Rights and the report that it issued about two years ago.[66] In spite of the emphasis, however, which the President has placed upon the recommendations of this report, none of the suggested legislation has yet been enacted and the present session of Congress is also indulging in various types of parliamentary maneuvering in order to prevent these matters from even being discussed.

The report on civil rights was a lengthy one, but it may be summarized briefly as a plea for the right of safety and security of the person, the right to citizenship and its privileges, the right of freedom of conscience and

---

[66] The President's Committee on Civil Rights was established by Harry Truman on December 5, 1946. In October 1947, *To Secure These Rights: The Report of the President's Committee on Civil Rights* was produced. Among other measures, the 178-page report proposed the establishment of a permanent Civil Rights Commission, a permanent fair employment practice commission, a Joint Congressional Committee on Civil Rights, and a Civil Rights Division in the Department of Justice. On July 26, 1948, President Truman ordered the desegregation of the federal work force and the armed services. He also sent a special message to Congress on February 2, 1948, to implement the Committee recommendations. Wikipedia contributors. "President's Committee on Civil Rights." *Wikipedia, The Free Encyclopedia*. Wikipedia, The Free Encyclopedia, 8 Sep. 2017. Web. 19 Sep. 2017.

expression, and the right to equality of opportunity.[67] In refusing to make an effort to achieve these goals, we belie both the Americanism of which we boast and the religion we profess, whether it be Christian or Jewish. Is it not hypocrisy to speak of Americanism when many Americans are deliberately disenfranchised? Is it not foolishness to proclaim the virtues of democracy to the Asiatic world that consists mostly of colored peoples, when on the basis of color, among other reasons, our democracy constantly practices discrimination? Washington gave us the classic phrase "to bigotry no sanction."[68] Lincoln reminded us that this nation "is dedicated to the proposition that all men are created equal."[69] How can we rejoice nationally in the birthdays of these two great men, as we shall soon do, and then completely ignore the ideals for which they stood![70]

And is it not hypocrisy for men to think of themselves as being devoted to Christian and Jewish principles, and then so pointedly ignore the Golden Rule and refuse to heed the prophetic challenge, "Why do we deal treacherously every man against his brother?"[71] Many Americans today are indeed living a lie and forget that until every vestige of hate and prejudice is removed from

---

67 "Security of the person is a basic entitlement guaranteed by the Universal Declaration of Human Rights, adopted by the United Nations in 1948... In general, the right to the security of one's person is associated with liberty," and includes various prisoners' rights. Wikipedia contributors. "Security of person." *Wikipedia, The Free Encyclopedia*. Wikipedia, The Free Encyclopedia, 25 Jul. 2017. Web. 19 Sep. 2017.

68 George Washington's August 21, 1790 letter to the Hebrew Congregation in Newport, Rhode Island is a "short but powerful statement from the first president of the United States reassuring one of the original colonial congregations that his nascent government guaranteed religious liberty for all. 'For, happily,' Washington wrote, 'the Government of the United States, which gives to bigotry no sanction, to persecution no assistance, requires only that they who live under its protection should demean themselves as good citizens in giving it on all occasions their effectual support.'" Paul Berger, "Solving the Mystery of Washington's Famous Letter,"*Forward*, 15 June 2011, forward.com/news/138689/solving-the-mystery-of-washington-s-famous-lette/. Accessed 19 Sep. 2017.

69 *The Gettysburg Address*, November 19, 1863, given at the dedication of the Soldiers' National Cemetery in Gettysburg, Pennsylvania.

70 From 1796, George Washington's birthday was celebrated on or around the 22nd. In 1968, "Congress introduced the Uniform Monday Holiday Bill in an effort to create as many long weekends as possible for U.S. workers. This law altered a handful of holidays to always fall on Monday, including moving Washington's Birthday to the third Monday in February, even though it would not fall on Washington's actual birthday." Some states also had been honoring Abraham Lincoln on his birthday, February 12, leading some to believe that the new Monday holiday was a celebration of both men. That idea had been discussed, but in fact was never enacted. On the contrary, the Washington-Lincoln Recognition Act of 2001 states that the legal public holiday Washington's Birthday shall be referred to solely as such, and that the President be requested to issue an annual proclamation recognizing President Lincoln's birthday. The Presidents Day moniker is mostly the result of commercial advertising." Tim Newcomb, "A Brief History of (What You Think Is) Presidents' Day," *Time*, 20 February 2012, time.com/3705195/presidents-day-history/. Accessed 19 Sep. 2017.

71 "Have we not all one father? Hath not one God created us? Why do we deal treacherously every man against his brother, profaning the covenant of our fathers?" (Malachi 2:10).

their hearts, or until the effect of someone else's hate and prejudice is eliminated from our community life, we are far from fulfilling either the American or the Judeo-Christian ideal.

There may be some, of course, who are opposed to civil rights legislation, who are sincere in their belief that this may not be the right way to attack the problem, however well intentioned it may seem. But for the most part, the arguments of those who oppose the civil rights legislation must be stamped as just so much witting or unwitting doubletalk.

The outstanding bit of double talk is that of states' rights. It may or may not be advisable for national legislation to enforce civil rights. It may possibly be better if each state handled the matter for itself; it may or may not be constitutional for the federal government to pass such legislation. But the test of the sincerity of states' righters is whether or not the individual states that are fighting to preserve states' rights have attempted to do anything themselves to make federal legislation unnecessary. And when we review what has happened throughout the South in recent months concerning civil rights, we can find many gains—but almost everything has had to be fought out in the federal courts and very little has been done by the states of their own accord. One of the most ironical cases of all occurred in South Carolina, where it was claimed to be a violation of the Bill of Rights to force the Democratic Party to permit Negro voting in the primary election, because the Democratic Party considered itself a private club. This would seem to be a fairly good answer to those who insist that they are all for a civil rights program, but feel obligated to protect the principle of states' rights.

It is also contended, possibly with a greater degree of sincerity, that civil rights legislation is meaningless because it is impossible to legislate people's emotions or to legislate prejudice out of existence. This must be admitted. The forces which make for prejudice in people are complex and deep-rooted and certainly cannot be wiped out with a flourish of a presidential pen. However, laws would make it clear that action against our fellow citizens based on prejudice is explicitly un-American, and would prevent the impression that our government gives such prejudiced action its tacit consent. In his book on anti-Semitism, *A Mask For Privilege*, Carey McWilliams pointed out some time ago that law can be a great weapon in the fight for tolerance.[72] Law is not a passive factor. Law is an active agent in the creation of customs and traditions. Today, law gives sanction in many cases to discrimination, and

---

72 "Carey McWilliams (1905–1980) was an American author, editor, and lawyer. He is best known for his writings about social issues in California, including the condition of migrant farm workers and the internment of Japanese Americans in concentration camps during World War II. For twenty years, he was the editor of *The Nation* magazine." Wikipedia contributors. "Carey McWilliams (journalist)." *Wikipedia, The Free Encyclopedia*. Wikipedia, The Free Encyclopedia, 3 Sep. 2017. Web. 19 Sep. 2017.

intensifies it; these are laws, McWilliams contends, that were for the most part created not by popular demand, but by unscrupulous politicians who were looking for issues with which to rouse the people, much as Hitler roused the Germans by inflaming them with anti-Semitism.

Early anti-Oriental laws in California, for example, were created not by popular demand, but by political agitation.[73] Once on the books, people were compelled to conform to these laws, and the habit of discrimination was set up and prejudice built up to a much greater degree than might otherwise have happened.[74] The Jim Crow movement in the South started in 1876, a time when the populist movement towards equality was at its peak, but the law strengthened segregation and created a pattern of conduct that taught people to be prejudiced.[75] It is McWilliams' conclusion, accordingly, that the law can be used positively as well as negatively, that sound laws can do much to raise the standard of thinking among us, even as bad laws have sometimes lowered it.

The American Jewish Congress[76] demonstrated this to some extent in a study on job discrimination in New York, where there is a state FEPC law.[77]

---

73 For American English speakers, "Oriental" has become an antiquated, pejorative, and disparaging term. Many Asian Americans in the anti-war movement in the '60s and early '70s identified the term with the Western process of racializing Asians as forever opposite "others." That distinction was not in public consciousness when this sermon was written in 1950.

74 "The California Alien Land Law of 1913 prohibited 'aliens ineligible for citizenship' from owning agricultural land or possessing long-term leases over it, but permitted leases lasting up to three years. It affected the Chinese, Indian, Japanese, and Korean immigrant farmers in California. Implicitly, the law was primarily directed at the Japanese. It passed 35 to 2 in the Senate and 72 to 3 in the Assembly... The law was meant to discourage immigration, primarily of Japanese immigrants, and to create an inhospitable climate for immigrants already living in California." Wikipedia contributors. "California Alien Land Law of 1913." *Wikipedia, The Free Encyclopedia*. Wikipedia, The Free Encyclopedia, 16 Aug. 2017. Web. 19 Sep. 2017.

75 "The origin of the phrase 'Jim Crow' has often been attributed to... a song-and-dance caricature of blacks performed by [a] white actor... in blackface, which first surfaced in 1832... As a result... [by 1838,] 'Jim Crow' had become a pejorative expression meaning 'Negro.' [When southern legislatures passed] laws of racial segregation—directed against blacks... at the end of the 19th century, they became known as Jim Crow laws." Henry Epps, *A Concise Chronicle History of the African-American People Experience in America: From Slavery to the White House!* (CreateSpace Independent Publishing Platform, 2012), 238.

76 "The American Jewish Congress, founded in 1918, is an association of Jewish Americans organized to defend Jewish interests at home and abroad through public policy advocacy, using diplomacy, legislation, and the courts. Through its emphasis on human rights for all Americans; on government protection of the weakest among us; and on a just society based on civil law and the Jewish concept of *Tzedek*—righteousness—the American Jewish Congress has made its mark on American society in general and Jewish well-being in particular." Wikipedia contributors. "American Jewish Congress." *Wikipedia, The Free Encyclopedia*. Wikipedia, The Free Encyclopedia, 2 Sep. 2017. Web. 20 Sep. 2017.

77 In 1941, President Roosevelt created the Fair Employment Practices Committee (FEPC) by an executive order, stating, "...there shall be no discrimination in the employment of workers in defense industries or government because of race, creed, color, or national origin." Wikipedia contributors. "Fair Employment

This study shows that most FEPC complaints stem from the initial refusal of the employer to conform to the law, because of previous habits he may have acquired or because of conventional patterns in the particular field of business. Once, however, employers have been compelled to cease their discrimination, they usually are satisfied with the results and make very few further attempts to get around the law. The law will not automatically cure misguided thinking, but it can be a help in establishing new habits of action and eliminating some of the evil results that a do-nothing policy has had for our minority groups.

As Jews, we are, of course, among those who stand to benefit from civil rights legislation. But whether it affects us or not, as Jews we should be expected to favor a move such as this which has the possibility of improving the standard of living for oppressed groups in our midst and of providing greater opportunities for life, liberty, and the pursuit of happiness. We could not possibly do otherwise if we take seriously the great traditions of our faith and its injunctions to love thy neighbor, to not oppress the stranger, and to remember that "ye were slaves" in Egypt. A statement issued recently by the Commission on Justice and Peace of the Central Conference of American Rabbis calls "upon our own Jewish congregants to set an example in this respect."[78] We can point with pride that often our congregations do set an example. In New Orleans a few weeks ago, one of the Reform temples was the only place in the community that would permit Dr. Bunche to address an unsegregated audience.[79] That took courage in a deep southern town like New Orleans. Nothing untoward, however, happened as a result. Perhaps others will thereby be encouraged to do likewise sometime in the future. This was certainly dealing a blow for justice and an excellent example of taking one's religion seriously. I hope that all our other congregations and congregants will measure up to this spirit in their actions. And I hope that we shall always

---

Practice Committee." *Wikipedia, The Free Encyclopedia*. Wikipedia, The Free Encyclopedia, 27 Aug. 2017. Web. 20 Sep. 2017.

78 "The Central Conference of American Rabbis (CCAR), founded in 1889 by Rabbi Isaac Mayer Wise, is the principal organization of Reform rabbis in the United States and Canada, and the largest and oldest rabbinical organization in the world." Wikipedia contributors. "Central Conference of American Rabbis." *Wikipedia, The Free Encyclopedia*. Wikipedia, The Free Encyclopedia, 23 Aug. 2017. Web. 20 Sep. 2017.

79 "Ralph Johnson Bunche (1903 or 1904–1971) was an American political scientist, academic, and diplomat who received the 1950 Nobel Peace Prize for his late 1940s mediation in Israel. He was the first African American to be so honored in the history of the prize. He was involved in the formation and administration of the United Nations. In 1963, he was awarded the Medal of Freedom by President John F. Kennedy." Wikipedia contributors. "Ralph Bunche." *Wikipedia, The Free Encyclopedia*. Wikipedia, The Free Encyclopedia, 10 Sep. 2017. Web. 20 Sep. 2017.

have in mind a thought from the Talmud with which the previously mentioned statement of the Central Conference of American Rabbis concluded:

> *The Talmud tells us that when God was ready to create the first human being, He gathered dust from every remote corner of the earth, and used the dust from everywhere to fashion Adam. This is in order that every kind and race of human being might know to the end of time that our destiny and fate are equal, even as our humble beginnings were equal.*

Dad—

I'd love to know the reaction of your Kentucky congregation to your strong statement on behalf of civil rights. I know you were unafraid to raise the subject even earlier (and further south) from your South Carolina pulpit. I also know you voted with your feet on this issue many times, including acting as a surreptitious poll inspector during your Lexington days and marching on Washington, D.C. in 1963. Bravo!

Blessings.
Yesh

West Hempstead, Long Island, New York, c. 1952

11. The Sabbath, A Reform Perspective

March 14, 1952

My father delivered this sermon shortly after arriving at the Nassau Community Temple in West Hempstead, Long Island, New York, where he spent most of his career. He offers a clear message to his new congregation about the importance of Sabbath observance. Because Reform Judaism had eliminated some traditional observances that were deemed unessential in modern times, many concluded that other fundamental rituals and commandments also had been eliminated—a common misconception that my father was addressing here. He felt it was every Jew's moral obligation to observe the Sabbath, perhaps as much to ensure the survival of Judaism as to obtain the personal benefits such observance might render the individual.

It is possible to pay tribute to the Sabbath in some fitting and joyful manner if the will to do so exists, and if we are concerned with Judaism and its future, we should have the will.

FOR OUR TORAH READING THIS EVENING we have read one of the earliest Biblical passages that deals with the Sabbath.[80] If you are at all observant, you will have noticed that the passage ends with verses which are also used as

---

[80] The weekly portion read in virtually all synagogues was *Ki Tissa*, in which God repeated the commandment regarding the sanctity of the Sabbath day: "Above all you shall keep my Sabbaths, for this is a sign between me and you throughout your generations, that you may know that I, the Lord, sanctify you" (Exodus 31:13).

part of the liturgy of the Sabbath evening service.[81] I touched upon modern Sabbath observance during our discussion of religious school matters several weeks ago, but since it is the theme of the Torah portion this evening, let us pursue it a bit further.

The Sabbath is the most important and perhaps the oldest religious observance in Jewish life. It is the only Jewish observance mentioned in the Ten Commandments, which is one of the oldest sections of the Bible.[82] It is the only day of the week that has a specific name in the Hebrew language. The other days in Hebrew are merely designated by their number in the week. And in the section read this evening and repeated on almost all Sabbaths, it is referred to as the sign of the covenant between God and Israel. In other words, Sabbath observance was the distinguishing characteristic of the faithful Jew.

I believe this ancient concept of the Sabbath still applies in large measure today. The Sabbath is a sort of barometer of Jewish life. So are a number of Jewish festivals, but none so tests Jewish sensitivities as the Sabbath. When feeling for the Sabbath is strong, the Jewish spirit is also strong. When it is weak, the Jewish spirit is also weak. Judaism without the Sabbath is a contradiction in terms. The poet Bialik called the Sabbath the cornerstone of Jewish life.[83] Achad Ha-am, the Hebrew writer, said words that may also be found in our prayer book: "Even as Israel has kept the Sabbath, so the Sabbath has kept Israel. Sabbath observance makes for Jewish survival." [84]

We have seen this in Jewish history. Jews have suffered in so many periods. The total pressure applied to Jewish life was such as could have

---

81 The reference is probably to the *V'shomru* prayer: "Thus shall the children of Israel observe the Sabbath, to make the Sabbath throughout their generations as an everlasting covenant."

82 "Remember the Sabbath day, to keep it holy. Six days shalt thou labour, and do all thy work; but the seventh day is a Sabbath unto the Lord thy God. In it, thou shalt not do any manner of work, thou, nor thy son, nor thy daughter, nor thy man-servant, nor thy maid-servant, nor thy cattle, nor thy stranger that is within thy gates; for in six days the Lord made heaven and earth, the sea, and all that in them is, and rested on the seventh day; wherefore the Lord blessed the Sabbath day, and hallowed it" (Exodus 20:8-11).

83 Chayim Nachman Bialik (1873–1934) was a "Jewish poet who wrote primarily in Hebrew but also in Yiddish. Bialik was one of the pioneers of modern Hebrew poetry" and came to be recognized as Israel's national poet. He said, "Sabbath is the cornerstone of Judaism, and it is not without cause that it is called the 'sign of the covenant' between God and the Children of Israel. In the Sabbath are enfolded many national and social concepts. If in the Ten Commandments is enfolded the whole Torah, then in the Sabbath are probably enfolded all the Ten Commandments." Wikipedia contributors. "Hayim Nahman Bialik." *Wikipedia, The Free Encyclopedia*. Wikipedia, The Free Encyclopedia, 19 Sep. 2017. Web. 20 Sep. 2017.

84 "Asher Zvi Hirsch Ginsberg (1856–1927), primarily known by his Hebrew and pen name Ahad Ha'am, was a Hebrew essayist and one of the foremost pre-state Zionist thinkers." Wikipedia contributors. "Ahad Ha'am." *Wikipedia, The Free Encyclopedia*. Wikipedia, The Free Encyclopedia, 3 Sep. 2017. Web. 20 Sep. 2017.

broken a stronger people, but Israel had a way of relieving this pressure. It was only psychological but it was effective. The change of mood and the change of pace on the Sabbath refreshed his spirit and built in him a sense of dignity, of renewed hope and faith, in a manner that could not be destroyed. He may have lived in the ghetto, bent and broken all the week, but on the Sabbath, he was a king who went forth to meet the Sabbath bride, and the sharp contrast with the rest of his existence strengthened him for the week to come.

There is a mistaken notion current among many Reform Jews that the Sabbath, as well as all other observances, is no longer very important to individual Jews, that each person is free to neglect it if he is so inclined, and that this neglect does not thereby violate the spirit of Reform Judaism. Nothing could be further from the truth. Reform Judaism has made changes in practice but not in principle. Reform Judaism has cast aside many of the Sabbath restrictions that are deemed impractical and meaningless in a modern world, but it has not cast aside the Sabbath altogether. The original spirit of the Sabbath, even with all the orthodox regulations, was a joyful one. In days gone by, even the restrictions were things joyfully observed. Today, life has changed. These restrictions tend to have an opposite effect and do not achieve the same result as in former times. Hence, Reform has made changes in order that the Jewish Sabbath not acquire the bleak and dismal characteristics of a seventeenth-century Calvinist Sunday. We do not want the Sabbath to seem forbidding and austere, and so those elements that in modern times have had that effect have been eliminated; but the things we can do to retain the sweet mystic quality of the Sabbath and keep its joyful religious overtones have been retained and improved upon in Reform Judaism. It is still the sign of the covenant between God and Israel, and the distinguishing mark of the good Jew.

Reform Judaism still recognizes the contribution that the Sabbath can make to strengthening our family life. We Jews have had a reputation for a strong home life. It is a deserved one. Jewish families that have kept close to Jewish traditions show less tendency to break than any other group. And the basic reason has been the religious observances in the home, such as the Sabbath, that have fostered a spirit of love and devotion in the home and cemented family ties. A prayer recited together with a child, a candle kindled with religious ceremony, the wine cup lifted for *Kiddush*—all create family moods and family memories that last throughout life.[85] The nostalgia of such memories also makes for a Jewish consciousness and a sense of Jewish identification that is difficult to shake off. And Reform Judaism still feels that

---

85 *Kiddush*, literally "sanctification," is a blessing recited over wine or grape juice to sanctify the Shabbat and Jewish holidays.

there is no better way to develop a joyful, positive attitude toward Judaism in ourselves and in our children than by bringing into the home some of the rich ceremonial life that is inherent in the acknowledgement of the Sabbath.

Reform Judaism also advocates synagogue attendance on the Sabbath. It still feels that living as good Jews makes necessary the quiet contemplation of Jewish values and ideals, which is what we do when we gather for prayer on Friday evenings. It helps broaden our Jewish knowledge, and, for many of us, our only source of Jewish knowledge is what we find in the synagogue. It strengthens and expresses our identification with the Jewish community, and we do draw strength and comfort from each other; otherwise, this congregation would never have been founded. And we particularly need the refreshing quiet of the sanctuary, as our prayer book words it, to offset some of the feverish activity of the rest of the week.[86]

The Jewish community in this country is suffering today from "active-itis." Organizations of all types are working at fever pitch. Committees are madly working on projects and meeting incessantly. Think of your own activities. Money for a multitude of projects is being squeezed out of the public. There is no doubt that most of this is good and necessary. But sometimes, we may well wonder whether we are not overdoing the mechanics of building Jewish organizations and are forgetting the primary goal of learning to live Jewishly ourselves as individuals. A synagogue cannot merely function as a money raising institution. The point of our projects and money raising must not be lost sight of. Our organizational activities have to be supplemented with periods of worship and study, and therefore, Sabbath worship is essential. It helps us keep things in proper perspective. In the long run, when we avail ourselves of the spiritual motivation and power that comes from the synagogue, the organizational work will also benefit and attain higher goals.

Reform Judaism also recommends a change of mood and change of pace whenever possible on the Sabbath. Reform has chosen to ignore many of the former restrictions on Sabbath activity, but it did not intend to make of the Sabbath just another day of the week. The keynote of Reform Judaism with regard to the Sabbath is change and recreation of body and spirit. In the Talmud, the Rabbis suggest the worker who spends his week in physical labor should on the Sabbath engage in the study of Torah; and the student who toils at his studies through the week should on the Sabbath seek other pleasures. These Rabbis were quite liberal in their interpretation and thus present pretty much the same point of view as Reform Judaism. Let the Sabbath be a change

---

86 *The Union Prayer Book*, 1937 edition, published by the Central Conference of American Rabbis to serve the needs of the Reform Judaism movement in the United States, was in use by Nassau Community Temple at this time.

11. The Sabbath, A Reform Perspective—1952

from the daily routine. The household activity and shopping routine of the week should be avoided. The Sabbath should be given over to things that are restful and relaxing and pleasing. There should be a touch of Jewishness in the home that ordinarily is not part of the weekday pattern. There should be a twenty-four-hour moratorium on hustle and bustle. That is the Reform prescription for the Sabbath and each one is the best judge as to how the Sabbath may best be observed by him, if he sincerely considers the question.

It is true that Sabbath observance, even in Reform manner, is at a low ebb today, and various factors in the environment tend to detract us even from considering the possibility of some Sabbath observance. But it is possible to pay tribute to the Sabbath in some fitting and joyful manner if the will to do so exists, and if we are concerned with Judaism and its future, we should have that will. Once a beginning has been made and a habit pattern established, it becomes easy from thereon.

There is a legend that two ministering angels—one good and one bad—accompany each Jew from the synagogue on each Sabbath. If the Jew comes home to a finely set Sabbath table prepared for Kiddush with Sabbath candles and if there is a good Sabbath meal waiting, the good angel says, "May the next Sabbath be also thus," and the evil angel is forced to say, "Amen." If, on the other hand, he arrives at a home with no Kiddush or Sabbath candles or Sabbath meal waiting, the evil angel says, "May the next Sabbath be also thus," and the good angel is forced to say, "Amen." It is all a matter of some slight effort and a bit of will, and we will be on our way to the fashioning of good Jewish homes which will be a source of joy and strength to us, our children, and all Israel.

Amen.

Dad—

Challah. Wine. Candles. White tablecloth. Polished *Kiddush* cups. The good china. Granny's cut glass decanter. The images linger. We were not always well behaved. Sometimes our foolish banter got under your skin. I hope you know that your most fervent wish—that our Shabbat observance make a meaningful and lasting mark on us, that we hand it down to succeeding generations, that we help perpetuate the Judaism you so fervently cherished— that all of this has come true, and that your wish is now my wish, my prayer that through my children and their children "*Am Yisrael chai*—the people of Israel live!"

Blessings.
Yesh

12. Holy, Holy, Holy

September 29, 1952

Yom Kippur Morning

In considering what holiness meant in our lives, my father, as a very rational and pragmatic person, emphasized earthly acts of goodness. He believed that by emulating God's qualities, people achieve holiness.

It is remarkable to note to what extent social ideals are involved in the Jewish concept of holiness. The primary interest of Judaism was not in the salvation of individuals in the next world, but in the individual as a member of society in this world.

LAST NIGHT, WE DISCUSSED THE MEANING of the piece of wood sculpture that hangs on the wall to my right.[87] This morning, let us think of its companion piece on the left. Both are expressive of fundamental ideals in our faith. The meaning of both should be understood by all of us. On the one side, we had *Adonoy echod*, the proclamation of the unity of God. Here we have, again in a crescendo of lettering, the proclamation of the holiness of God. Starting with a small and incomplete rendering of the Hebrew word *Kadosh/*Holy, the design rises to a climax at the top with the word *Kadosh* spelled out in dramatic fullness. *Holy, Holy, Holy* is the message of this piece, and it is something with which you should not be altogether unfamiliar, since it forms an important part of our morning services. You heard it this morning, and

---

[87] This was the second of two sermons describing art by A. Raymond Katz, "a WPA muralist, illustrator, and modernist painter especially known for paintings with Jewish themes and narrative American scene works." "Alexander Raymond Katz, Hungarian/American (1895–1974)," *RoGallery.com*. rogallery.com/Katz_A_Raymond/Katz_A_R-bio.htm. Accessed 19 Sep. 2017.

you will hear it again later in the day as part of our *Kedusha* or Sanctification, the proclamation of God's holiness.

"Holy, Holy, Holy," reads the full phrase, "is the Lord of hosts, the earth is full of his glory." This verse comes from the book of Isaiah, chapter 6, when Isaiah describes the vision where he was called by God to go and speak to the people of Israel. In his vision, Isaiah felt himself in the presence of God, surrounded by seraphim using this phrase to proclaim to each other the holiness of God. In his commentary on this passage, Hertz says that this cry out of eternity proclaiming the ineffable holiness, supreme majesty, and universal sovereignty of God, has been called the quintessence of all the teachings of the prophets.[88] It is the quintessence of the teachings of all true religion.

But let us come down a bit more to earth. What do we actually mean when we speak of being holy? What are the implications when we proclaim, "Holy, Holy, Holy is the Lord of hosts"? It is not easy to fully explain this thought. There seem to be two different qualities that make up our understanding of the holiness of God. It is in the explanation of the first of these that we find the greater difficulty, because it is an idea that does not lend itself to an effective description in words; it is something which must rather be felt. To explain it to someone who has not directly experienced it would be like describing beautiful colors to one who has never been able to see, or the meaning of music to one who has never been able to hear. Words alone are insufficient. It is the feeling that comes when we gaze upon some beautiful or awe-inspiring phenomenon of nature and somehow sense the invisible yet real and eternal force which seems to pervade the whole universe. We have a perception of might, of majesty, and of mystery. We also feel how small and insignificant is man in the face of the greatness of it all. It is the feeling expressed by the psalmist when he exclaims,

> *When I behold the heavens, the work of Thy fingers,*
> *The moon and the stars, which Thou hast established;*
> *What is man that Thou art mindful of him?*
> *And the son of man that Thou thinkest of him?*

But this is not all. Even as we think of the dependence and insignificance of the human race as contrasted to the vastness of the universe, this perception of holiness must at the same time be mixed with quite the opposite

---

[88] "Rabbi Joseph Herman Hertz, (1872–1946) was a Jewish Hungarian-born rabbi and biblical scholar. He held the position of Chief Rabbi of the United Kingdom from 1913 until his death in 1946... He edited a notable commentary on the Torah, popularly known as the Hertz Chumash, used in synagogues and classrooms throughout the English-speaking world." Wikipedia contributors. "Joseph Hertz." *Wikipedia, The Free Encyclopedia*. Wikipedia, The Free Encyclopedia, 22 Jul. 2017. Web. 20 Sep. 2017.

emotion. After his self-abasing query "what is man?", the same psalmist goes on to say,

> Yet Thou hast made him but little lower than the angels and hast crowned him with glory and honor. Thou hast made him have dominion over all the works of Thy hands, and Thou hast put all things under his feet.[89]

Together with our insignificance, we sense at the same time the miracle of life, its dignity, its sanctity, and the power of the human spirit, and we ascribe its source as God.

The second aspect of holiness is a bit easier to describe. When we speak of the holiness of God, we mean to express His complete freedom from every imperfection that might possibly be found in man. We speak of the ideals of ethical perfection, of goodness, of purity, and of righteousness all combined into one: the ideal of personal character and social achievement which no human being or society has yet attained, but which the religious person recognizes as the most desirable goal of human life.

God, then, is holy in the double sense that He personifies the mystery and majesty of the universe, and that He personifies moral and ethical perfection. And now the question must still be answered: "What is the implication of this thought about the holiness of God for ordinary human beings?" And this implication we find expressed best in the Book of Leviticus, chapter 19, which we read this afternoon at the beginning of what is called the Holiness Code.[90] It lays out what may perhaps be considered the keynote of Jewish ethics: "Speak unto the congregation of the children of Israel and say unto them, 'Ye shall be holy, for I the Lord Thy God am holy."

God is holy, and consequently, man must be holy. Man is not only to worship God, but what is of greater importance, he is to imitate Him. That is the primary teaching of Judaism. God is the ideal pattern whose characteristic of holiness man is slavishly to copy.

But, of course, we may well ask, "How can man be holy as God is holy? What does it mean to copy Him?" Certainly, men cannot hope to imitate God's infinite majesty and eternity. Man can sense the mystery of life, but we cannot imitate its creation. The Jewish answer, however, is that to be holy, man must live with the constant awareness and reverence for the sacredness

---

89 Psalm 8:6-7.

90 "'The Holiness Code' is a term used in biblical criticism to refer to Leviticus chapters 17–26; it is so called due to its frequently repeated use of the word 'Holy.' Critical biblical scholars have regarded it as a distinct unit, noting that the style is noticeably different from the main body of Leviticus. Unlike in the remainder of Leviticus, the many laws of the Holiness Code are very closely packed together and described very briefly." Wikipedia contributors. "Holiness code." *Wikipedia, The Free Encyclopedia*. Wikipedia, The Free Encyclopedia, 22 Jun. 2017. Web. 20 Sep. 2017.

of human life and the significance of human personality, which man senses when he has the type of experience we spoke about a few moments ago. The rabbinic interpretation of "Be ye holy because I the Lord your God am holy" is:

> *If ye sanctify yourselves, I account it unto me as if ye had sanctified Me, but if ye do not sanctify yourselves, I account it as if you had not sanctified Me. If you hold your own human life as sacred, then you sanctify God and are holy as He is holy.*

Not only by his attitude toward life but, especially, also by imitating God's ethical qualities does man make himself holy. "Be like God," said the rabbis. "As He is merciful and gracious, so be thou merciful and gracious." Scripture commands, "Walk ye after the Lord your God."[91] But the Lord is a consuming fire; how can men walk after Him? But the meaning is by being as He is—merciful, long-suffering, loving. Mark how, on the first page of the Torah, God clothed the naked, Adam; and on the last, He buried the dead, Moses. He heals the sick, frees the captives, does good to his enemies, and is merciful both to the living and the dead.[92]

Holiness, therefore, according to Judaism, has never been so much an abstract or mystical idea as a principle that regulates the daily actions of all men. Holiness does not mean a flight from the world, a life of asceticism or self-mortification. Men who sit on flagpoles or torture themselves in one way or another are not holy by Jewish standards. Holiness does not imply renouncing the human relationships of family and position in society, but refers rather to the spirit in which the obligations of life itself are managed. And this is well illustrated in this Holiness code to which we have referred. The words, "Ye shall be holy," do not stand isolated by themselves in the text. They are immediately followed by concrete examples of the type of conduct which holiness implies. In the afternoon reading, we are told to be reverent toward parents. We are told to be considerate of the underprivileged. We are told not to withhold the wage of a laborer. We are told to love our neighbor and to have consideration for the stranger. And in a section not included this afternoon, we are warned with regard to good business ethics, and are given suggestions which were applicable in olden times, at least, as to how to create a righteous social order in which there would be a better distribution of the wealth of the nation and no exploitation of the less fortunate.

It is remarkable to note the extent to which social ideals are involved in the Jewish concept of holiness. The primary interest of Judaism is not in the salvation of individuals in the next world, but in the individual as a member

---

91 Deuteronomy 13:5.

92 Talmud: Shabbat 133b.

of society in this world. Men can become holy only through their relationship to the community at large. No man, according to Judaism, can live as a hermit and through his purity attain salvation and be considered a holy man. Such thoughts are foreign to Judaism. Jewish ethics involve man in relationship to his family, to his fellow man, and to his country. One Jewish philosopher pointed out that whenever the ideal of holiness is spoken of in the Torah, the plural is invariably used: "Ye shalt be holy," not "Thou shalt be holy." This, he says, is because mortal man can attain holiness only when cooperating with others in the service of a great ideal. Man is holy only as his life is devoted to the good of his fellow men.

This Jewish concept of holiness still has a place in this modern world. The world is desperately in need of an interpretation of religion such as this, which directs the energies and thoughts of men toward laboring for a better life on this earth, instead of thinking overly much of the next world. Men need to make ever-greater conscious efforts to live holy lives in the best sense of the word as we have just described it. The message of Judaism today is still "Holy, Holy, Holy is the Lord of hosts," and "Be ye holy for I the Lord thy God am holy." Every human life is sacred, it tells us, and every man entitled to the consideration and sympathy of his fellowmen. Every person, regardless of accident of birth or position, is endowed with the divine spark and possesses a soul and personality that it is sacrilege to injure. The particular economic prescriptions of the Bible may be out of date, but the underlying principle still holds that no man shall be ground into the dust and that we are all responsible for one another.

If we do not take such ideals seriously, we cannot lay claim to being truly religious or imitators of God's holiness. Then, indeed, we lay ourselves open, rather, to the charge that the prophet brought against Israel in the prophetic reading for this morning:

> *Ye fast not this day to make your voice heard on high! Is not this the fast that I have chosen, to loose the fetters of wickedness, to undo the bands of the yoke, to let the oppressed go free... Is it not to deal thy bread to the hungry and thou bring the poor that are cast out into thy house.*[93]

This is the test of our religion. This is holiness. The psalmist says, "Let us worship the Lord in the beauty of holiness."[94] If this be our understanding of holiness, then we could worship God in no finer way, and no greater beauty could be created.

---

93 Isaiah 58:4-7.

94 Psalm 96:9.

Dad—

Holiness seems like such an unachievable goal, and at the same time you give us the message that it is simple and easily in reach through everyday acts of human kindness. Jews, unlike followers of many other religions, do not seek salvation in a world to come. We raise ourselves by our good deeds in the here and now. What a great reason to be Jewish! Perfection may be out of reach, but perfect moments are abundant.

(Ha! Dad, no sooner did I write this than the doorbell rang with two Jehovah's Witnesses trying to interest me in salvation. I had the opportunity to practice what you preach by having a loving conversation with them. Yes! Holiness! It is simple and easily within reach! Thank you.)

Blessings.
Yesh

13. A Liberal Faith

September 26, 1955

This sermon lays out my father's case for why Jewish survival is so necessary. He felt that while many of the world's religions share common tenets, often derived from Judaism, the unique message that Judaism provides to the world is too precious to lose. He found this message compelling enough to deliver versions of it on Yom Kippur morning in three successive pulpits. First offered in Columbia, South Carolina in 1947, then the following year in Lexington, Kentucky, and finally in West Hempstead, New York in 1955, this sermon describes three characteristics—theological, social, and psychological—that mark Judaism's particular wisdom.

Judaism is not just another religion that we have become associated with by the accident of birth. Rather, it is a philosophy of life and a faith that we must share out of full conviction.

AS JEWS, ALL OF US ARE PROUD that we are the members of a people that has given religion to the western world. Whatever our state of knowledge may be with regard to the finer points of our faith, all of us do know, at least, that Judaism first proclaimed the doctrine of monotheism. Judaism first interpreted morality as a divine commandment to man. Judaism is the mother of the two other great monotheistic faiths, Christianity and Mohammedanism. We have, indeed, fulfilled the prophetic ambition to be "a light unto the nations," and the nations readily recognize the Jewish roots of their religious faith.[95]

---

[95] "Light unto the nations" (Hebrew: *Or LaGoyim*) is a term originated by the prophet Isaiah; it may express the universal designation of the Jewish People as a mentor for spiritual and moral guidance for the entire world. "I the Lord have called unto you in righteousness, and have taken hold of your hand, and submitted you as the people's covenant, as a light unto the nations" (Isaiah, 42:6).

Because of these achievements of the past, the thought may perhaps arise that Judaism has fulfilled its mission, that there is no religious work left to do that cannot be done equally as well by the faiths that it has already fostered. Since so many people accept monotheism and since we all speak in terms of "Love thy Neighbor," there is, perhaps, no longer any specifically Jewish task to be concerned with and no longer any important basic differences between Judaism and the other major religions.[96] What differences that exist are surface differences of approach. Ultimately, we all arrive at the same goal.

Accordingly, even those of us who are thoroughly happy in our Judaism and would never make a conscious effort to destroy it may sometimes feel that if Judaism gradually and peacefully disappeared, the world would suffer no great religious loss. After all, its fundamental teachings have been passed on to the future through other religious groups.

However, the differences that remain between Judaism and other groups may not be overlooked so glibly. There are religious values in Judaism that the world still sorely needs, particularly in these critical times, and we as Jews would do well to be aware of them and to proclaim them. Some Jewish leaders even speak in terms of a missionary effort to reach other people who may be spiritually in sympathy with us. We all ought to be committed to the belief that Judaism today serves as a liberal faith for men to live by, and that it may offer solutions to some of the world's problems.

The distinctive characteristics of Judaism were once described by Rabbi Joshua Liebman, of blessed memory, as falling into three categories.[97] He said that we might sum up the virtues of the Jewish approach to life in terms of its remarkable theological wisdom, its remarkable social insight, and its remarkable psychological penetration. I should like to touch briefly on each of these this morning.

The theological wisdom of Judaism may best be seen in its lack of dogmatism. Judaism confesses honestly that finite man cannot know all that there is to know about the infinite God. It recognizes the limitations of human knowledge and permits man to use his reason to continue the search after truth and to become ever more enlightened. The Bible always has been an authoritative book in Judaism, but even the Bible itself recognizes the process of growth in religious thinking and changing conceptions of God. For example, Moses is

---

96 Leviticus 19:18 says, "...thou shalt love thy neighbour as thyself: I am the Lord." This quote is repeated in the New Testament: "'Love your neighbor as yourself.' There is no commandment greater than these" (Mark 12:31).

97 "Joshua Loth Liebman (1907–1948) was an American rabbi and best-selling author. He is best known for his book *Peace of Mind*, published in 1946, which sought to reconcile religion and psychiatry and spent more than a year at #1 on the *New York Times* Best Seller list." Wikipedia contributors. "Joshua L. Liebman." *Wikipedia, The Free Encyclopedia*. Wikipedia, The Free Encyclopedia, 9 Sep. 2017. Web. 21 Sep. 2017.

reported to have had a different understanding of God than the Patriarchs'. In Exodus 6, God spoke unto Moses and said unto him, "I am the Lord, and I appeared unto Abraham, unto Isaac, and unto Jacob as El Shaddai, but by my name Adonoy I made Me not known unto them." Thus, a new facet of divinity was revealed to Moses.

Each prophet also viewed God from his own perspective. To Amos, He was a god of justice; to Hosea, a god of love; and to Isaiah, a god of righteousness and compassion. In post-Biblical days, the rabbis of the Talmud reinterpreted the Bible in their own manner—to the extent that it was said that Moses one time came down from heaven and listened to Rabbi Akiba teach in the school—and did not even recognize his own Torah![98] And after the days of the Talmud came the teaching of the religious philosophers, and the mystics, and today the modernists—all of whom fit into the framework of Judaism without the sectarian fragmentation that characterizes other religious groups. Even in its most rigid form, Judaism allows for variations in interpretation; tradition and reason both have played significant roles in its development. This flexibility in Judaism makes unnecessary those bitter conflicts between science and religion such as *Inherit the Wind* now reminds us of on Broadway; Judaism is able to take the findings of science and to use them rather than quarrel with them.[99]

Judaism's emphasis is not on abstract dogma but rather upon man: his way of life and his conscience. Judaism has been a faith in which the emphasis has been on deed rather than creed. What man *believed* did not come first, but what man *did*. We read from the Torah this very morning that "the word is nigh unto thee in thy mouth and in thy heart, that thou mayest *do* it."[100] The doing is all-important and the believing is secondary. One ancient rabbi even dared picture God as saying, "Would that ye would forsake me, if only you would keep my commandments." And indeed, how much better off this world would have been if through the centuries there had been a greater concern for godly conduct rather than the creeds that men have professed!

This flexibility in dogma has contributed to a second virtue in Judaism: its social insight. The social insight of Judaism is perhaps best reflected in its concept of salvation. Because Judaism is basically tolerant of variation in religious belief, it does not proclaim salvation as the exclusive property of

---

98 The Talmud is a central text of mainstream Judaism. It takes the form of a record of rabbinic discussions pertaining to Jewish law, ethics, philosophy, customs, and history.

99 *Inherit the Wind*, a play by Jerome Lawrence and Robert Edwin Lee, debuted in 1955. It is a fictionalized retelling of the 1925 Scopes "Monkey" Trial, in which John T. Scopes was convicted of breaking Tennessee state law by teaching Darwin's theory of evolution to a high school science class.

100 Deuteronomy 30:14.

one particular creed. A particular belief does not guarantee salvation of the soul; nor does the accident of birth or adherence to a different religious group deny it. Rather, Judaism proclaims that the pious of all nations have a share in the world to come.[101] There are, indeed, special demands upon the Jew, but righteous living brings its reward to Jew and non-Jew alike.

The Jewish understanding of salvation is significant for another reason also. Salvation in Judaism is not a self-centered concept. Many other groups instill in their followers a concern for their own individual souls in the afterlife. In Judaism, salvation has a social emphasis. It is something that concerns not merely the individual alone, but humanity as a whole. And it concerns not so much life after death, as man's victory in this life over human defects, over sinfulness, ignorance, selfishness, and all human failings that make for an imperfect society. And it is, furthermore, not something that we sit back and wait for. Salvation comes from God, but it must be achieved also through the effort of man, who must pitch in as copartner with God in wiping out the obstacles that stand in the way of a better humanity and a better world. Thus, Judaism is not a "pie in the sky" type of religion!

The social insight of Judaism is also reflected in what Rabbi Leo Baeck called its "ethical optimism."[102] Judaism recognizes that there is evil and suffering in the world, and it is neither indifferent nor resigned to it. It faces the world with a commandment from God to change it, and with confidence that man is capable of realizing in himself the good that he sees in God. Man can shape his life for good and it is his religious duty to do so. One might have expected Jews, because our bitter experience in history, to have been among the world's greatest pessimists and to have lost faith in the possibility of redeeming mankind; but Judaism does not yield to pessimism, regardless of circumstances. It maintains its faith in man's essential goodness and in the ultimate triumph of this goodness. It continues to look forward to a Messianic age when such evil will be overcome, and it continues to look upon its task in the world as one of sanctifying God by overcoming evil and realizing good. The vision of the end of days has been the motivating force in Jewish history and a factor making for survival. This way of thinking is in striking contrast to the pessimistic view that man is a hopeless sinner entangled in original sin for which he was not even responsible; that man is not capable of achieving salvation for himself but is dependent upon the grace of God—for which he may only hope but of which he cannot be sure because it

---

101 Sanhedrin 105a.

102 Leo Baeck (1873–1956) was a twentieth-century German rabbi and a leader in Progressive Judaism movement. "There is only one complete and flawless optimism, and that is ethical optimism" (Baeck, *The Essence of Judaism*, 1905).

is arbitrarily bestowed at God's will; that man stands alone in a hostile world, trapped by the problems of his existence, powerless to do anything about them. This was not only the belief of ancient thinkers, unfortunately, but is the trend among many noted modern religious thinkers as well.

The accomplishments of a society as well as of an individual may be determined to a great extent by the attitude with which it faces its problems. If we approach our lot with pessimism, then we handicap ourselves at the outset in dealing with the challenges that confront us. If we are to survive the crisis of the atomic age, there is a crying need for the tolerance, the concern for our fellowman, and the confidence that emanates from Judaism.

Finally, the psychological penetration of Judaism is evident from a comparison of Judaism with the patterns that psychiatrists today say make for mental health among individuals and groups. Judaism somehow seems instinctively to have inclined towards these patterns, even in the days before there was any inkling of the science of psychiatry. Psychiatric subjects are complex and non-experts should hesitate to discuss them. However, this relationship of religion to psychiatry was a favorite field of study of Rabbi Liebman, whom I previously mentioned, and I bring you briefly some of his thoughts on this subject.

Judaism, he points out, has shown psychological wisdom by avoiding doctrines that might make for a sense of guilt or a sense of frustration in man. Judaism, for example, has never espoused as great virtues the doctrines of "turning the other cheek"[103] or "loving thine enemy."[104] In Judaism, there has always been room for anger as well as love. In Judaism, there has been room for righteous indignation as well as profound compassion. This is not a defect in Judaism, as some may be tempted to say. Our society theoretically calls for a perfect love in men's hearts. It asks men to turn the other cheek and love their enemies, and a paradox has resulted. Our own generation has seen not love but concentration camps and crematories and war. Rabbi Liebman attributes this to the doctrine of unattainable perfectionism, and describes the process as follows: If you tell people that you must achieve perfect, unblemished love, man says to himself, "Superb ideal. I wish I could reach it." But he cannot reach it since he is merely human with human emotions and imperfections. Therefore, because he cannot reach it, he becomes obsessed with guilt in one form or another. The guilt becomes hate. Hate is repressed and then leads to an explosion such as the violence of a decade ago. A society that

---

[103] "Turning the other cheek" is a phrase in Christian doctrine that refers to responding to an aggressor without violence. The phrase originates from the *Sermon on the Mount* in the New Testament.

[104] In the *Sermon on the Plain* in the Gospel of Luke, Jesus says: "But I say unto you which hear, love your enemies, do good to them which hate you" (Luke 6:27).

does not allow any room in the world for the passions and instincts of man begets a split personality, and the anger, which has not been given a creative outlet, breaks out with the savagery that has plagued our civilization. Judaism allows for outrage, for indignation. And righteous indignation is something the world needs more of. Turning the other cheek, after all, is to countenance an injustice.

Nor does Judaism try to repress the normal and natural emotions of man. Judaism does not favor the ascetic. It is man's obligation to enjoy life, and religion's function to help him do it properly. An ancient sage once said, "He who sees a legitimate pleasure and does not avail himself thereof is an ingrate against God who made it possible."

The Jewish religion does not care for frustrated personalities who have withdrawn themselves from life's battles. It has never seen a conflict between the flesh and spirit. It avoids overemphasizing either, approving of both in proper balance. Man is to neither thwart his body nor give in to it, but rather to sanctify it. Marriage is not considered a concession to the flesh but a sanctification, and love becomes a high adventure of the human spirit.

All this has not been an outline of Judaism. It has been only brief mention of significant highlights which give you perhaps some indication of the trend of Jewish thinking and which I hope demonstrate the continuing importance of the message of Judaism in the world today. We have only skimmed the surface, but I hope it has been sufficient to convince us that Judaism is not just another religion that we have become associated with by accident of birth. Rather, it is a philosophy of life and a faith which we must share out of full conviction. In our Torah reading this morning, we read, "I call heaven and earth to witness against you this day that I have set before you life and death, the blessing and the curse; therefore choose life that thou mayest live."[105] Judaism is life. Let us choose it in pride and joy, and proclaim it as a saving message to the world.

---

105 Deuteronomy 30:19.

Dad—

You take pride in our differences. We are not like the other nations, religions, or peoples. We bring a unique vision to the planet. The fact that many Jews and non-Jews alike see us as "just another religion" doesn't make it so. On the contrary, as you have often preached, it's important not only to point out Jewish distinctions, but to celebrate and—more importantly—to preserve them. We are a fungible, evolving faith. Our propensity is to optimistically work to repair the world. Our philosophies are healthy and life-sustaining. We are here to support one another and to enjoy life. Our evolving voice must be sustained to enhance life in all generations.

Blessings.
Yesh

14. Mid-East Crisis

November 16, 1956

Given the seemingly perpetual conflict between the Arab nations and Israel, it's fascinating to read real-time accounts of now-historic battles. This sermon provides perspective on the 1956 Suez Crisis. It's heartening to look back with the knowledge that Israel has survived such crises, even as it is discouraging to recognize the repetitive nature of these events.

It is only a little more than eleven years since the downfall of Hitler, but now, after a short period of comparative calm, again the Jew fights for his very survival.

I FEEL LIKE A RADIO ANNOUNCER saying that the "program originally scheduled for this time will not be heard." The topic that I announced for this evening was the discussion of a book by Maurice Samuel in connection with the observance of Jewish Book Month.[106] However, under the influence of a meeting that I attended during the past week, I have decided to put this off in order to speak to you of something much more pressing. The man that I listened to was Avraham Harman, formerly the Israeli consul-general in New York.[107] At present, he is still in the Israeli diplomatic service, and in this country now on a special mission for Israel. This past week, he brought to the New

---

106 "Maurice Samuel (1895–1972) was a Romanian-born British and American antigentilist novelist, translator, and lecturer." It's likely that the topic of Israel/Arab conflict would have been addressed that evening even had the topic not been changed, since Samuels had recently published a book entitled *The Professor and the Fossil*, a study of the works of Arnold Toynbee that Samuels felt misrepresented Jewish history from biblical times down to the modern conflict between the Arabs and the State of Israel. Wikipedia contributors. "Maurice Samuel." *Wikipedia, The Free Encyclopedia.* Wikipedia, The Free Encyclopedia, 23 Jul. 2017. Web. 21 Sep. 2017.

107 Avraham Harman (1914–1992) was an Israeli diplomat.

York Board of Rabbis a first-hand summary of the situation in the Mid-East that everybody ought to hear.[108]

He perhaps did not say very much that was absolutely new to us, but the way he put his facts together, the urgency of his presentation, his reflection of Israeli desperation, and the manner in which he seemed to suffer out every word that he spoke lent emphasis to what he said, and put these facts in a new light. When Israel first moved into Egypt, every one of us was concerned with the morality of the act, its legality, and its effect on public relations. Perhaps we still are. For that reason, if for no other, it would be well for us to review the situation. This review that I give you is for the most part the picture as brought to us by Avraham Harman, although I shall occasionally perhaps draw on other sources as well.

It is only a little more than eleven years since the downfall of Hitler, but now, after a short period of comparative calm, once again the Jew fights for his very survival. Israel considers the situation in the Middle East not merely a struggle for its own protection, but one of primary importance for all Jews, wherever they may be: it will affect the Jews of Eastern Europe who have somehow managed to remain Jews through four decades of communism, the Jews of North Africa, and yes, even the Jews of America who will be uplifted or depressed by what happens to Israel.

Furthermore, the problem of the Middle East is not a problem of the relationship between Jews and Arabs. This is only a symptom. Nor is it a problem of settling the dispute with regard to the Suez Canal.[109] This, too, is only a symptom. The basic problem is the threat to the security of the Middle

---

108 The New York Board of Rabbis is an organization of Orthodox, Reform, Conservative, and Reconstructionist rabbis in New York State and the surrounding portions of Connecticut and New Jersey.

109 The Suez Canal, originally constructed between 1859 and 1869 (widened between 2014 and 2016), is an "artificial sea-level waterway in Egypt, connecting the Mediterranean Sea to the Red Sea through the Isthmus of Suez... The canal offers watercraft a shorter journey between the North Atlantic and northern Indian Oceans via the Mediterranean and Red Seas by avoiding the South Atlantic and southern Indian Oceans, in turn reducing the journey by approximately 4,300 miles... [In 1956,] because of Egyptian overtures towards the Soviet Union, the United Kingdom and the United States withdrew a pledge they had made to support the construction of the Aswan Dam. Egyptian President Gamal Abdel Nasser responded by nationalizing the canal and transferring it to the Suez Canal Authority. On the same day that the canal was nationalized, Nasser also closed the Straits of Tiran to all Israeli ships." Wikipedia contributors. "Suez Canal." *Wikipedia, The Free Encyclopedia*. Wikipedia, The Free Encyclopedia, 2 Sep. 2017. Web. 21 Sep. 2017.

On October 29, 1956, Israel, followed by the United Kingdom and France, invaded the Egyptian Sinai. "The aims were to regain Western control of the Suez Canal and to remove Egyptian President Gamal Abdel Nasser from power. After the fighting had started, the United States, the Soviet Union, and the United Nations forced the three invaders to withdraw. The episode humiliated Great Britain and France and strengthened Nasser." Wikipedia contributors. "Suez Crisis." *Wikipedia, The Free Encyclopedia*. Wikipedia, The Free Encyclopedia, 15 Sep. 2017. Web. 21 Sep. 2017.

14. Mid-East Crisis—1956

East and the security of the entire world arising from Hitlerian ambition for power. This is to be found today in Nasser's Egypt, and the efforts of Russia to extend her sphere of influence. Egypt has been the primary aggressor in every phase of the Middle East conflict. The other nations have merely been following her leadership.

This drive for power on the part of Egypt is not an imaginary one. Hitler had his *Mein Kampf* and Nasser has his *Philosophy of a Revolution*, a book in which he clearly sets forth, as did Hitler, his whole plan of aggressive expansion.[110] Regardless of what Nasser may say for purposes of public relations, his true aims are a matter of record, and his book reflects these aims just as clearly as *Mein Kampf* reflected the goals of Nazism. He is concerned with empire building and the domination of the Arab world from the Atlantic to the eastern ends, and just as was the case with Hitler, there are no humanitarian goals involved. This is not a revolution to better the miserable conditions in which most of the Arabs live today, but one merely for the sake of power itself. And once Egypt made an arms deal with Czechoslovakia and the Soviets in 1955, this intention to dominate had to be taken very seriously.[111]

First came the deal that brought to Egypt not only weapons but Russian technicians to help the Egyptians master them. Then came the seizure of the Suez Canal, which is not to be considered merely an angry reaction to American refusal to help with the Aswan Dam, but something that had been planned for a very long time.[112] Simultaneously, Nasser turned his attention to

---

110 Gamal Abdel Nasser Hussein (1918–1970) was the second President of Egypt, serving from 1956 until his death. Nasser's nationalization of the Suez Canal and his emergence as the political victor from the subsequent Suez Crisis substantially elevated his popularity in Egypt and the Arab world. Nasser resigned following Egypt's defeat by Israel in the 1967 Six-Day War, but he returned to office after popular demonstrations calling for his reinstatement. Historians describe Nasser as a towering political figure of the Middle East in the twentieth century.

111 Secretary of State John Foster Dulles and President Dwight Eisenhower told Nasser "that the United States would supply him with weapons only if they were used for defensive purposes and accompanied by U.S. military personnel for supervision and training. Nasser did not accept these conditions; he then looked to the Soviet Union for support. Although Dulles believed that Nasser was only bluffing and that the Soviet Union would not aid Nasser, he was wrong—the Soviet Union promised Nasser a quantity of arms in exchange for a deferred payment of Egyptian grain and cotton. On September 27, 1955, Nasser announced an arms deal, with Czechoslovakia acting as a middleman for the Soviet support." Wikipedia contributors. "Aswan Dam." *Wikipedia, The Free Encyclopedia*. Wikipedia, The Free Encyclopedia, 19 Sep. 2017. Web. 21 Sep. 2017.

112 The Aswan Dam is an embankment dam built across the Nile at Aswan, Egypt between 1898 and 1902. Since the 1960s, the name commonly refers to the Aswan High Dam. "Construction of the High Dam became a key objective of the Egyptian government following the Egyptian Revolution of 1952, as the ability to control floods, provide water for irrigation, and generate hydroelectricity were seen as pivotal to Egypt's industrialization." The High Dam was constructed between 1960 and 1970, and has had a significant effect on the economy and culture of Egypt. Wikipedia contributors. "Aswan Dam." *Wikipedia, The Free Encyclopedia*. Wikipedia, The Free Encyclopedia, 19 Sep. 2017. Web. 21 Sep. 2017.

stirring up trouble in Algiers and to a network of pacts with other Arab states against Israel.[113] The last phase of these Arab alliances, the Jordan-Syria-Egyptian pact, was completed only about four weeks ago under the leadership of Egypt. And now the time was almost at hand for direct assault upon Israel, and Israel was not alone in evaluating the situation in this manner. Israel, unfortunately, is astride the great land routes that link the Arab kingdoms together. All through history this geographical situation had been a problem, and now again, because it stands at the crossroads of the Middle East, this area is the focal point of eyes lusting for power.

Along with all of this diplomatic maneuvering, two other factors impacted the situation. One was Egypt's constant insistence that in spite of the armistice, she remained in a state of technical war with Israel. The Israelis were hard-pressed, however, to note the difference between a state of war that was technical and a state of war that was not technical. Because of this "technical" state of war, Egypt felt justified in excluding Israeli shipping from the Suez Canal. Nor did it permit ships to come into the port of Elath in the Gulf of Akaba in the Negev. Israel, the country that could least afford it, was compelled to move its shipping around the continent of Africa. At the same time, a boycott enforced by the Arab world meant that all the natural markets for Israeli goods were closed to it. Thus, although the state of war was technical, the economic war was very real and the goal was the bankruptcy of Israel. It was a one-sided, real war that was being waged.

The second factor in this one-sided war was the *Fedayeen*.[114] These were Egyptian-trained and Egyptian-controlled raiders of Israel's territory and the murderers of Israeli civilians. That these were not merely unorganized robber gangs is seen from the fact that when it suited Egypt's convenience, there were no *fedayeen* raids; but when Egypt willed it, they were on again. Thus, when the Suez Canal matter was before the Security Council and Egypt did not want to complicate it by news concerning *fedayeen* raids, there were none. Immediately after the Security Council debate was ended, Nasser felt free to order the *fedayeen* into renewed action, and the raids began again. These *fedayeen* raids were the prelude to a planned big thrust into Israel, and if there was ever any doubt about that, it was dispelled when documentary evidence

---

113 Nasser supported the Algerian independence movement, both politically and financially. Algeria gained independence from France in 1962.

114 In 1955, Nasser "employed a new tactic to prosecute Egypt's war with Israel." Egypt decided to dispatch Arab terrorists, or *fedayeen* ("one who sacrifices himself"), trained and equipped by Egyptian Intelligence, to engage in hostile action on the border and infiltrate Israel to commit acts of sabotage and murder. Dominic Caraccilo, *Beyond Guns and Steel: A War Termination* Strategy (Santa Barbara: Praeger, 2011), 113.

was discovered in the Gaza Strip.[115] And not only were the documents evidence, but the military buildup in the Gaza Strip and Sinai Peninsula was also evidence. The reason Israel was able to capture so much Egyptian equipment is because Egypt had readied itself to attack Israel and its supply was plentiful close to the Israeli borders.

Faced with the continuing one-sided war, faced with a refusal to sit together and talk about a lasting peace, faced with the constant attack upon its borders and its citizenry by the *fedayeen*, faced with the knowledge that Russian help was building Egypt's military power, realizing that all that had happened up to that time pointed to a move against Israel, and supplied with intelligence reports that the move was now in readiness, Israel had only two choices: seize the initiative herself, or wait for Egyptians armed with Russian guns, tanks, and planes to move into Israel and bomb her cities. Nasser had not really even tried to conceal his intentions. Whatever he may have been saying in English for worldwide consumption, in his own Arabic press he had been boasting that he had completed a ring of steel around Israel which had converted it into a concentration camp, and he also had proclaimed in Arabic, just prior to the Israeli invasion, that "the Day of Israel is near."

Israel feels that the surface legalities of the situation were meaningless, because for them, it was a matter of life and death. There can no more be a continued one-sided war than there can be a one-sided peace. Neither the United Nations nor the United States were helping Israel, and the *fedayeen* were being ignored. No nation on earth was committed to help Israel in case of attack. While Israel had to beg for arms and buy what little it could manage to get at regular prices, Nasser was getting plenty of arms free or extremely cheaply. Nasser was not getting arms for internal policing or self-defense. He was openly talking about genocide and destroying the Jews. Was every nation on earth to have the right of self-defense but Israel?

Strangely enough, though Egypt was preparing to attack, it was taken by surprise at the Israeli counterthrust. And strangely enough, the Arab world did not join Egypt in rising against Israel. Nasser asked Jordan to help, but Jordan answered back, "What will you be able to do for us, if Israel attacks us?" Apparently, if Egypt had gained the upper hand, the other Arabs would have jumped in for the kill, but upon seeing Egypt get cuffed about, they decided discretion was the better part of valor.

---

115 "The Gaza Strip, or simply Gaza, is [an exclave region of the State of Palestine] on the eastern coast of the Mediterranean Sea that borders Egypt on the southwest for 11 kilometers (6.8 miles) and Israel on the east and north for 51 kilometers (32 miles)." Gaza is part of the Palestinian territories. Wikipedia contributors. "Gaza Strip." *Wikipedia, The Free Encyclopedia*. Wikipedia, The Free Encyclopedia, 28 Aug. 2017. Web. 21 Sep. 2017.

Israel today is convinced that what was done was necessary for her own self-preservation. Israel is further convinced that in doing what she has done, she contributed to peace of the world, if the world will only know how to use this opportunity wisely. Israelis feel, however, that we do not recognize an opportunity when we have it, and that we are making the same mistake made in Hitler's time—letting the aggressor become strong instead of dealing with him while he is weak.[116] They cannot understand our policy of saving the Nasser regime, of permitting Egypt to go back to the point from which Israel pushed them back. They cannot understand the policy that will permit *fedayeen* to go to work again.[117] They believe that what we are doing serves only Nasser and Khrushchev, and not world peace.[118]

Now that the crisis has been precipitated, what does Israel want of American Jewry? She wants the realization that Israel is faced with a life and death struggle. She wants the understanding that Israel's moral case is strong and not weak. She wants help from America in defining a bit more precisely and accurately the term *aggression*. This word so far has not received any precise definition from the UN, and it remains a crucial question as to when a nation may be branded an aggressor. In Israel's mind, economic warfare and border violations and murder constitute aggression. Self-defense does not.

Israel also wants help on the economic front. And in this light, every member of the New York Board of Rabbis has been pressed to appeal tonight from their pulpits for the generous purchase of Israel Bonds. This will provide urgently needed funds for the defense of Israel, and even more than that, it will be a vote of confidence in Israel on the part of American Jewry. It will encourage them and strengthen the Israelis with the knowledge that they are not a deserted people and that we understand their plight. In 1955, it was pointed out by Levi Eschol, the Finance Minister of Israel, that $43 million of bonds were sold, while from the German government, $90 million in reparations were collected. Six million dead Jews thus contributed twice as much as six million live Jews to the cause of Israel. Israel deserves our help. She fights our battle, too. That is a statement we must take on faith. I don't want to see

---

116 "As Israel's Ambassador to Washington, Abba Eban, put it: 'Can Israel wait like a rabbit for the snake to get large enough to devour her?'" David Nichols, *Eisenhower 1956* (New York: Simon & Schuster Paperbacks, 2012), 27.

117 Not wanting to fuse Soviet expansionism with Arab state nationalism, the U.S. refrained from opposing both the Soviet Union and Egypt. The U.S., therefore, chose a path of cooperation with the lesser of two enemies, Egypt.

118 "Nikita Sergeyevich Khrushchev (1894–1971) led the Soviet Union during part of the Cold War. He served as First Secretary of the Communist Party of the Soviet Union from 1953 to 1964, and as Premier from 1958 to 1964." Wikipedia contributors. "Nikita Khrushchev." *Wikipedia, The Free Encyclopedia*. Wikipedia, The Free Encyclopedia, 19 Sep. 2017. Web. 21 Sep. 2017.

14. Mid-East Crisis—1956

the day when it may be proved by disaster. I don't think such a day will come. The situation is tense, but we need not be pessimistic. Israel has already demonstrated her capacity for resistance and her will to live. With God's help and with our help, Israel *shall* live.

Dad—

You begin your narrative with "Eleven years after the downfall of Hitler..." It is understandable, with the Holocaust still ringing in your ears, that you should frame this sermon from beginning to end with reference to Hitler and the death of six million Jews. You use the threat of annihilation as a reasonable justification for Israel's attack on Egypt.

In every generation, there are those who have risen up against our people. Why do you suppose that is? Does our moral code so threaten them? Do we appear too strong, as in Pharaoh's eyes? Or too weak, as in the eyes of a common bully? Are we the go-to scapegoat in every era of national turmoil? Yes, we defended ourselves. Or no: as seen from the other side, we were once again aggressors. The results are the same—death, destruction, increased enmity, and temporary relief from the threat du jour.

> Esa einai el heharim, me'ayin yavo ezri?
> I lift my eyes up to the mountain—whence cometh my help?

I'm sure some help cometh from the Lord, and I'm sure some cometh from the United States, but I'm not seeing a solution here.

Maybe that's the way things are. That's the human condition—one of continual turmoil, hate, war. I'm getting that impression. I'm thinking the Torah is just a series of battles that are there to remind us that that is who we are, who we have always been, and who we will ever be. Bummer. It doesn't seem like a sustainable strategy, so I suppose our 3,000-year history is a miracle in itself!

Blessings.
Yesh

15. Jewish Peoplehood in America

October 5, 1957

Yom Kippur Morning

The following sermon is a product of its times. It reflects an era that was a good deal less pluralistic than today, a time when political correctness was unheard of, and a day in which sensitivities about fully speaking one's mind were less prevalent. Therefore, my father's exposition on the distinguishing characteristics of Judaism among the three dominant religions in 1950s American society may seem chauvinistic by today's standards. Some may find this a bit jarring. Regardless, my father unhesitatingly makes the case that Judaism is important, relevant, and unique—qualities the religion arguably maintains to this day. He extols the need, as he often did over the years, for Jews to connect to their common history, language, and homeland, and not to succumb to conformity with the prevailing society.

Judaism is certainly very much at home in the American environment and rejoices in the freedom which gives opportunity for expression as never before, but it must use this freedom to preserve its uniqueness and universality and not sacrifice them in a desire to be completely like unto our neighbors.

IN HIS BOOK ENTITLED *PROTESTANT, CATHOLIC, AND JEW*, Will Herberg presents an analysis of the tremendous increase in religious affiliation in present day America.[119] His thesis, which has been referred to again and again

---

[119] "Will Herberg (1901–1977) was an American Jewish writer, intellectual, and scholar. [He was] a social philosopher and sociologist of religion, as well as a Jewish theologian... His 1955 book *Protestant, Catholic, Jew: An Essay in American Religious Sociology* ...has been described as 'one of the most influential

from almost every pulpit, is a must-read for anyone who is interested in the subject. The major point that he makes is that America, the great melting pot for many peoples, has developed religiously speaking into a triple melting pot. Over the course of time, we have tended to eliminate all differences and barriers that have existed among the various ethnic groups that have come to this land save one, and this one we have rather encouraged to remain. The *religious* difference has been preserved. Religiously, America has not served to fuse everyone into a single pattern, but has rather encouraged three different forms—Catholic, Protestant, Jewish—any one of which is considered to be normal and appropriate on the American scene. As a matter of fact, not to be identified as either Catholic, Protestant, or Jew is somehow not to be fully part of the American way of life.[120] Rightly or wrongly, there is a tendency to regard all people not committed to one of the major faiths as being disloyal to American principles. Atheists, agnostics, and humanists are at a disadvantage today, as we may note particularly in the numerous controversies that arise on the question of religion in the schools.

For us as Jews, this has had an interesting consequence. There was a time about a generation ago when our young people, in their effort to make of themselves good Americans, often felt that they had to reject the faith of their immigrant fathers because that faith connoted for them something foreign which was not at home in the new land. But now this same urge to conform to the American scene leads in the opposite direction, because today, conformity to the American pattern causes acceptance rather than rejection of religious

---

books ever written about American religion.'" Wikipedia contributors. "Will Herberg." *Wikipedia, The Free Encyclopedia*. Wikipedia, The Free Encyclopedia, 17 Sep. 2017. Web. 21 Sep. 2017.

120 The U.S. Census Bureau no longer surveys for religion. However, according to the Current Population Survey of March 1957, a Bureau-directed monthly survey of 35,000 households, Americans of 14 years and above stated their religion as following: White Protestant 57.4% , Black Protestant 8.8%, Catholic 25.7%, Jewish 3.4%, Other religion/not reported 2.2%, No religion 2.7%. Total 100%.

The US population was 170 million in early 1957. While Jews have always made up a small percentage of the population, they were nonetheless considered to be one of the big three religions of the country. Today, the U.S. population is over 326 million. The number of Jews has remained fairly stable, causing the percentage of Jews in the U.S. to drop. Nonetheless, Jews remain the second most popular religious affiliation after Christians. Today, one might say the three big religions in the United States are all forms of Christianity, followed by Judaism, and then Islam. Since the 1950s, the American religious landscape has changed significantly in four ways: 1) the adherents of religions other than Christianity are increasing every year; 2) the number of mixed-religion households is on rise (due to inter-faith marriages); 3) among religions, the composition of various denominations or sub-groups is changing and they are also becoming more important due to their socio-political activities; and 4) the number of Americans unaffiliated with religion is also growing. Zahid Bukhari, "A Question on Religion in the US Census," *Georgetown University School of Foreign Service*, acmcu.georgetown.edu/a-question-on-religion. Accessed 21 Sep. 2017.

affiliation. Being American today seems to make religious identification mandatory.

Many good things, in addition to the increase in religious enrollment, have resulted from this development. Not least among these is the greater degree of religious tolerance and a stronger feeling of common purpose among the three great religions. But Will Herberg points out drawbacks as well. On the one hand, the taint of foreignness has been eliminated from the three faiths, and this removes a formidable obstacle to their transmission and preservation. But on the other hand, the Americanization of religion has meant a distinct loss of the sense of religious uniqueness and universality. Each faith, he says, as far as the masses are concerned, tends to regard itself as merely an alternative form of being religious in the American way. We tend to emphasize our common ground and to suppress our distinctive characteristics. We tend to make a super-religion of Americanism with the three major religious groups as subdivisions. This results in a distortion of the authentic character of each faith in itself. Thus, even in the expression of religious difference, there seems to be an element of conformity that takes away from each faith something of its uniqueness and peculiar meaning.

I shall not touch upon this problem as it affects the branches of the Christian faith, but let us consider it to some extent at least as it pertains to Judaism. Judaism, particularly in our Reform interpretation, agrees that there must be adjustment to locale and time, but it cannot continue in a meaningful way if it's completely overpowered and overshadowed by conformist Americanism. Judaism is certainly very much at home in the American environment and rejoices in the freedom which gives opportunity for expression as never before. However, it must use this freedom to preserve its uniqueness and universality and not sacrifice them in a desire to be completely like unto our neighbors.

One aspect of uniqueness in particular that tends to suffer on the American scene and which is fundamental to our faith is our concept of the peoplehood of Israel and its role in the world. We speak very often about the fashioning of an American Judaism, which is all to the good, but that Judaism should not be an all-American Judaism to the neglect of our historic ties and eternal values. Politically, we are citizens of America and happy that it is our good fortune to be so, but spiritually, our scope is broader than America. We are part of a people with deep roots in time and widely scattered in space. We are not an American denomination, but a branch of a worldwide spiritual community. The memories of Americanism go back to Valley Forge or Plymouth Rock, but the memories of Judaism go back to Abraham and Sinai and are shared by fellow Jews throughout the globe.

The element of peoplehood is one of the basic ingredients of Judaism. Our peoplehood constitutes one of the major differences between ours and the Christian faith. The Christian fellowship is based upon a church. It is an organized association of men drawn from one people or many peoples held together by a common creed or religious discipline. History has made of Judaism, on the other hand, the religion of a single people, the Jewish people. A people is not an association of individuals. A people is a chain of generations united by a common history and a common cultural origin that can be traced to a common land. It has been rightly observed that the connection between the generations of a people is just as intimate as that between the generations of a family. The soul of a people and the soul of a family belong equally to the individual. One can resign from a church, but one cannot resign from the Jewish people.

Christianity is concerned with history only to the extent that a single episode in history is the basis of its faith. Judaism, in contrast, is concerned with all of history because it is a faith that emerged out of the total history of a people rather than out of the story of a single man. That episode of history that is most significant to Judaism was the covenant at Sinai, but the significance of this covenant was not in the immediate moment. Rather, it was the result of historical events concerning the people of Israel up to that moment; and it was a compact which committed a people to be the servants of God beyond the moment—not merely the generation that stood there at Sinai, but also for those who are here this day, as we have just read from the Torah.

The significance of Judaism today remains that it is the faith of a people who have chosen to be a holy people and a kingdom of priests. It is true that as Jews, our religious interests are of prime importance. The people of Israel without religion is a purposeless entity. But on the other hand, without the people of Israel, our religion is a disembodied soul. Without a sense of peoplehood and spiritual unity with fellow Jews of past and present and even the future, Judaism has its foundations pulled out from under and comes toppling down.

How can we keep our sense of peoplehood alive in the face of an environment that tends to make us feel self-sufficient as an American Jewish community and weakens our family ties? There are several things that can help. First, it is important for us to saturate ourselves with the knowledge of Jewish history. History to the Jew is as vital as the catechism to the Christian faith. Eleanor Roosevelt said the other day, on returning from Russia, that Americans needed to study more history. Only then, she said, would we understand the world better and handle our political problems more maturely. The Jew, likewise, needs a sense of history to understand and appreciate his faith the more. Through understanding and identifying with the heroic story of the Jewish past, we shall acquire a sense of belongingness to the Jewish people that we shall never lose.

We need, secondly, to cultivate as much as possible the Hebrew language, and to use it at least to some extent as a medium of prayer, if not more. It is the Hebrew language that holds the idiom of our faith. It is in Hebrew that the Bible was written and is best understood. It is the one language that we share an allegiance to with all Jews of whatever type they may be or where they are from. It is the reminder of our common heritage as Jews, as no other symbol can be.

Finally, we must retain our interest in the land of Israel as something special. We cannot agree that the Jewish community of Israel is just another Jewish community of no more interest or consequence to us than any other. The Jewish settlement of Israel is more than a place of refuge. Jews have found refuge in many lands through the years, not the least among them being this very land where there are more Jews than Israel probably can ever hope to hold. But Israel is the land where our faith was forged. It is the repository of our most sacred memories as a people. It was rebuilt under the inspiration that only such a land of historic memory can fire. It is a nation in which the principle of Jewish peoplehood functions—not merely in an abstract spiritual manner, but in a concrete, challenging form. It is a very tangible reminder of the spiritual bond that exists among the Jewish people. For these reasons, Israel is something special. We are not citizens of Israel. We owe it no political loyalty as American Jews, but we are spiritually concerned with it. Jewish peoplehood is openly on display there, and we should accept this land where Jewish peoplehood is underscored as a reminder of our kinship to Jews the world over, even as we pray that our own Jewish community where religion is underscored will be a reminder to them of the spiritual character which they must in turn be careful not to neglect.

The Jew must always have the courage and conviction to be himself. In lands of persecution, we have feared that the Jew would be physically destroyed. In lands of freedom, the pressures upon our faith are more subtle, even though the opportunity to live it fully is present without restriction. It is possible for the essentials of our faith to be almost imperceptibly diluted in our natural desire to be like others among whom we live. The Jew, however, was never known as a conformist. He was always the great protestant of history. It is precisely this characteristic that can also be our finest contribution to America. We do not necessarily serve the country best by casting aside our uniqueness. We may, perhaps, best serve by retaining our basic character, and by contributing not only to the religious consciousness of our land, but to its religious conscience. There may be times when it serves a far better purpose to preserve our integrity and stand apart. Our highest loyalty is to God, and it is the vocation of the Jewish people to practice such loyalty to God.

Dr. Julian Morgenstern, speaking to the Hebrew Union College student body, once said,

> *We are a people with a God-appointed destiny which we cannot avert either through fear or through frenzied choice. We have been drafted by God for an eternal service which we dare not evade. We are the prophet people of history... Be this service what it may, brief or enduring... easy or exacting, let us serve with faith, with integrity and courage... hearing constantly ringing in our ears the heartening words of our Eternal Comforter... But thou Israel, My servant, Jacob, whom I have chosen, seed of Abraham whom I do love; thou whom I have drawn from the ends of the earth and from its borders have called thee and said unto thee, My servant art thou; I have chosen thee and have not rejected thee, fear not for I am with thee.*[121]

Dad—

In confirmation class, a half a century ago, you, as our rabbi and teacher, tried valiantly to teach us the meeting of peoplehood: that Judaism is not just a religion, and certainly not a nation or ethnicity. It might have helped if you had handed out copies of this sermon that you had written five years prior. Understanding what we were *not* would have been a great first step in learning what we *were*. We were not just another version of our Catholic and Protestant friends and neighbors. (And, yes, that was about all we had to compare ourselves to back then, before the proliferation of faith communities in the United States.) Even today, a greater sense of belonging to the peoplehood of Jews might stimulate increased thirst for our history, language, and homeland (or vice versa).

Blessings.
Yesh

---

[121] Rabbi Julian Morgenstern, Ph.D. (1881–1976), instructor in Bible and Semitic languages, was the first native-born American and alumnus of Hebrew Union College to become its president.

16. Mr. Sputnik
October 18, 1957

One of my father's tendencies, which both mystified and amused his family, was to consistently see the world through his rabbinical filter. On October 4, 1957, the world was dramatically changed by the Soviet Union's successful launch of the first man-made object to circle the earth in space—Sputnik. Most Americans reacted to this with fears of Soviet domination, criticisms of American science education, and other political arguments. For my father, this was just another occasion to remind his flock of the supremacy of God and moral law, higher even than the orbit of a Russian satellite hurtling through the heavens.

And the answer is not in rivalries that produce competition among nations..., but... in the realization that the future of mankind depends not on the intercontinental missile or the rocket to the moon, but rather on the weapon mentioned by our rabbis: the weapon of Torah, the force of moral law.

IT WAS JUST TWO WEEKS AGO THAT MR. SPUTNIK made his unexpected appearance and the world passed into a new age, an age in which man may soon see himself freed from the boundaries of this Earth and shall be able to pass into interplanetary space.[122] Of all the achievements of man, this is certainly the most fantastic. The scientific age has produced many marvels—the steam engine and the gasoline engine, the submarine by which we dive

---

[122] Sputnik 1 was the first artificial satellite to be put into Earth's orbit. It was launched into an elliptical low-Earth orbit by the Soviet Union on October 4, 1957. The unanticipated announcement of Sputnik 1's success "precipitated the Sputnik crisis in the United States and ignited the Space Race, a part of the larger Cold War. The launch ushered in new political, military, technological, and scientific developments." While the Sputnik launch was a single event, it marked the start of the Space Age. Wikipedia contributors. "Sputnik 1." *Wikipedia, The Free Encyclopedia*. Wikipedia, The Free Encyclopedia, 15 Sep. 2017. Web. 21 Sep. 2017.

beneath the sea, the planes which span the continents and the oceans in the air, and atomic energy with its unlimited possibilities of providing power. But surely the creation of a satellite that flies steadily about the earth miles above us, the intimation that it gives us of soon being able to reach other planets, this is the most astounding, the greatest miracle man has achieved, the nearest we have come to encroaching upon the powers of the divine.

And yet it seems to me that such a momentous event has by no means produced the kind of excitement we might have expected. There was more reaction to Milwaukee winning the World Series than to the announcement of a man-made satellite running around the earth.[123] This may be because man is getting rather blasé about his scientific achievements and takes everything in stride regardless of how impressive it may be. Or it maybe because this new development is so overwhelming, man is numbed by its magnitude and senses his own littleness in comparison to the power he has found himself capable of unleashing. Surely what reactions we have had to Mr. Sputnik fall short by far in measuring up to the significance of the moment.

The average man probably is conscious mostly of the destructive potential of the satellite, and rather than worrying about it, tries either to shut it out of his mind altogether or says, as I heard one man say, "Mr. Sputnik is above us. Let's all have fun."

The politicians all are confused and contradict each other at every moment. The outs find it a convenient opportunity to criticize the defense policies of the ins, and the ins make light of Sputnik, saying that what has happened will very shortly be surpassed by experiments in America still in preparation.

The scientists had yet another reaction. They are rightly quick to criticize the government policies impeding scientific development in our country.[124] In fact, Dr. Elmer Hutchisson, the Director of the American Institute of Physics, is quoted in *The New York Times* saying that the nation's youth must be taught to appreciate the importance of science, or the American way of life is doomed to rapid extinction.[125]

---

123 "The 1957 World Series featured the defending champions, the New York Yankees, playing against the Milwaukee Braves... The Braves won the Series in seven games... Of the previous ten World Series, the Yankees had participated in eight of them and won seven. This was also the first World Series since 1948 that a team from New York did not win." Wikipedia contributors. "1957 World Series." Wikipedia, *The Free Encyclopedia*. Wikipedia, The Free Encyclopedia, 27 May. 2017. Web. 21 Sep. 2017.

124 This comment may be referring to the post-World War II period when U.S. Senator Joseph McCarthy and governmental investigative committees engaged in political repression as well as a campaign spreading fear in order to root out communist sympathizers in the United States, including "revolutionary" thinkers among the scientific community.

125 Physicist Dr. Elmer Hutchisson (1902–1983) was a professor at the University of Pittsburgh, and the Director of the American Institute of Physics from 1957 to 1964. "Concerned with 'scientific illiteracy in an

And yet another kind of reaction was quoted in the press as coming from such a man as Will Durrant.[126] He admitted not being too excited about the new satellite, and said with a philosophical shrug,

> *I suppose it's something of importance from a national defense point of view. But to a philosopher, these physical changes aren't too interesting. People will go on living about the same way as they have before. Food and sex are basic and the most important human goals, whether we live in this world or some other one.*

Thus, the average man, the politician, the scientist, and the philosopher, and what each has to contribute to the situation, is possibly deserving of some thought, but there is, I think, a religious reaction to Mr. Sputnik that is far more significant for mankind than any of these.

Abraham Heschel, whom you have heard of on other occasions, wrote a book on the Sabbath several years ago, and it is amazing how some of his remarks in that book seem to fit the very situation we now speak of.[127] Judaism, he says, is a religion of time aimed at the sanctification of time, and what we do with time is more important than what we do with space. [He says:]

> *Technical civilization is man's conquest of space... To enhance our power in the world of space is certainly one of our tasks. The danger begins when in gaining power in the realm of space we forfeit all aspirations in the realm of time. There is a realm of time where the goal is not to have but to be, not to own but to give, not to control but to share, not to subdue but to be in accord. Life goes wrong when the control of space becomes our sole concern.*[128]

Ralph Waldo Emerson was not the mystic theologian that Professor Heschel is, but in a different way, he expressed somewhat the same thought about time.[129] When the first railroad successfully spanned the continent and

---

age of science,' he established the Center for History of Physics and its Niels Bohr Library, and founded the *Journal of Applied Physics*, of which he was editor from 1937 to 1953." "Elmer Hutchisson," *WNYC*, www.wnyc.org/people/elmer-hutchisson/. Accessed 21 Sep. 2017.

126 William James Durant (1885–1981) was a prolific "American writer, historian, and philosopher. He is best known for *The Story of Civilization*, eleven volumes written in collaboration with his wife Ariel Durant and published between 1935 and 1975." Wikipedia contributors. "Will Durant." *Wikipedia, The Free Encyclopedia*. Wikipedia, The Free Encyclopedia, 21 Sep. 2017. Web. 21 Sep. 2017.

127 "Abraham Joshua Heschel (1907–1972) was a Polish-born American rabbi and one of the leading Jewish theologians and Jewish philosophers of the twentieth century." Wikipedia contributors. "Abraham Joshua Heschel." *Wikipedia, The Free Encyclopedia*. Wikipedia, The Free Encyclopedia, 22 Jul. 2017. Web. 21 Sep. 2017.

128 Abraham Joshua Heschel, *The Sabbath* (1951), 3.

129 "Ralph Waldo Emerson (1803–1882) was an American essayist, lecturer, and poet who led the Transcendentalist movement of the mid-nineteenth century. He was seen as a champion of individualism and a prescient critic of the countervailing pressures of society, and he disseminated his thoughts

he was asked what he thought of it, he said, "It will certainly help man travel faster, but will it make him better?" Mr. Sputnik may be more dramatic than a railroad, but for religion, Mr. Sputnik, like the first railroad, merely accentuates the question, "How is man to handle the power and the knowledge that he acquires?" Speed and distance are exhilarating and desirable, but does not life indeed go wrong when the control of space becomes our sole concern?

The question is not a new one, brought to our attention only in the modern world of science. The question is one that is as old as man. The Torah portion of this week, the first in the Torah, speaks of the creation of the world, and already alludes to it.[130] We read of the creation of the world and then of the creation of man. Man is placed in the Garden of Eden where life is perfect and there are no problems, but man ignores the command of God and so is driven out of the garden, and to prevent his return, a revolving sword of flame is placed at the entrance.[131] The writer of the story does not, of course, use the word "utopia," but he nevertheless has written the story to explain the problems of society, the presence of pain and toil and conflict; and in his own unsophisticated way, he has suggested that man has deprived himself of the pleasure of living in a utopian society because of his own disobedience of God's law.

Later, in their own reading and interpretation of this chapter, the rabbis underscored this meaning. In the *Midrash*, they speak of Adam standing by the entrance to the Garden of Eden. When he noticed the revolving sword guarding it, they say, he cried out, "What will save my children from this revolving weapon of flame?" The answer came back to him: "The weapon of Torah." Man's future and man's salvation, the rabbis thus pointed out in a truth that remains valid, depends not on anything physical or spatial but upon his intelligent use of the weapon of moral law.

The revolving sword of flame is now a revolving satellite moving about the earth. But if we are wondering how to cope with it, the answer is the same now as it was in ancient times. Its challenge is no different than that which man has faced all through the ages. If there is a difference, it is only that the challenge is more crucial and more immediate because of the greater power and speeds and distances that man now finds himself involved with, and the energies that he can loose but not necessarily control. And the answer is not in rivalries, which produce competition among nations in scientific research,

---

through dozens of published essays and more than 1,500 public lectures given across the United States." Wikipedia contributors. "Ralph Waldo Emerson." *Wikipedia, The Free Encyclopedia*. Wikipedia, The Free Encyclopedia, 19 Sep. 2017. Web. 21 Sep. 2017.

130 *Parashat Bereishit*, Genesis 1-6:8.

131 Genesis 3:24.

the ability to manipulate great forces, and directing great missiles; but in broader cooperation, the reduction of national pride, the realization that the future of mankind depends not on the intercontinental missile or the rocket to the moon, but rather on the weapon mentioned by our rabbis: the weapon of Torah, the force of moral law.

We need not be altogether pessimistic. We are now in the midst of an international geophysical year. The scientists of the world with the blessing of their governments have joined in mutual cooperation to explore the secrets of the universe and search out new knowledge, and they are pledged to share what they find. If we can achieve such cooperation in the finding of knowledge, why should it not be possible to carry on similar cooperation in the application of this knowledge for the good of humanity and not its hurt? We have been banded in a United Nations where many political problems have been discussed and at least some shooting wars avoided. If only this process can continue until the habit is sufficiently fixed that there shall always be discussion and the shooting become altogether obsolete. The surface signs of cooperation, however, do exist, and we need to exert ourselves earnestly to expand them. Standing as we do on the threshold of amazing new adventures for mankind, it seems hardly likely that anyone will run the risk of ending it all by intentionally calling down destruction.

Let us pray only that we may be spared the effect of unintentional blunders that get out of control. In next week's portion of the Torah, there is another story that has bearing on our situation today: we are told of mankind's very first venture into space.[132] Men united their efforts in order to build themselves a tower which would penetrate into the heavens. They failed and God scattered them, we are told, over the face of the earth. But why did they fail? In uniting their efforts and resources, surely mankind was doing something worthwhile, something we are desperately trying to achieve today. But we are told man failed because of the motives that were involved. Man wanted to penetrate space in order to get himself a name. It was the spirit of arrogance and rebellion against God that moved them.

Our penetration of space today is not by means of a tower, but by means of rockets and satellites. However, the same moral applies to us. If there is arrogance involved in our achievements, then destruction will result and we shall be scattered. Above all, we must remain humble in our accomplishments. We must yet remember that if Mr. Sputnik is above us, God is also above him

---

[132] *Parashat Noach*, Genesis 6:9–11:32. After recounting the familiar story of Noah, the weekly portion describes how the earth was repopulated through Noah's three sons. The descendants of Noah remained a single people with a single language for ten generations. They eventually returned to evil ways by uniting in an idolatrous religion that led them to build a "tower with its top in the heavens"—the so-called tower of Babel.

and us together. Indeed, the more we venture forth into the unknown, the vaster and the more unknown the rest of the universe becomes and the more humble ought man to be. If we put our triumph over space in proper perspective, and if our achievements make us more conscious of the mystery of the universal and divine law which makes such a thing as a satellite possible and predictable, if this be what Mr. Sputnik will define, then what we do shall possibly be for the benefit of man and his ultimate glory. May it be our will and the will of God that it shall be so.

Amen.

Dad—

You look at the entire span of humanity—from Eden, to Babel, to Hiroshima, to outer space. Every step of the way humans have faltered, and yet you stand tall in your humility to remind us of the supreme mystery of the universe, divine law, and our ultimate salvation that can only come from the unity that divine awareness brings to us. You pray that God's will be our will. You quote Heschel: "The goal is not to have but to be..." These are words that nearly sixty years later are just landing in my ears, words that have become familiar in recent years, even as their attainment has been elusive. I pray with you that I learn to be content with being, that I resist the urge to have and to control. Let me find ways to live more in harmony with nature, with the well-being of my body, and with love and generosity of spirit for every human being and for all life on this small and precious planet.

Blessings.
Yesh

17. The Strange Call of the Shofar

September 15, 1958

Rosh Hashanah Morning

As a *ba'al tekiah* (shofar sounder), I naturally have a particular interest in this sermon. In it, my father studies the various uses of the ram's horn—both holy and unholy—to illustrate the potential for holy and unholy behavior in everyone.

The man who has mastered and elevated his emotions, who puts forth the effort to make the most of his natural endowments, who pursues goals in life which ennoble and give it purpose—that man has transcended his animal state, and, like the shofar, has been transformed into an instrument whose notes are in the service of God.

THE MOST DISTINCTIVE RITUAL involved in the observance of Rosh Hashanah is the blowing of the shofar. So basic is this rite that in earliest times, this holy day was not even known as Rosh Hashanah. It was known as *Yom Zichron Teruah*, the day of remembering the shofar blast, a name which has been replaced in popular usage but which still survives in our prayer book.

Traditionally, the use of the shofar is explained by the fact that it is considered a reminder of the story of Isaac which we read from the Torah this morning.[133] Because Abraham is finally commanded not to sacrifice Isaac but to offer a ram in his stead—the ram which had been opportunely entangled in the thicket by his horn—we blow the ram's horn as a reminder of the faith of Abraham, the obedience of Isaac, and the providence of God in intervening

---

[133] Genesis 22.

on behalf of Isaac. It is that providence which the devout worshiper has always relied upon as his deeds were examined by the celestial court on this day of judgment, and the shofar blast that reminded him of it filled him with religious fervor.

We as Jews are rather used to hearing the piercing blast of the shofar at this sacred service, but I can conceive of a stranger looking upon it with a bit of wonderment. It is all the more strange that the shofar should be used in a religious ceremony when we consider its background, for the shofar was the ancient signal horn used in time of war. A blast of the shofar called upon the columns of the ancient tribes to move forward or to halt. It signaled attack or retreat. When the Temple in Jerusalem was built, the use of iron was forbidden because the sword, an instrument of war, was also made of iron. By the same process of reasoning, we should have expected the shofar, used as a war signal, to be barred from religious use—but somehow the shofar transcended its profane usage and did take its place as a highly significant religious symbol. So much so that the psalmist was moved to declare, "Happy is the people who knoweth the sound of the *Teruah*; they walk, O Lord, in the light of Thy countenance."[134] And we should note that the verse does not say merely the *sound* of the shofar, but mentions specifically the *Teruah*, the tones of the shofar that had especially to do with sounding the alarm for battle.

The rabbis of old showed their awareness of this strange fact in the comment they made upon this verse. They asked:

> *Do not all the nations know the sound of the Teruah? They all have horns and trumpets and clarions. Why is it said of Israel, "Happy is the people who knoweth the sound of the Teruah; they walk, O Lord, in the light of Thy countenance."*

And they gave the answer: "Because Israel knows to use the Teruah to woo the favor of God." Thus, they pointed out that Israel had transformed the Teruah. It had elevated the use of the shofar. It had taken an instrument that could be used for purposes that were unholy, and directed its use to a purpose that was godly.

Knowing this background of the shofar, we can better understand its message to us today. Every individual may be compared in a sense to the shofar. Every individual is like an instrument that can potentially express itself in a variety of ways. We can permit ourselves to live out our days on a level that is ungodly, or we can elevate ourselves to a higher personality that will woo the favor of God. The sound of the shofar on Rosh Hashanah is a call

---

134 Psalm 89:16.

17. The Strange Call of the Shofar—1958

not to rest on the lower levels of human behavior, but to aspire toward our highest potential.

When man was created, the Bible tells us, he became a living soul—a *nefesh chaya*. But the word *chaya*, which means living, also means an animal, a beast. And the rabbis pointed out that the biblical verse could also be interpreted as meaning that man was created with the soul of a beast, an animal like all other animals, with all their evil potentialities. On the other hand, we find in the Psalms a more complimentary evaluation of man:

> *Thou hast made him but little lower than the angels,*
> *And hast crowned him with glory and honor.*
> *Thou hast made him to have dominion over the works of thy hands;*
> *Thou hast put all things under his feet.*

Here is a description of the man who has raised himself up, who is not on the level of an animal but who, as the psalmist continues, "has dominion over the beasts of the field, the birds of the air, and the fish of the sea."[135] These two estimates of man in our sacred literature do not necessarily contradict each other. They indicate feelings of Judaism that man has potentialities that can carry him to either extreme. Man is, indeed, born into the world like an animal, but there is a divine spark in him. Man has choice. If he wills it, he will function in this world as he came into it, an animal living on a biological level. But if he wills otherwise, even though he came into the world as an animal, he may transform himself into a great person, little lower than the angels.

Life is a constant challenge to choose wisely between these opposite directions in which we can travel. The man who lives merely for the satisfaction of his physical appetites, for whom material comforts form the highest good of life, and for whom the pursuit of pleasure is the highest value—that man lives a life no different than and not better than an animal.

The man who never takes time out for the pursuit of knowledge, who gives no thought to community service, whose life is devoted to making as much money as possible so that he can indulge himself as much as possible without ever a moment for a book or for music or for art or for prayer—that man has not chosen to allow the divine spark to function within him. But the man who has mastered and elevated his emotions, who puts forth the effort to make the most of his natural endowments, who pursues goals in life which ennoble and give it purpose—that man has transcended his animal state, and like the shofar, has been transformed into an instrument whose notes are in the service of God.

---

[135] Psalm 8:8-9.

When we speak of mastering our emotions, this does not mean that Judaism wants us to repress them altogether. Judaism sees no inherent evils in the natural instincts and emotions of man— far from it. Judaism asks only that man be critical of his instincts and emotions and subject them to an ethical standard, that he permit himself emotional expression which is enriching and deny himself that which is degrading, that he not respond to life compulsively and instinctively like an animal, but that his reactions reflect meaning and insight. Judaism never preaches asceticism, only that man fit his actions into a framework of human dignity and harmonize the animal in him with the divine.

Thus, some religious doctrines may look upon the sexual instinct as basically an evil and marriage a concession to the flesh. Judaism sees evil only when sex is abused and exists outside the framework of marriage that is faithful and family life that is pure. Some religious doctrines idealistically say that it is wrong to hate, putting all their emphasis on the need to love. Judaism realistically says that we cannot be one-sided in our emotional life. Hatred is not an evil when directed toward evils that must be combatted. As far as Judaism is concerned, there is no instinct or emotion with which nature has endowed man that is in itself good or evil. It is man that gives it moral coloring, depending upon the direction that he gives to his emotion. Love may be a virtue, but it too can be an evil when what we love is unworthy of being the object of our emotion. It is what we love that makes love either good or bad. Joy also can be good or bad. It is selfish when we are absorbed solely with the thought of our own good fortune, but it becomes unselfish when we are moved to share our joy with others less fortunate. Sorrow can be good or bad. It can be selfish if we remain overly long unconsoled and concerned only with our own hurt, but it is ennobling if it makes us sympathetic to the wounds of others. Thus, whatever natural instinct or emotion of man we may consider, the direction we give it is of utmost importance. Judaism calls upon us not to let our emotions rule over us indiscriminately, but to elevate them in a manner which leads man to the fulfillment of his potential as a unique creation of God, who can become but little lower than the angels.

In speaking of the call to each of us to reach our potential, a Hasidic story inevitably comes to mind. It is a story told about the famous Hasidic rabbi, Reb Zussya of Annapol.[136] He is reported to have said tearfully on Rosh Hashanah:

On the Day of Judgment, I shall not be asked why I was not a Moses, because I am not Moses. I shall not be asked why I did not become a Rabbi Akiba,

---

[136] Rabbi Meshulam Zussya (1718–1800) of Annapol, a village in west-central Poland, was an "Orthodox rabbi and an early Hasidic luminary." Wikipedia contributors. "Zusha of Hanipol." *Wikipedia, The Free Encyclopedia*. Wikipedia, The Free Encyclopedia, 15 Sep. 2017. Web. 21 Sep. 2017.

because I'm not Rabbi Akiba. But woe is me! For I shall be asked, "Why were you not Zussya of Annapol?" And to that I shall not be able to answer.

Many of us tend to excuse our shortcomings using comparisons to others. We tell ourselves we have not the saintliness, the talents, the intellect that some other people have. We are just average men and women, and this talk of being but little lower than the angels is not for us. We must remember the implication of the words of Reb Zussya. Only a comparatively few people, after all, are endowed with the qualities that come with genius or the characteristics that accompany greatness. Only a few of us are destined to fame or renown. But each one has his own individual character and capabilities, whatever they may be. These he is expected to develop to their highest. No man is expected to develop capacities that he does not possess. No man is asked in judgment, "Why did you not become a Moses or an Akiba?" He is asked only, "Why did you not become yourself? Why are you not Zussya of Annapol or Yankel of Long Island? Why are you not as good as *you* can be? Why have you not developed your own potentiality to the fullest possible extent?" The spark of the divine is not restricted, and it burns strongly within every one of us if we choose to keep it alive. And when he responds to it, even an average man achieves greatness and is little lower than the angels.

This is the thought that is inherent in the symbolism of the shofar, and it is to arouse this thought that the shofar calls. In the words of the great philosopher Maimonides, it says to us:

Awake, ye sleepers, from your sleep, and ye who are in a trance, rouse yourselves. Consider your actions and turn back in repentance. Remember your Creator. Be not as those who forget reality in their hunt after shadows, and waste their whole year in empty things which can neither help nor deliver. Look to your souls and improve your ways and your deeds. Let each one forsake his evil ways and thoughts which are not good.[137]

Let each one of us strive to be his best. Let us, indeed, not be as those who forget reality in their hunt after shadows. Let us make way for the divine that is within us, and on this solemn occasion, let us resolve so to live that our true capabilities shall not be stifled, and the possibilities of a better, nobler, and more purposeful life shall be realized.

Amen.

---

[137] Moshe ben Maimon, acronymed Rambam for "Rabbeinu Moshe Ben Maimon" ("Our Rabbi/Teacher Moses Son of Maimon"), and Latinized Moses Maimonides, a preeminent medieval Sephardic Jewish philosopher and astronomer, "became one of the most prolific and influential Torah scholars and physicians of the Middle Ages... He worked as a rabbi, physician, and philosopher in Morocco and Egypt." Wikipedia contributors. "Maimonides." *Wikipedia, The Free Encyclopedia*. Wikipedia, The Free Encyclopedia, 17 Sep. 2017. Web. 21 Sep. 2017.

Dad—

Ah! Three years before I became a *Ba'al Tekiah*—a "carrier of the sound of the shofar"—I must have heard these words. What impression could they have made on a ten-year-old? Now, decades later, having sounded these ancient calls countless times, having learned slowly to transform these notes from performance into prayer, I now hear your words anew. I have always known the shofar blasts to be the "Jewish alarm clock" awakening our slumbering souls, and this message makes it that much more clear from and to what we may be awakening.

You speak of how we might be judged. The question I may be asked is, "Why was I not Yeshaya?" You had the courage to be Sidney—God bless you for that. Thank you for inspiring me to search more deeply for the divine that is within me in order to fulfill my role in life as Yeshaya.

Blessings.
Yesh

18. The Complete Jew

September 23, 1958

Kol Nidre

This sermon emphasizes two important traditional Jewish values—study and charity—and concludes with one of my father's favorite parables, one that reflects the humility with which Sidney Ballon led his life.

And now as I conclude, may I say that very often after a sermon of a somewhat personal nature as this, there are people who turn to their neighbor and say, "That was good. He certainly gave it to them." The truth is, however, I did not give it to them. I gave it to you and I gave it to myself.

IN THE TRADITIONAL PRAYER BOOK, for this most solemn occasion of Yom Kippur Eve, the *Kol Nidre* service begins with the statement, "In the heavenly court and in the court on Earth with the permission of God and the permission of this congregation, we give leave to pray with transgressors."

Our reform prayer book has left these words out, and I wonder if it was not because some editors with a sense of humor thought to themselves, "Who else is there that we can pray with, if not with transgressors." Judaism believes that only God is perfect, and people, being what they are, all fall short of the ideal somewhere along the line. "No man liveth that sinneth not."[138] If we were to try to organize for prayer this evening a congregation of Jews without any

---

[138] From King Solomon's prayer at the dedication of the Temple, 1 Kings 8:46: "If they sin against Thee—for there is no man that sinneth not—and Thou be angry with them, and deliver them to the enemy, so that they carry them away captive unto the land of the enemy, far off or near."

failings, we surely would not be able to get a *minyan* together, and I venture to confess not even a rabbi to lead them.[139]

Judaism tells us that the perfect man does not exist, but this is not to say that we as individuals have a right to take refuge in this thought and thus excuse ourselves for anything that we may do that is short of the ideal. Even as we recognize the inevitability of human failings, we nevertheless are obligated to reproach ourselves for our failures and to improve ourselves as much as we possibly can. Yom Kippur asks us to make honest confession. Our prayer book, particularly in the passage *Al Chet Shechatanu*, lists the sins of which frail man may easily find himself guilty.[140] I should like to spend a few minutes with you in this Yom Kippur spirit, but I shall dwell not on *Al Chet Shechatanu*, on the sins we have committed, but rather *Al Hamitzvos*, on the virtues that we have turned away from and should be striving to fulfill.[141]

Several years ago, a sociological study of the Jews of the towns of Eastern Europe was published under the title of *Life is With People*. A comment in this book tells us that "...the word Yiddishkeit—Jewishness—carries, as an aura, the veneration of learning, [and] the acceptance of obligation..." Here, indeed, are two characteristic Jewish virtues, which we Jews in modern times ought to be more concerned with. In days gone by, a man's rating as a Jew approximated his rating as a Jewish scholar. A Jew without learning was an incomplete Jew, and if a Jew was not learned himself, he at least had a healthy respect for those who were. Many factors entered into determining the social status of the Jew, but the more removed he was from Jewish learning, the more *prost*—ordinary—he was considered. Wealth was not despised; our people admired success in business. But the primary value in Jewish life was learning. In the world of Eastern Europe, when someone said of another, *"Er is a shayneh yid* (He is a beautiful Jew)," it was a supreme compliment. It involved a beauty that did not depend on physical appearance, but on inner content. Men of learning were automatically classified as *shayneh yiden*, even if they didn't have a dollar. Men of money might attain the same classification, but it did not come automatically because they had money. It depended

---

139 A *minyan* (lit. Hebrew: "to count") in Judaism refers to "the quorum of ten Jewish adults required for certain religious obligations," especially public prayer. Wikipedia contributors. "Minyan." *Wikipedia, The Free Encyclopedia*. Wikipedia, The Free Encyclopedia, 5 Sep. 2017. Web. 21 Sep. 2017.

140 The central prayer on Yom Kippur, the Day of Atonement, is a confession of sins committed both individually and as a community. Each line of the prayer begins with "*Al chet shechatanu*, for the sin which we have committed."

141 *Mitzvos* (*mitzvot* in modern Hebrew), plural of the Hebrew *mitzvah*, "commandment," "refers to a moral deed performed as a religious duty. As such, the term *mitzvah* has also come to express an act of human kindness." Wikipedia contributors. "Mitzvah." *Wikipedia, The Free Encyclopedia*. Wikipedia, The Free Encyclopedia, 11 Jun. 2017. Web. 21 Sep. 2017.

entirely on how the money was used. If a man did not have learning, he at least had to spend his money in accordance with the ideals of the Torah, which was the object of learning; he had to live in accordance with its teaching. Men of learning were treated with *derech eretz*.[142] Men of learning were listened to in matters of Jewish content, community life, and even politics, and their advice was sought out.

Today, I am afraid that some of the same anti-intellectualism that has infected the general community, the same disparagement of "eggheads," has to a great extent infected Jewish life as well.[143] We live today in an environment that glorifies the business world and worships the dollar. To acquire wealth rather than knowledge is the ideal toward which we strive, and if knowledge is acquired, its value is judged by how much income it will ultimately produce. This attitude, unfortunately, has serious byproducts. It influences our efforts in Jewish education with respect to our children, and it causes us to neglect our own adult Jewish development. We are satisfied today, most of us, with altogether too little in the way of Jewish knowledge for our children, and the smattering of education we do give them must not conflict with the convenience of the mother, the whims of the child, or with a hundred other outside interests the child is involved in. As for adults, Jewish learning is for the rabbis, and rabbis are impractical people whom everybody asks in amazement, "What was it that made you want to be a rabbi?" And even learning in rabbis is not altogether appreciated in the congregation of today. Although many duties are imposed on the rabbi, few people are concerned whether he has time to fulfill the duty to study, and if he takes the time to do so, he is often considered to be taking advantage of the congregation.

I think it fitting, my friends, to remind ourselves on this night of Yom Kippur that on the scale of Jewish values, a man is measured by his mind and his heart, and not the bulk of his pocket; and that one of the virtues of the good Jew is a proper appreciation of intellectual attainment and a proper regard for those positions in Jewish life which imply such attainment.

The other quality of a complete Jew that we previously mentioned is the acceptance of obligation. In the Jewish home in Eastern Europe, as described in *Life is With People*, there always was a collection of *tsedoko* boxes in which at

---

142 *Derech eretz* (Hebrew, literally: "the way of the land") often is broadly translated as "decent, polite, respectful, thoughtful, and civilized behavior... 'behaving like a *mentsh*' (refined human being)." In this context, it suggests the respect given to deserving individuals. Wikipedia contributors. "*Torah im Derech Eretz.*" *Wikipedia, The Free Encyclopedia*. Wikipedia, The Free Encyclopedia, 17 Sep. 2017. Web. 21 Sep. 2017.

143 The term egghead, an anti-intellectual epithet, "reached its peak currency during the 1950s, when vice-presidential candidate Richard Nixon used it against Democratic Presidential nominee Adlai Stevenson," loser to Dwight D. Eisenhower in 1952 and 1956. Wikipedia contributors. "Egghead." *Wikipedia, The Free Encyclopedia*. Wikipedia, The Free Encyclopedia, 31 Aug. 2017. Web. 21 Sep. 2017.

appropriate times coins might be dropped.¹⁴⁴ Some of these boxes survived even in this country and perhaps even within your own memory. In times of joy and times of sorrow, particularly before the lighting of the Sabbath candles—now too often the forgotten art—an offering was placed in these boxes that ultimately found itself used to help the poor, to support the synagogue and *yeshivos*, to build the Holy Land.¹⁴⁵ Even the poor who received charity were, according to the *Shulchan Aruch*, expected to give to others out of what they received themselves.¹⁴⁶ The Jew was helped to give this *tsedoko* graciously because he was more conscious in those days of the Jewish philosophy of life. It is a philosophy that teaches us that whatever we have is not ours. We find it in our *Union Prayer Book* for the Sabbath in the words, "We are but stewards of whatever we possess… May we never forget that all we have and prize is but lent to us, a trust for which we must render account to Thee."

Even the wealthiest is not to be smugly self-satisfied with his own achievements. Material possessions are acquired with the help of God and with the will of God and still belong to God; and it is our obligation to give back in humble appreciation at least a portion of what is, after all, not really ours. This is the Jewish spirit.

Our society today is not geared to the tin box type of *tsedoko*. Our social organization is much more complex than it was in the towns of Eastern Europe, but the principle endures. It is still our obligation to share humbly for the purpose of helping our fellowmen and advancing Jewish causes. The box for the poor has grown into the Federation of Jewish Philanthropies. The box for the Holy Land has grown into the United Jewish Appeal. The box for the synagogues and *yeshivos* has grown into temple dues and contributions to our national religious institutions such as the Union of American Hebrew Congregations¹⁴⁷ and the Hebrew Union College.¹⁴⁸ Of course, there are many

---

144 *Tsedoko* (*tzedakah* in Modern Hebrew) "[literally means] righteousness but [is] commonly used to signify charity." Wikipedia contributors. "Tzedakah" *Wikipedia, The Free Encyclopedia*. Wikipedia, The Free Encyclopedia, 6 Mar. 2017. Web. 21 Sep. 2017.

145 *Yeshiva* (Hebrew, literally: "sitting"; pl. *yeshivos*, or *yeshivot* in Modern Hebrew) is a Jewish educational institution that focuses on the study of traditional religious texts, primarily the Talmud and Torah.

146 The *Shulchan Aruch* (Hebrew, literally: "Set Table") is the most authoritative legal code of Judaism, authored by Yosef Karo in 1563. Wikipedia contributors. "Shulchan Aruch." *Wikipedia, The Free Encyclopedia*. Wikipedia, The Free Encyclopedia, 9 Sep. 2017. Web. 21 Sep. 2017.

147 The Union of American Hebrew Congregations (UAHC), now named the Union for Reform Judaism (URJ), is an organization which supports Reform Jewish congregations in North America.

148 The Hebrew Union College-Jewish Institute of Religion (also known as HUC, HUC-JIR), with "campuses in Cincinnati, New York, Los Angeles and Jerusalem… is the oldest extant Jewish seminary in the Americas and the main seminary for training rabbis, cantors, educators, and communal workers in Reform Judaism." Wikipedia contributors. "Hebrew Union College-Jewish Institute of Religion." *Wikipedia, The Free Encyclopedia*. Wikipedia, The Free Encyclopedia, 29 Aug. 2017. Web. 21 Sep. 2017.

other community causes that might be mentioned, but how many of us in this land of wealth manage to lose ourselves in the crowd. Perhaps we cannot contribute significantly to every appeal that comes our way, but we might very well ask ourselves on this holy night, "Have we assumed our fair share of the burden? Have we approached the ancient biblical prescription for tithing— the giving of one-tenth of one's income back to God? Have we demonstrated to proper degree that we have a social conscience?"

Tonight, it is perhaps appropriate to add an extra word about our own synagogue. As you entered this evening, your eye undoubtedly caught the display that demonstrates what is being proposed by our architects with regard to the new temple we have been planning for so long. I ask you tonight, my friends, do you really want this temple? Of course, if you are at all interested in serving the Jewish community adequately, you do. Of course, if you are at all concerned about our poor school and teenage facilities and the consequent problems, you do. Of course, if you want a house of worship that will indeed be invested with purity and sanctity, you do. But you will have to remember that it must take effort and sacrifice, that we must all participate according to our abilities and cannot wait for others to do it for us. Temples are not built by people who abdicate their responsibilities, who are offended when the officers who do their work for them remind them of their obligations. Temples are difficult to maintain when Jews come to them only when the children are of the right age, or when they are in for a bar mitzvah and out right afterwards. If a congregation is to be here when you "need" it, it has to be maintained at all times. If the religious training you give your child is to be meaningful, you must demonstrate its meaningfulness by your own loyalty before and after the formal education of your child. The sage Hillel,[149] in *Sayings of the Fathers*, said "Do not withdraw thyself from the congregation."[150] The good Jew, the complete Jew, heeds very seriously this ancient admonition.

There is yet one more virtue that I want to consider with you this evening, and if I need any excuse for selecting this particular one above all other possibilities, other than the fact that my mood impels me to do so, I can find it also in the *Sayings of the Fathers*. There we find the words of Shammai: "Set a fixed

---

149 Hillel (according to tradition ca. 110 BCE–ca. 10 CE) "was a Jewish scholar and founder of a dynasty of patriarchs who were the spiritual heads of Jewry until the fifth century." "Hillel," *Encyclopedia of World Biography* (The Gale Group, 2004), www.encyclopedia.com/people/philosophy-and-religion/judaism-biographies/hillel. Accessed 21 Sep. 2017.

150 *The Sayings of the Fathers* (*Pirkei Avot* in Hebrew) is a "compilation of the ethical teachings and maxims" of Mishnaic-period rabbis (c. 10–220 CE). "It is part of didactic Jewish ethical Musar literature. Because of its contents, it is also called *Ethics of the Fathers*." Wikipedia contributors. "Pirkei Avot." *Wikipedia, The Free Encyclopedia*. Wikipedia, The Free Encyclopedia, 28 Aug. 2017. Web. 21 Sep. 2017.

time for the study of Torah, say little and do much, and receive all men with cheerful countenance."[151]

The first two parts of this statement are in the very same spirit as my previous remarks with regard to the veneration of learning and the acceptance of obligation. Set a time for study and do much. What Shammai has linked with this is the very suggestion that I want to leave with you as my final thought for the evening. Thus, I but follow the precedent of Shammai, when to my previous admonitions I also add the instruction: "*Haray mikabail es kol ha-adam bsayven panim yafos.* Receive all men with a cheerful countenance."

This is a very simple thought and a very elementary bit of advice, but how often we act as if we had never heard of it. This is, to be sure, a world full of various pressures and frustrations, and we often, indeed, do not deserve to be too harshly judged if our tempers are short and our words are sharp. But we must have a sense of humor about things and a sense of proportion. How often I meet people with long faces—not long with sorrow, not long with pain, but just long because they have forgotten to smile. Very often, if they could manage the smile, the fancied problems that exist between them and another person would vanish with the frown, and the real problems, indeed, would be more easily settled. Did somebody aggravate us? A smile will lessen the aggravation. Did something happen in temple that annoys us? A sense of humor can bring tremendous relief. To walk about with a long face, to snap at people because they do things differently than we might have, to condemn because of human error, to resign and to sulk is not only to go contrary to the advice of our rabbis but to invite ulcers as well.[152]

During the past summer, a friend sent me, in jest, a printed card on which was written: "When I do something right, no one remembers. When I do something wrong, no one forgets."

When we are tempted to criticize, let us stop to remember the good of the past. It is not that criticism is bad and must never be offered, but criticism, too, should be *yesurim shel ahava*—chastisements of love—and can be offered with a cheerful countenance.

The psychologists tell us that when we tear our neighbors down, we do so because of our own sense of insecurity and in an effort to build ourselves up. Perhaps we would be less prone to excitement if we could remember that the way we criticize reveals even more about ourselves than about the person

---

151 "Shammai (50 BCE–30 CE) was a Jewish scholar of the first century. An important figure in Judaism's core work of rabbinic literature, the *Mishnah*," he frequently was at odds with Hillel. Wikipedia contributors. "Shammai." *Wikipedia, The Free Encyclopedia.* Wikipedia, The Free Encyclopedia, 6 May. 2017. Web. 21 Sep. 2017.

152 Until the mid-1980s, the conventional wisdom was that ulcers form as a result of stress. A relatively recent theory holds that bacterial infection is the primary cause of peptic ulcers.

we criticize. If I may be permitted to quote the Sayings of the Fathers yet once again: "Let the honor of thy neighbor be as dear to thee as thine own and suffer not thyself to be easily angered."

And now as I conclude, may I say that very often after a sermon of a somewhat personal nature as this, there are people who turn to their neighbor and say, "That was good. He certainly gave it to them." The truth is, however, that I did not give it to them. I gave it to you and I gave it to myself. The Hasidic rabbi of Sanz used to say,

> *In my youth when I was fired with the love of God, I thought I would convert the whole world to God. But soon I discovered that it would be quite enough to convert the people who live in my town. I tried for a long time but did not succeed. Then I realized that my program was still too ambitious and I concentrated on the persons in my own household. But I could not convert them either. Finally, it dawned on me: I must work on myself, so that I may give true service.*[153]

And so, in the spirit of the rabbi of Sanz, let us, on this night of forgiveness and confession, not concern ourselves futilely with the faults of our neighbor. Let us each—you and I included—begin working upon that inadequate person over whom we do have the greatest influence: our very own selves.

Dad—

Humor and above all—humility. You lead by example. Rather than castigate your congregation for their sins, you freely admit your own. You accentuate the positive (commandments) rather than harp on transgressions. You remind them of what is truly important "on the scale of Jewish values," and of the insignificance of material possessions. You remind them of the power of a simple smile. How elegant!

Lastly, you tell an anecdote that has always lingered in my mind, one that simultaneously empowers all who hear it even as it, once again, demonstrates your humility. Who hasn't aspired to change the world, overlooking the real challenge to change oneself?

Blessings.
Yesh

---

[153] Chaim Halberstam (1793–1876) of Sanz (also Zans), Poland, was a "famous Hasidic Rebbe and the founder of the Sanz Hasidic dynasty." Wikipedia contributors. "Chaim Halberstam." *Wikipedia, The Free Encyclopedia*. Wikipedia, The Free Encyclopedia, 27 May. 2016. Web. 21 Sep. 2017.

19. Ignorance of Judaism

January 22, 1960

This is one of my father's most common sermonic themes. He comes back to it again and again throughout his career. Clearly, his most frustrating and perplexing challenge in the pulpit was dealing with the perceived ignorance and apathy among Reform Jews about their history and heritage.

To be a Reform Jew... does not mean indifference or drifting. It implies intelligent appraisal and meaningful renewal of our Jewish life. For this, adequate Jewish knowledge is essential.

IN THE TORAH PORTION OF THIS WEEK, WE BEGIN THE STORY of the enslavement of the Jews in Egypt.[154] How did it happen that these Jews were enslaved? The original settlers had been welcomed to Egypt as the family of the wise Joseph, whose skill as administrator for Pharaoh had saved the land from famine. Now, the descendants of Joseph and his brothers were being degraded. The Bible tells us how it could happen. It reads, "Now there arose a new king over Egypt who knew not Joseph."[155] The biblical writer thus ascribed the difficulties of the Hebrew people to ignorance. The new Pharaoh was ignorant of the past, and he did not know of the contribution of Joseph and his people.

Ignorance continues to be a problem for the Jewish people to this very day. Much of the anti-Jewish feeling that is expressed is a product of ignorant minds—ignorance about Jews and Judaism. One way we attempt to counter anti-Jewish feeling today is by enlightenment, trying to bring knowledge of the Jew and Judaism to the masses of people. For example, the Jewish

---

154 *Shemot*, Exodus 1:1-6:1.

155 Exodus 1:8.

Chautauqua Society program, which is sponsored by the National Federation of Temple Men's Clubs, works with colleges and church groups.[156]

But there is today a different twist to the problem of ignorance with which we should be even more concerned. (Here again, I should add that the National Federation of Temple Men's Clubs are becoming most active in the battle against this other aspect of ignorance.) The ignorance that I wish to underscore this evening has nothing to do with anti-Semites, but is rather the ignorance of Jews and Judaism that exists among ourselves. The pharaohs that know not Joseph are not our only problem today. It is the Jews who know not Joseph, the Jews who are ignorant of their heritage and the Jewish past, with whom we must be concerned.

We Jews have become very self-satisfied because of the constant improvement that we have noted in Jewish life over the past years. We are in the midst of a so-called religious revival which has led to greater numbers of Jews becoming affiliated with synagogues and an ever-increasing number of new congregations as well. As Maurice Samuel has pointed out, three or four decades ago, Jews were asking, "Why should we be Jews?" But today, a new pleasure in Jewish identity has eliminated this question. We no longer are apologetic about our Jewishness, and the State of Israel, especially, has contributed to our pride. But the extent of our Jewish knowledge, nevertheless, remains shallow and sketchy. I used the term "Jews who know not Joseph" as a figure of speech, but we may take it literally and ask how many are not familiar even with the simple facts of a biblical personality like Joseph. Our tradition has always been that the Torah *sedra* of the week be read three times.[157] *Shnayim mikra v'echod l'targum*—twice in Hebrew and once in translation.[158] But how much Bible do we read on any regular basis today, and how do we let the Bible contribute to our daily living and our daily attitudes? What do

---

156 "The Jewish Chautauqua Society was the interfaith education program of the Men of Reform Judaism, a U.S. nonprofit organization. It [sought] 'the dissemination of knowledge of the Jewish religion by fostering the study of its history and literature, giving popular courses of instruction, issuing publications, establishing reading-circles, holding general assemblies, [etc.].'" The National Federation of Temple Men's Clubs, also known as the National Federation of Temple Brotherhoods and now called the Men of Reform Judaism, was founded in 1923 as part of the Reform Jewish movement. Wikipedia contributors. "Jewish Chautauqua Society." *Wikipedia, The Free Encyclopedia*. Wikipedia, The Free Encyclopedia, 19 Jan. 2017. Web. 21 Sep. 2017.

157 The weekly Torah portion (*Parashat ha-Shavua*, popularly just *parashah* or *parsha* and also known as a *Sidra* or *Sedra*) is a section of the Torah.

158 "According to the *Gemara* in Tractate *Berakhot* 8a:, Rav Huna bar Yehuda says in the name of Rabbi Ammi, 'One should always complete the reading of one's weekly Torah portion with the congregation, twice from the *mikra* (i.e. Torah) and once from the *Targum* (Aramaic translation and explanations).'" Wikipedia contributors. "Shnayim mikra ve-echad targum." *Wikipedia, The Free Encyclopedia*. Wikipedia, The Free Encyclopedia, 11 Sep. 2017. Web. 21 Sep. 2017.

we know of the Hebrew language? And to go further: what of Jewish history and Jewish practice or Jewish theology?

The pathetic state of Jewish knowledge was reflected recently when the book *Exodus* hit the bestseller lists. It was a thrilling book and a wonderful contribution to the understanding of what is happening in Israel today. But it was amazing to note that for so many, what *Exodus* had to say was so new. There was nothing new in *Exodus*. Anyone with knowledge of the Bible and history would understand the devotion the Jew has for the Holy Land. Anyone familiar with modern Jewish history would know about the social and economic factors that stimulated the Zionist movement. Anyone who has kept abreast of Jewish current events knows about all the horrors and the achievements of which *Exodus* speaks—but this was a revelation to so many. They had no prior understanding of the Jewish past and the Jewish spirit. Thank God for *Exodus*, but it was disturbing to see that so many found its story so new.

This is quite a contrast with the attitudes toward learning that traditionally prevailed among our people. In Jewish life, study was at least as important as prayer. Knowledge ranked equally with worship as an essential of the good Jewish life. According to the rabbis, a synagogue may be converted into a schoolhouse but a schoolhouse should not be given up for a synagogue; the rule was that one might increase the sanctity of a holy place, but one must not decrease it. Study thus seems to be even more important than prayer. "*Talmud Torah kneged kulam*," they said. Study of the Torah is the greatest of all virtues. The prayer book refers to the words of Torah as our true life and length of days, and the *Ethics of the Fathers* tells us, "An ignorant man cannot be a pious man."[159] These ideals have gotten away from us in the present. Environmental pressures have caused us to relax our standards, and we have fallen away to an appalling degree.

Part of the cure of any bad situation, however, is to be aware of the problem. If we are not aware of our sickness, we shall seek no cure. But today, we can at least point to a growing awareness of the disease of ignorance in Jewish life; and consequently, more and more effort, small though it may still be, is being expended to remedy the problem. Our children, at least, are being exposed to Jewish education to a greater extent than ever before in this country, and when we have, for example, a *bar mitzvah* service as we do this evening, it is more likely than not that a significant period of preparation preceded it. It is not merely a matter of calling a boy up to the Torah. But we

---

[159] "Hillel used to say: A brutish man cannot fear sin; an ignorant man cannot be pious, nor can the shy man learn, or the impatient man teach. He who engages excessively in business cannot become wise. In a place where there are no men strive to be a man" (*Pirkei Avot* 2:6). www.myjewishlearning.com/article/pirkei-avot-ethics-of-the-fathers-5/. Accessed 21 Sep. 2017.

need to become ever more aware of two things in particular. One, the education of our children needs to become much more intensified and their period of study lengthened. Even for our children we do not do enough. And two, Judaism cannot be taught only on the basis of educating the child. It is too deep and there is too much to do. Just as we try to give our children Jewish knowledge on a regular basis, so now should we also do this for adults. It takes a mature mind to come to a full understanding of Judaism, and it takes educated parents to educate our children.

For us as Reform Jews in particular, this education is necessary. There is an altogether erroneous impression that being a Reform Jew means that we can tolerate lower standards of religious interest and religious knowledge. For some strange reason, it is expected that no demands need be made upon Reform Jews. Say you are Reform and anything goes. Nothing could be further from the truth. To be a Reform Jew is a great challenge. If we are going to break with traditions of the past, we must know what we are breaking from. And we must know how to fashion intelligently and in a good Jewish spirit what we propose to substitute for that which we reject. Reform does not mean indifference or drifting. It implies intelligent appraisal and meaningful renewal of our Jewish life. For this, adequate Jewish knowledge is essential.

There are hopeful signs that we may yet be moved to follow the right path. We have brought many back to the synagogue, and now we must work to bring them back to the ideal of Torah. And even though today there are many Jews who know not Joseph, we dare hope that patient and faithful leadership will yet redeem them and lead them through the wilderness so that they will again embrace the Torah at a new Sinai.

And now, Jerry, as you become *bar mitzvah* this evening, we hope that we have recruited you into the ranks of those who will be faithful to Judaism and zealous for its advancement. We hope that the bare beginnings of Jewish study that you have achieved will continue, and that in years to come, you will become something that is as yet altogether too rare in Jewish life: a layman with deep knowledge and understanding of his faith.

Our best wishes to you for the future.

19. The Ignorance of Judiasm —1960

Dad—

Ignorance and apathy is a common theme among your sermons. In this essay, you have emphasized the ignorance part of the equation.

Decades ago, when I attended "Junior Congregation" with my children, every Shabbat morning we read the words you quote, "*Talmud Torah kneged kulam.*" You translate that, "Study of the Torah is the greatest of all virtues." I'm actually surprised that you didn't complete that teaching: "because it leads to all the other mitzvot."

Study and knowledge lead to action and are essential for young and old alike. Despite your best efforts, there was a considerable gap in my Jewish education. I feel I am always playing catch-up. I pray that these words inspire my children to close the gap for themselves and for their children more readily than did I.

Blessings.
Yesh

20. The Melody of Faith

September 30, 1960

Kol Nidre

For most people, the evocative melody of the *Kol Nidre* chant is much more meaningful and powerful than the words. The *Kol Nidre* words are brittle, empty of meaning in themselves; yet the melody is so alluring we drink it in. My father posits that our lives, too, may seem meaningless without infusing them with the melody that Judaism provides.

We simply do not give our religious feelings a chance. We are content with the notions of religion gained in childhood, and make no effort to cultivate a religion of maturity.

THERE IS AT LEAST ONE SERVICE DURING THE YEAR when the congregation can be counted upon to be present with a high degree of promptness. And that is the service of this evening. The reason for the comparatively few latecomers is the fortunate custom of having the *Kol Nidre* chanted as the introduction to our evening's worship. The *Kol Nidre* melody is such a captivating one. It so perfectly expresses the mood of this sacred night, which ranges from brooding over our human failings to a spirit of resolution and aspiration with respect to our future, that our people simply will not miss it. The high point of our service comes not as a climax to the evening, but rather at its beginning.

There is a peculiar disparity, however, almost a sharp contradiction between the warm, mystical melody of the *Kol Nidre* and the cold legal tone of its text, which is a formula for the annulment of vows.[160] You have no doubt

---

[160] There are variations in the translations of the original Aramaic text. The following text comes from the *Jewish Encyclopedia*: "All vows, obligations, oaths, and anathemas, whether called *'onam,' 'onas,'* or by

already noted that our *Union Prayer Book* omits the text of the *Kol Nidre*, and we have in its place only an English paragraph, which attempts to interpret the spirit of the melody rather than translate the original words.[161] The reason for this is that the words were considered a problem. They did not seem to have any meaning for us. But do not think that the displeasure with the words of the *Kol Nidre* is merely a Reform quirk of modern times. Even in medieval days, there was opposition to the *Kol Nidre* among leading rabbis who questioned its meaning and who felt it might be misinterpreted by our enemies. But the *Kol Nidre* has remained a part of our service regardless of the problems, and it is the magnificent melody, of course, which has redeemed it from meaninglessness and enabled it to survive.

I find something symbolic in this redeeming relationship that the melody of *Kol Nidre* has to its text. It seems to me that the same relationship exists between religion and life. There are many people—and I daresay some are even here tonight, although we are all gathered for a religious service—there are many who question the value of religion and are not altogether convinced that it has an important place in life. You may belong to the synagogue, and you may come to an occasional service, especially on the High Holy Days, but the nature of our times is such that a touch of doubt remains, and you wonder why, after all, you should be so concerned with religious pursuits. The *Kol Nidre* symbolizes the answer. Religion is the melody that gives life its sense and purpose.

As we reflect with our proud intellect upon the problems of human existence, there are often moments of despair when it seems that life and the world is devoid of meaning. "What is man?" we may ask. And the cold rational answer is that from the standpoint of biology, man is a kind of higher animal, but an animal nonetheless. The psalmist long ago bemoaned the fact that "the days of our years are threescore and ten, and it is speedily gone and we fly away."[162] Regardless of what man achieves in this world, regardless of his

---

any other name, which we may vow, or swear, or pledge, or whereby we may be bound, from this Day of Atonement until the next (whose happy coming we await), we do repent. May they be deemed absolved, forgiven, annulled, and void, and made of no effect; they shall not bind us nor have power over us. The vows shall not be reckoned vows; the obligations shall not be obligatory; nor the oaths be oaths."

161 "All prayers which the children of Israel offer unto Thee, O our Father, that they may depart from sin, from guilt and from wickedness, and follow the ways of Thy Torah, the ways of justice and of righteousness; yea, all the resolutions which we make from this Day of Atonement until the coming Day of Atonement—may they be acceptable before Thee, and may we be given strength to fulfill them. We have come to seek atonement and to ask Thy pardon and forgiveness. Turn us in full repentance unto Thee, and teach us to undo the wrongs which we have committed. Thus will Thy great and revered name be sanctified among us."

162 Psalm 90:10.

20. The Melody of Faith — 1960

position, regardless of how much he would like to remain alive, he is inevitably doomed to give up what he has and sacrifice it all in the frustration of death.

And while he yet lives, how often he must endure pain and suffer in body and soul. He suffers from his own physical failings. He suffers from the loss of dear ones. He suffers the brutality of his fellow man. We behold intolerance and persecution, war and extermination. And we are tempted to cry with Koheleth, "Vanity of vanities. All is vanity."[163] We look out into the universe and it seems so coldly mechanical and impersonal. The floods and winds do not seem to care for man. The immutable laws of nature are no respecters of persons. Space seems endless and hostile, and we ask, "Can there be any intelligence to it? Is it not all a vast machine which is the product of cosmic accident? Where is God? Can He possibly exist? Need we be concerned with Him? What sense does it all make?"

These are the words without the melody. But if we would only listen to the melody that our tradition plays for us, what by itself seems senseless would be redeemed and given meaning. Man may, indeed, be a mortal animal; but our faith tells us, in the words of the closing service tomorrow, that man has been distinguished from the very beginning and has been singled out. Man may, indeed, appear small, but nevertheless, the psalmist exclaims:

> *Thou hast made man but little lower than the angels and hast crowned him with glory and honor. Thou hast made him to have dominion over the works of Thy hands; Thou hast put all things under his feet.*[164]

Man may, indeed, be an animal, but he is capable of achievement. Man is but a speck of dust in the universe, but his mind penetrates to the distant stars. And it is not only the power of his hands and mind in which he may glory, but also the power of his spirit. Man has the choice between good and evil. He has a moral sense. He can live with greatness. Our faith tells us that man is made in the image of God. This is not a statement about the shape of man's body; it is a challenge to man not to be bound by the limitations of the animal kingdom, but rather to transcend them and aspire to the godly virtues of goodness and truth.

Man does suffer on earth, and he often will cry, as did Job, "Make me to know why Thou dost contend with me."[165] But his faith tells him that sacrifice

---

163 Ecclesiastes 1:2. Koheleth, meaning "Gatherer" but traditionally translated as "Teacher" or "Preacher," is the pseudonym used by the author of the book Ecclesiastes, one of the 24 books of the Hebrew Bible. The title *Ecclesiastes* is a Latin transliteration of the Greek translation of the Hebrew.

164 Psalm 8: 6-7.

165 Job 10:2.

and sorrow can also release positive forces that enable him to achieve heights he would otherwise not have dreamed of. Many are the wounded souls who, defying their fate, became the benefactors of mankind. Many are those whose experience gained through pain gave them insight and understanding to be a comfort to others. The Jewish people has confronted the pitfalls of history only to be endowed with a stronger determination to live on and bear witness to the moral potential of man and the divine power which gives meaning to existence. Man often suffers. But, though like Jacob of old he may wrestle through a night of darkness, with patience and courage he can, also like Jacob, finally behold the dawn and wrest a blessing from his adversary.

The universe seems mechanical, and yet from another point of view this is but the evidence of a divine orderliness before which even the scientist stands in humble reverence. It is only the amateur scientist who does not confess to a religious awe as he contemplates the mystery of the universe. Einstein called the appreciation of this mystery the very essence of religious feeling. Many are the great names of science who, though they may not always subscribe to some of the conventional religious doctrines, nevertheless affirm that we must reckon with the design and the creative force that manifests itself through all their research. The true scientist is not arrogant about what he knows, but rather humbled by what there is left to learn. For every bit of mystery that is unraveled, he notes a greater mystery beyond. The psalmist long ago perceived that "the heavens declare the glory of God and the firmament revealeth His handiwork," and the modern scientist does not profess to contradict.[166]

Only those who look upon the world and the human condition in it with such a religious spirit feel that life is not meaningless after all, but a glorious challenge filled with purpose. Just as the *Kol Nidre* cannot stand without its melody, so our existence also depends for its meaning upon our ability to respond to the melody of faith.

Why is it, however, that so many cannot arrive at a full appreciation of this religious melody? Why is it that a rabbi is so often called upon to justify a religious attitude toward life? I think it is because the melody of religion is comparable to music in general. The capacity for religious feeling is as varied as the capacity to appreciate good music. There are some who seem to be born with such ability and quite naturally find themselves with a fine musical ear. But most people have only a potential which cannot be reached without practice and effort, and there are even some who are unfortunately tone deaf altogether and will never appreciate the beauty of an opera or a symphony.

---

166 Psalm 19:2.

20. The Melody of Faith — 1960

So it is with religion. There are, indeed, those who instinctively react to life with religious feeling. They confront life with humility and reverence. They do not necessarily refrain from questioning, and often find themselves in a struggle with their doubts and their conflicts, but somehow, like Job, they manage to fight their way from doubt to stronger faith. They hear the melody and they respond to its beauty. And there are also those unfortunates who are religiously tone deaf. They simply do not have the capacity for feeling or the imagination that can lift them out of their self-centered existence and enable them to look out upon broader horizons. Archibald McLeish once said that the greatest flaw of modern civilization is its inability to feel and imagine such as earlier civilizations have done.[167] It is this lack of feeling and imagination that is also the cause of our religious weakness and our rampant materialism.

Most of us, however, I believe do possess the potential, but are lacking in practice and in effort. We simply do not give our religious feelings a chance. We are content with the notions of religion gained in childhood, and make no effort to cultivate a religion of maturity. Or we arrogantly think that we have the capacity to think through the complex questions of human destiny by ourselves, and fail to seek the guidance of great spirits. We have a superficial knowledge of science and believe that this is the last word on human life, or we ask for scientific proof for truths that are outside of the realm of science and can only be apprehended by the intuitions of the heart. We refuse to expose ourselves regularly to a religious atmosphere or give ourselves the opportunity for repeated religious experience. On the basis of only snap judgments and a bowing acquaintance with the synagogue, we decide religion is irrelevant to life and there is no need for faith.

In a comment on prayer, Rabbi Jacob Weinstein once wrote:

> *The more you experience, the more meaning you find in these expressions of universal human sentiments [found in the prayer book]. Nor need you sacrifice your intelligence, your freedom of inquiry or judgment to gain this faith. You need only to sacrifice your smart-aleckness, your brittle sensualism, your all-pervasive, all absorbing materialism, your nose-to-the-grindstone absorption in the trivia of life. Open yourselves to the great organ of our music, to the effulgent radiance of our Sabbath candles, to the blessed insights of our Torah... and you will find the faith which made our fathers sing unto the Lord.*[168]

---

167 Archibald MacLeish (1892–1982) was an American poet, a writer, the Librarian of Congress, and the recipient of three Pulitzer Prizes. He authored the book and play J.B. which is a modern interpretation of the Job story.

168 Rabbi Jacob Joseph Weinstein (1902–1974) was a leading spokesman for Reform Judaism, a past president of the Central Conference of American Rabbis, and the spiritual leader of Kehilat Anshe

We have tonight partially fulfilled what Rabbi Weinstein has asked of us. We have listened particularly to the great organ of our music and perhaps to the greatest bit of synagogue music of all, the melody of *Kol Nidre*. Surely you must have responded at least to this with some surge of feeling. Think back now upon that moment. Try to fix it in your mind, and let its influence persuade you to seek out many more such moments throughout the year to come. Just as we must expend effort and practice to become skilled in music or in any of the arts, so let us in days to come practice that we may become skilled in the art of religion. Just as we must listen to the great masters if we want to improve our musical taste, so let us listen regularly to the great religious masters as they speak to us through the prayer book and Bible and other sacred writings that we may heighten our appreciation of religious experience. And in so doing, may we all find the insight that shall help us walk the path of life with courage, with dignity, and with faith.

Amen.

Dad—

Thank you for rendering such a beautiful metaphor—Judaism as the melody that brings richness and meaning to life. I feel blessed to hear your words. We may wonder at those who have no knowledge or capacity to allow this melody into their lives, whose abandonment of their tradition deprives them of this measure of purpose and meaning.

You suggest that an appreciation of Judaism need not be inborn, that if we are willing we can develop it, and that, like Job and Jacob knew, it is not easy, but that the toil, the struggle with doubt, is all manageable and rewarded with growing faith. Sometimes we are closest to the Divine in the midst of that dark struggle. I pray that I never lose the will to be a God-wrestler.

Blessings.
Yesh

Mayriv Temple in Chicago from 1939 to 1967.

21. Baal Shem Tov

October 1, 1960

Yom Kippur Morning

Through this biographical sketch of the Baal Shem Tov, we learn about the roots of Hasidism, its differences from modern day Hasidism, and its theology that elicited humility, joy, and enthusiasm.

The test of true service of God is humility. The necessary attitude for it is joyfulness. Man speaks to God through prayer, but this worship must always be cheerful, and sadness is a hindrance to devotion.

THIS YEAR HAS MARKED THE 200TH ANNIVERSARY of the death of that famous personality, Israel Baal Shem Tov, Israel Master of the Good Name.[169] It is appropriate to make mention of him to you on this sacred Day of Atonement because he was the founder of the movement of Hasidism, which had as its objective the making of every day of one's life a day of at-one-ment with God.[170] Most of us, I imagine, when we hear the term Hasidism, have an immediate association in our mind with Williamsburg and a picture of

---

169 Rabbi Yisroel (Israel) ben Eliezer (c.1700–1760), often called the Baal Shem Tov or the acronym Besht, was a rabbi and mystic. He is considered to be the founder of Hasidic Judaism.

170 Hasidism, from the Hebrew *hasi dut*, meaning "piety" or "loving-kindness," is a "branch of Orthodox Judaism that promotes spirituality through the popularization and internalization of Jewish mysticism as the fundamental aspect of the faith... It was founded by the Baal Shem Tov as a reaction against what was perceived by some as overly legalistic Judaism. Hasidic teachings cherished the sincerity and concealed holiness of the unlettered common folk, and their equality with the scholarly elite. The emphasis on the Immanent Divine presence in everything gave new value to prayer and deeds of kindness, alongside rabbinical supremacy of study." Merrimack Valley Havurah, "Hasidic Judaism," merrimackvalleyhavurah.wordpress.com/about/denominations/hasidic-judaism/. Accessed 21 Sep. 2017.

extremist Orthodox Jews with long coats and beards.[171] Many of us may look askance at the type and feel disturbed. But the truth of the matter is that Hasidism, at one time, represented an important reform movement in Judaism. Therefore, as Reform Jews ourselves, we should feel a bit of sympathy with its intention, which was to bring new vitality into Jewish life. I do not mean to say that Hasidism is any sense similar to the Reform Judaism of today. Far from it. But it was a reform movement, and although it soon deteriorated and fell victim to a number of abuses, it left a significant impression and influence on Jewish life, and it possessed certain characteristics which may well be seriously considered even today, regardless of the branch of Judaism we espouse.

Its founder, the Baal Shem Tov, was born in 1700, and many are the legends and stories of miraculous events that were told by his followers about his birth and his childhood. As a child, he did not take kindly to formal schooling but was often found meditating in the woods. As he grew up, he gave the appearance of being ignorant and lazy, but he would study in the synagogue at night when no one could see him, and he maintained his scholarship. He was popular with people. He had a warm, sympathetic approach to the masses, and it was his ambition to help and instruct those who were even humbler and poorer than himself. He was often used as an arbitrator in disputes because people trusted him. He saw a glimmer of goodness and nobility in all men, and after listening to him, the humblest felt an unconscious pride and dignity in their lives. He did not leave any writings, but he taught in pithy sayings and parables which were readily understood and remembered and were handed down by his followers.

He was forty-two years old when, it is said, he revealed his true character and mission to some chosen friends and began spreading his doctrines. He formed a little band of followers and traveled about considerably, preaching his interpretation of Judaism. His status as a teacher and reformer was justified by any number of miracles that, it is claimed, he performed. To one disciple, he is said to have revealed secrets that could come to him only by divine revelation. When the Baal Shem desired to cross a stream, it is said that he merely spread forth his mantle on the waters and walked across. Many other such events are reported. The telling of these stories helped establish his authority, and because of the nature of the times in which he lived and

---

171 Williamsburg is one of the neighborhoods New York City's borough of Brooklyn. "It contains the headquarters of one faction of the Satmar Hasidic group, [numbering about 73,000.] ...Beginning in the late 1940s, the area received a large concentration of Holocaust survivors, many of whom were Hasidic Jews from Hungary and Romania... The rebbe of Satmar, Rabbi Joel Teitelbaum... was known for his fierce anti-Zionism and for his charismatic [but abrasive] style of leadership." Wikipedia contributors. "Williamsburg, Brooklyn." *Wikipedia, The Free Encyclopedia*. Wikipedia, The Free Encyclopedia, 18 Sep. 2017. Web. 21 Sep. 2017.

the place in which he taught, these stories gained believers. Jews were still living under medieval conditions. They were cut off from the rest of the world and found refuge only in the study of their own law. Unfortunately, in some rabbinical circles, the study of the law, instead of remaining a sincere search for God's word, became a dry intellectual exercise. Instead of providing truth and inspiration, it provided only a means of subtle debate; scholars delighted in outdoing each other in *pilpul*, splitting hairs in debate.[172] Religion became a matter of complicated legal cases and innumerable ordinances, and the emotional aspects and the feelings of men, matters of faith and love, were neglected.

But the Baal Shem Tov gave a special priority precisely to these noble religious emotions, and in the locality in which he lived, it so happened that he found a ready response.[173] The Jews in the area near the Carpathian Mountains were not as learned in the Law as elsewhere. They did not care about the finesse with which their Polish rabbis could carry on a Talmudic argument. They revolted against the emphasis on Talmudic debate and the glorification of the Talmudic scholar. For them, the ideal was not a life spent over the folios of the Talmud, but rather the singing of hymns, preferably pouring out of doors or under the green trees of the forest. The differences the Hasidim saw between themselves and other Jews are reflected in one of their legends. On the evening before the Day of Atonement, the Baal Shem, contrary to his usual manner, was depressed and weeping. At the end of the day he became his cheerful self again. When asked for an explanation, he said the Holy Spirit had revealed to him that heavy accusations were being made against the Jewish people, and heavy punishment was ordained. "The anger of heaven," he said, "was due to the rabbis, who in their Talmudic debate had distorted the true meaning of the Law. They were accused in heaven by the great rabbinical scholars who had originally produced the Talmud." Therefore, the Baal Shem shed tears, and his prayers were successful. The judgment was annulled.

The main objective of man, according to Hasidism, is the service of God. And God can best be served when we realize that His living presence is in every aspect of existence. He did not merely create the world and watch it from afar; He is part of everything in the world. There is no place that God does not enter. Every manifestation of nature reveals His presence, and every

---

172 "The Hebrew term *pilpul* (from "pepper," loosely meaning "sharp analysis") refers to a method of studying the Talmud through intense textual analysis in an attempt to either explain conceptual differences between various rulings or to reconcile any apparent contradictions presented from various readings of different texts. *Pilpul* has entered English as a colloquialism used by some to indicate extreme disputation or casuistic hairsplitting." Wikipedia contributors. "Pilpul." *Wikipedia, The Free Encyclopedia*. Wikipedia, The Free Encyclopedia, 18 Sep. 2017. Web. 21 Sep. 2017.

173 About 1740, the Besht established himself in the Ukrainian town of Mezhebuzh.

human effort bears witness to Him. It is necessary for man to remember that God is with him always and everywhere, for because God is everywhere, it is possible for man to serve Him even in trifles. Because God is in everything, there is actual or potential good in everything and everybody. And because there is this potential good in everybody, one must not despair because of the sinfulness of man. No one is irredeemable, and in a moment of repentance he can lift himself up to God again. The reflection of man may be obscured by sin, but the true believer hopefully strives to restore the likeness of God in man.

The Baal Shem understood "service of God" to mean not merely fulfilling the precepts of the law, which he did not reject, but also having a certain attitude toward life in general. The important thing is not how many injunctions are obeyed, but the spirit in which we obey them. Since God is in everything, the very activity of life is a manifestation and a service of the Divine. Even eating and drinking and sleeping are not merely means of keeping alive, but are in themselves a service of God. All pleasures are manifestations of God's love and should be spiritualized and ennobled. Worldly matters and religious matters are not separate. Worldly matters are also an aspect of God, and man must serve God by ennobling them.

The service of God must be accompanied by three major virtues. They are *Shiflus*, *Simcha*, and *Hihlahavus*—best translated as humility, joyfulness, and enthusiasm. The test of the true service of God is that it leaves behind a feeling of humility. Before you can find God, you must lose yourself. If a man, said the Baal Shem, be conscious of the least pride or self-satisfaction after prayer, if he thinks that he has earned a reward by the ardor of his spiritual exercises, then let him know that he has not prayed to God but to himself. And what is this but disguised idolatry? Furthermore, humility connotes not only modesty but also considerateness and sympathy. It implies not only thinking humbly about oneself, but also the other side of the coin: thinking highly of one's neighbor and having love for one's fellow man. Our fellow man has goodness in him. Therefore, it is our duty not to judge that which may seem evil in him, but rather to help him realize the good in him. We must think humbly of ourselves, but be ready to think good and slow to think evil of another—very good counsel even for ourselves today. "God does not look on the evil side," said one *Zaddik*.[174] "Therefore, who am I that I should dare to do so." Each man in this world is unique, and none else is like him. In each man

---

174 *Zaddik* (also *tzadik*), is a righteous and saintly person by Jewish religious standards; he also is the spiritual leader of a modern Hasidic community. The root of the word is *tzedek*, which means "justice" or "righteousness." In Hasidic Judaism, the institution of the *tzaddik* assumed central importance.

is a priceless treasure that is in no other. One must honor each man for his hidden value that only he and none of his comrades has. Another *Zaddik* said,

> If a man sees that his companion hates him, he shall love him the more. For the community of the living is the carriage of God's majesty, and where there is a break in the carriage, one must fill it, and where there is so little love that the joining comes apart, one must love more on one's own side to overcome the lack.

The same Zaddik, before a journey, called to a disciple to sit with him in his carriage. The disciple was hesitant and replied, "I fear that I shall make it too crowded for you." Whereupon the Zaddik answered, "So we shall love each other more; then there will be room enough for both of us."

The test of true service of God is humility. The necessary attitude for it is joyfulness. Man speaks to God through prayer, but this worship must always be cheerful, and sadness is a hindrance to devotion. God is not a melancholy deity rejoicing in tears and concerned only with penance for sin. We must heed the words of the psalmist: "Serve the Lord with gladness. Come before Him with singing."[175] Once you believe that you are truly the servant and the child of God, how can you fall again into a gloomy condition of mind? Every kind of asceticism was opposed by the Baal Shem. There never was an extreme amount of asceticism in Judaism, but some had crept in, particularly in Kabbalistic circles, and Hasidism condemned it. Excessive fasting and doing penance were considered machinations of Satan to drive us into gloom and despondency, whereas God must be served only with a happy and confident disposition. *Simcha* was the condition of service of God, and God is to be approached with a glad and singing heart.[176] This explains the legacy of beautiful melodies and dances that have come to us from the Hasidim, for these served to express their cheerfulness and their joy in God's creation. And may we also add cautiously that they were not averse to stimulating this joy by an occasional *L'chaim* over some hard drinks.[177]

The final characteristic we would mention is *hishlahavus*, Hasidic enthusiasm, or perhaps better, ecstasy. In Hebrew, this word carries the implication of kindling or setting afire. A religious act must not be a lifeless mechanical performance. If so, it is valueless. We have not done our duty. We are not nearer the attainment of oneness with God just because we have gone through the whole round of laws prescribed in the codes. Every religious action must have enthusiasm. You can have this enthusiasm only if your

---

175 Psalm 100:2.
176 *Simcha* in Hebrew means gladness, or joy.
177 *L'Chaim* in Hebrew is a toast meaning "to life."

worship is motivated by love. If one prays out of fear, this enthusiasm will be stymied. We worship out of love when the inspiration of the service is an end in itself, and we have not prayed for the sake of reward either in this world or the world to come. We worship out of love when our service is not the mere repeating of the routine of the day before, but when we look upon ourselves as penitents and feel that we are lifting ourselves more and more each day toward the divine. The repetition of prayers did not disturb the Hasidim, because in their ecstasy, each prayer caught fire again and again and was not found to be boring, which is sometimes the modern cry. To the man in ecstasy, even what repeats itself is eternally new. A *Zaddik* once stood at his window in the early morning and cried out, "A few hours ago it was night, and now it is day—God brings up the day." He marveled at each new dawn, at the constant re-creation of the day. It was the same performance, but each time met with fresh enthusiasm. He was a soul afire with God's singing. And the dancing and the singing we spoke of a moment ago was not only an expression of joy, but also an almost involuntary expression of ecstasy as the Hasid was carried away in his worship. And so it is with prayer. When the peak of such enthusiasm is attained, there is nothing that can intrude upon the mood of the one possessed by it.

The Hasidic movement still exists today, but it is a relic of another time and another place. For reasons we shall not now go into, it deteriorated and fell away from its high ideal. We cannot expect it to revive itself and again sweep the masses. It belonged to a different age and a different mood. But it did contain within itself some significant basic religious elements that have a certain relevance for us even today. These are the things that I have already tried to point out to you, and I need elaborate no further. These qualities of Hasidism speak for themselves. If we on this Day of Atonement, when we ostensibly seek to draw nearer to God, if we could capture but a fraction of the motivation to serve God that was characteristic of the Hasidim at their best, but a fraction of their humility and their joy and their enthusiasm, our lives would be richer, our relationship with our fellow man would be improved, and God would be more discernible in our midst.

21. Baal Shem Tov—1960

Dad—

You speak of the Baal Shem Tov and of the early Hasidim with admiration and longing for a Judaism founded in humility, joy, and ecstasy. I imagine how pleased you might be to know of my enthusiastic participation in the neo-Hasidic experience of today's Jewish Renewal movement. This group inspires me to seek God's presence in every mundane act of daily life. It inspires me to look for *b'tzelem Elohim*—the image of God in every person, to approach prayer with *kavanah*—reverent intention, and to be grateful for every new day. Indeed, though I may have captured only a fraction of the Hasidic spirit, all that you once suggested opens before me—a richer life, improved relationships, and a greater sense of God's presence.

For this I am grateful.

Blessings.
Yesh

Nassau Community Temple, c. 1952. Left to right: Jeff, Jean, Doug (Yesh), Sidney, Martha (Muff)

Nassau Community Temple, December 10, 1960, Doug's (Yesh's) Bar Mitzvah

22. The Wisdom of the Heart

September 20, 1961

Yom Kippur Morning

We live in an information age. We seek more and more data and tangible evidence to guide our lives. Yet well before our so-called information age, my father sought to turn our attention from our overdeveloped brains to our underdeveloped hearts. He wanted us to pay attention to what our hearts were telling us, and to hold onto these promptings as valid reflections of a true reality that we might easily ignore.

Trust these intuitions of the heart as a clue to ultimate truth and allow the memory of them to sustain you in later moments when you may possibly be susceptible to doubt and questioning.

THERE IS NO HOLY DAY ON OUR RELIGIOUS CALENDAR that is more emotionally charged than the Day of Atonement that we now observe. It begins with the awesome tones of the *Kol Nidre* chant. It continues through a day of fasting, of solemn prayer and meditation on life and death. It ends in a spirit of deep humility with the concluding service of *Ne'ila*.[178] And from beginning to end there is a feeling of being in the presence of what a noted religious philosopher has called the *mysterium tremendum*, a term which practically explains itself, the great mystery, the indescribable and unknowable power that permeates the universe. In fact, it was after visiting a Yom Kippur service in a North African synagogue that Rudolf Otto conceived of the idea of the *mysterium tremendum*, which he called the central factor of all

---

[178] *Ne'ila* (lit. locking, as in locking the gates of prayer) is the concluding service on Yom Kippur, the time when final prayers of repentance are recited.

religion.[179] There is a touch of mystery inherent in Yom Kippur. Everyone present in the synagogue, I venture to say, senses it to some extent at least, and it is even possible to have one's entire life changed by it.

One man whose life was changed by his Yom Kippur experience was Franz Rosenzweig.[180] I wonder how many of you have heard of him. Franz Rosenzweig was a young German Jew with a brilliant mind. He possessed a deep knowledge of philosophy, but knew very little about Judaism. One day, he came to the conclusion that he wanted to become a Christian, and he was encouraged in this by several friends. But he decided to go about this in a strange way. He said he did not want to enter Christianity as a pagan, but rather like its founders—as a Jew. He therefore decided to subject himself to a Jewish experience in preparation for his becoming a Christian, and so on the High Holy Days of 1913, he attended services in a synagogue. His attendance on Yom Kippur was supposed to be a sort of leave-taking of his people, after which he was to be converted. He was truly converted on that day. It was, however, a total conversion to Judaism. When the *Ne'ila* service had ended and the final cry of *Shema Yisroel* was pronounced, Rosenzweig was wholeheartedly a part of the congregation, and he joined with them in this declaration of faith.[181] He had been recaptured by the magnetic mood of the day, and sometime later in a lecture, he said,

> Anyone who has ever celebrated Yom Kippur knows that it is something more than a mere personal exaltation or the symbolic recognition of a reality such as the Jewish people—it is a testimony to the reality of God which cannot be controverted.

In the years subsequent to this significant visit to Yom Kippur services, Rosenzweig became one of the most creative Jewish thinkers of the century. His faith remained firm and unshakable, even through long suffering from the effects of a crippling paralysis that caused his death in his early forties.

Another man whose life was profoundly changed by a Yom Kippur service was not Jewish at all, but rather a young French Catholic who had been planning on entering the priesthood. His name was Aimé Pallière, and in his autobiography entitled *The Unknown Sanctuary*, he tells us of a strange incident that kept him from fulfilling his plan.[182] In 1902, at age seventeen, while

---

179 Rudolf Otto (1869–1937) was a German Lutheran theologian and a scholar of comparative religion.

180 Franz Rosenzweig (1886–1929) was a German Jewish theologian and philosopher.

181 *Shema Yisroel* (or *Sh'ma Yisrael*) ("Hear, [O] Israel") are the first two words of a verse of Torah that encapsulates the monotheistic essence of Judaism: "Hear, O Israel: the Lord is our God, the Lord is One" (Deuteronomy 6:4).

182 Aimé Pallière (1868–1949), originally a French Catholic, became a Noahide, a non-converting adherent to Judaism.

he was on vacation, he just happened to be passing by a synagogue with a friend. His friend had heard that the Jews were observing a great festival that day and suggested they go into the synagogue. Pallière had been raised in a very religious atmosphere and a pious Catholic would not ordinarily go into a synagogue, but he nevertheless yielded to the suggestion.

It was the time of the *Ne'ila* service, and that unique moment changed his life. Pallière tells us that he cannot fully explain what happened to him. He calls it an unfathomable enigma. Actually, there was no sudden flash of transformation, but the effect of that moment influenced his thinking and feeling to such an extent that his whole life took a different turn. Pallière had no background whatsoever in Jewish matters. He could not understand the service or interpret what was going on. For the moment, it was a confusing experience, but the electricity of the occasion communicated itself to him. What he sensed particularly, he says, was the mystery of Israel as reflected in two characteristics. One is the form of collective priesthood that is basic to Judaism; that is, the equality of all Jews. All Jews are priests.[183] The second is the spirit of expectancy, the faith in the future, which is the special seal of Judaism. Judaism is an ancient religion; but he noted that it does not look to the past, but in a living and dynamic manner still hopes for achievement in the future.

On that day, Pallière said, he first beheld the people to whom the nations had been ungrateful, who had survived despite all things. While the other great peoples of antiquity had disappeared from the face of the earth, Israel had been preserved for providential ends. Aimé Pallière did not formally convert to Judaism, but his visit to the synagogue on Yom Kippur, the insight that he gained at that *Ne'ila* service, moved him to study Judaism thoroughly, to love it, and to live it to the same extent as if he had, indeed, been fully a Jew.

We who sit here tonight in this sanctuary will probably not find the direction of our lives so dramatically changed by this Yom Kippur service. But even if we are not like Rosenzweig and Pallière in that respect, I believe that we are like them in that we, too, on Yom Kippur, sense something of the mystery of God and Israel. For us also, Yom Kippur is a moment of truth when our emotions overcome our sophistication, when our enslavement to cold reason is temporarily suspended, when there is a surge of faith within us and we feel that somehow we have glimpsed something holy and meaningful, have drawn near to the sacred and divine.

And assuming all this to be true, I present you with a simple plea this evening. Believe in yourself at this moment, and do not later repudiate what

---

[183] "And ye shall be unto Me a kingdom of priests, and a holy nation. These are the words which thou shalt speak unto the children of Israel" (Exodus 19:6).

you now feel. Do not think that this reaction to Yom Kippur is mere sentimentality or the result of nostalgia. Do not be ashamed of it or embarrassed by it. Do not reproach yourself for having been touched by the seemingly irrational, but rather accept these intuitions of the heart as a meaningful experience. Trust these intuitions of the heart as a clue to ultimate truth, and allow the memory of them to sustain you in later moments when you may possibly be susceptible to doubt and questioning.

In this scientific age, so many of us tend to disparage our religious emotions and believe only in what we can prove by the logic of the intellect or the testimony of the five senses. But man's intellect and senses do not necessarily tell us all that there is to know about reality. The admonition of the poet is in order:

> O WORLD, thou choosest not the better part!
> It is not wisdom to be only wise,
> And on the inward vision close the eyes,
> But it is wisdom to believe the heart.[184]

In this scientific age, we are so enamored of the achievements of man's mind and the truly magnificent progress that has been made in adding to our knowledge of physical things, that even in religious matters, intellectual proof is expected. We ask, "How do you know? Can you prove it?" But religious problems cannot be handled in quite the same way as the problems of the physical world. We cannot depend altogether on rational proof. We cannot prove in a scientific sense the answers to the religious questions of God and immortality and human destiny and such. We can only, even as we do on Yom Kippur, stand in awe before the mysteries of life and place some trust in the revelations of the heart. This is not to say that reason is to be excluded from our religious searching. Certainly in Judaism, reason is never repudiated—but reason must be supplemented and cannot by itself help us find our way.

Many are the mysteries which reason cannot now and never will be able to unravel alone. There is the mystery of why there is anything in existence at all. There is the mystery of our own individual, unique, never-to-be duplicated self. There is the mystery of what is life, what really is man who is able to conceive of beauty, goodness, and truth. There is the mystery of the universe, its order and regularity, its infinite space. And there is, indeed, the not insignificant mystery sensed by Pallière in the synagogue: that the people of Israel, who have lived through centuries of hardship and frustration, have been able to recover from the cruelest tragedy imaginable and go on new achievements. Einstein once said that to feel the mystery of all existence is the

---

184 George Santayana (1863–1952), "O World, Thou Choosest Not."

fairest experience of man. "He who knows it not and can no longer wonder, no longer feel amazement, is as good as dead..."[185] But our intellect will not answer the questions this experience of mystery poses. The answers—or, more accurately, some small insight into the answers—can come only from the revelations of the heart. It comes, as Abraham Heschel says, only in the *feeling* that all existence is embraced by some spiritual presence we call God, although we cannot always describe it or define it.

Professor Harry Overstreet has told the story of how he once stopped at a collector's shop in Tucson, Arizona, where many kinds of minerals and stones were on display.[186] In the course of his visit, he was taken into a small room where rocks were laid out on shelves. They were quite ordinary looking rocks. Had he seen them elsewhere, he probably would not have given them a second glance. But the man in the shop closed the door so the room was in total darkness and then turned on an ultraviolet lamp. Instantly, these ordinary rocks became transformed and brilliant colors of indescribable beauty were seen upon them. It made Overstreet realize what hidden realities there are all around us, not perceptible by our ordinary vision, but in need of some special power to make them evident.

This day of Yom Kippur releases such a special power which enables us also to sense the presence of hidden realities that are not always evident to our senses. Just as the colors remained inherent in the rock when the ultraviolet was dimmed, so what we feel here tonight remains real and true though our emotions may wane when we turn again to our daily routine. May we find lasting inspiration in the experience of this day. May its recollection be a support to us through the year to come, and may we so live as to reflect a constant awareness of the reality of God among us.

Amen.

---

185 "The fairest thing we can experience is the mysterious. It is the fundamental emotion which stands at the cradle of true art and true science. He who knows it not and can no longer wonder, no longer feel amazement, is as good as dead, a snuffed-out candle. It was the experience of mystery—even if mixed with fear—that engendered religion. A knowledge of the existence of something we cannot penetrate, of the manifestations of the profoundest reason and the most radiant beauty, which are only accessible to our reason in their most elementary forms—it is this knowledge and this emotion that constitute the truly religious attitude; in this sense, and in this alone, I am a deeply religious man. I cannot conceive of a God who rewards and punishes his creatures, or has a will of the type of which we are conscious in ourselves. An individual who should survive his physical death is also beyond my comprehension, nor do I wish it otherwise; such notions are for the fears or absurd egoism of feeble souls. Enough for me the mystery of the eternity of life, and the inkling of the marvelous structure of reality, together with the single-hearted endeavour to comprehend a portion, be it never so tiny, of the reason that manifests itself in nature." Albert Einstein, *The World as I See It* (Secaucus, New Jersey: The Citadel Press, 1999), 5.

186 Harry Allen Overstreet (1875–1970) was a popular American author who wrote about modern psychology and sociology.

Dad—

This is breathtaking! I love your allowing God to be reduced to a "great mystery." Our childish notions of God are a constant barrier to opening ourselves up to the mystery that ever lurks behind that particular three-letter word. There is an indescribable, ineffable power that fuels all of existence. Mostly, we walk through life blindly accepting our reality as the ordinary and inevitable state of being. Why question the universe? Every once in a while, such as on Yom Kippur as you suggest, we are touched by the great mystery. We marvel at the miracle of life, even if just for a few moments. The blessing you wished for your congregation is to harness that and allow it to inform the rest of their lives. Thank God and thank you that in a small way I have received that blessing.

Now my prayer is to pass it on.

Blessings.
Yesh

23. Blowin' in the Wind

September 19, 1963

Rosh Hashanah Morning

The following sermon is one of the few from a half-century ago that I can legitimately say I remember hearing! Reflecting and responding to the increased consciousness of civil rights that grew out of the August 1963 March on Washington, my father spoke on the topic a few weeks later on Rosh Hashanah morning. While he was acutely aware of the tempo of his times, he was hardly a fan of the popular music of the younger generation. So for him to demonstrate that he was not only aware of the voice of Bob Dylan, but also clearly moved by the message, was particularly memorable for his teenage son.

As is often the case throughout reading these archives, one cannot help but notice that the language, especially regarding race, was very different in that era. Despite what is now outdated terminology, the sincerity of my father's plea for equality among all people is unmistakable.

How could we possibly retain our integrity as Jews if we did not become involved in this effort to advance the cause of justice for others today, when we have so long pleaded for it and yearned for it so deeply for ourselves in the past?

THERE ARE MANY TOPICS THAT ARE FITTING for discussion from the pulpit on the sacred occasion of Rosh Hashanah, but it seems to me that on this particular Rosh Hashanah, there is one that is inescapable. On this day of judgment when we search our conscience with respect to our moral behavior as individuals, when we pray that all hate and oppression shall vanish from the earth, when we speak of the coming of God's kingdom and the time when all men will be united in brotherhood and peace, surely we cannot help but make mention of the challenge which presently confronts us: the establishment of justice and freedom of opportunity for the Negro citizens of our country. During the past year, the effort of the Negro to lift himself up and to acquire in full the human rights to which any citizen in a democratic country is entitled has quickened its pace in spectacular fashion and has developed the full force of a revolution. Whatever our attitude may have been in the past, however much or little attention we may have paid to the problem in previous years, this revolution has gathered momentum. It is a quiet revolution for the most part, but occasionally violence breaks forth and it has its potential dangers. It has spread throughout the nation. It is in our own backyard, and it dare not now be ignored.

Just about three weeks ago, there took place in Washington one of the most spectacular public demonstrations in all of history. The March on Washington was held to petition for freedom and jobs for those of the Negro race and to ask that Congress pass pending legislation on civil rights. I was happy to be there to participate in it and to witness it, but you hardly need any description of it from me. The newspapers reported it in full and television gave everyone in the nation an opportunity to see what took place, even without taking the trip. This is one of the great occasions when television compensated for the many hours of nonsense with which it normally fills the air.

I doubt very much whether anyone would really have believed or could really have appreciated what took place in Washington on that unique day were it not for television—it made it possible for all to see for themselves this magnificent challenge to the conscience of America. There were many who questioned the wisdom and propriety of this march. They were afraid of the possible violence that might result. They thought it was not proper to pressure Congress in this manner. They had visions of a vast, unruly throng lingering in Washington and bringing chaos to the nation's capital. Even many ardent sympathizers with the cause were opposed. It was a great tribute to the earnestness, sincerity, and responsibility of Negro leadership and the understanding of Washington officials that none of these fears were realized. The march took place in peaceful dignity. Congress could look upon it only as a heartfelt petition that every American has a right to submit to his legislators, and the mass of petitioners went out of the city even as they came in—orderly and quietly except for the songs that spoke their spirit.

Next to the mood of these marchers, what was most impressive was their wide variety. This was no protest merely by professional battlers for Negro rights. This was a broad cross-section of the nation. It was thrilling to see the multitude of young people, both Negro and white, and this gives us hope for the future. And what I particularly want to call your attention to at this time is the tremendous interest that was shown by the religious groups of our country, on the part of both clergy and the layman—Catholic, Protestant, and Jew. This interest has been somewhat tardy in expressing itself, but at last, it has slowly built up great strength. There is great satisfaction in noting that prominent among the religious organizations present was the representation of our own Union of American Hebrew Congregations (UAHC), with its banners in Hebrew as well as in English. And don't take too seriously the congressman questioning the number of clergymen at the march. He said it only meant that there had been a great amount of clerical garb rented by costume supply houses. Even if this were so, collars do not tell the story. The Central Conference of American Rabbis (CCAR) reports that about 75 Reform rabbis alone were present—and they did not have any collars.

Why were we there as Jews—not only the UAHC and the CCAR, but the Synagogue Council of America and other organizations? The answer was there to be seen on one of the Hebrew-English placards carried by the Union, which recalled the commandment of the Torah: "*Ukrawsem Dror Baw-aretz l'chol yoshveha*—Ye shall proclaim freedom in the land to all the inhabitants thereof."[187] The commitment of Judaism to racial justice needs hardly to be argued. Judaism was born when our people were fresh out of slavery, and the memory of that experience never faded. It was reflected in the words of Torah, "*Tzedek, tzedek, tirdof*—Justice, justice shall ye pursue"[188]; in the chastisement of the prophet, "Are ye not as the Ethiopians unto me, O children of Israel, saith the Lord"[189]; in the poetry of the psalmist, "Righteousness and justice are the foundations of God's throne"[190]; in the preaching of the rabbis, "The sword comes into the world because of justice delayed"[191]; in the Jewish version of the Golden Rule, "What is hateful to you, do not do to your fellow man."[192] This, of course, is only a meager sampling of what Judaism has to say about social justice and the dignity of man. But even if it had no more to say, there is the historical Jewish experience: oppression in so many times and places has sensitized us to the wrong that man often does his fellow man, and has made us, above all, a people who realize that the security of no man is safe when the security of any man is threatened.

---

187 Leviticus 25:10.

188 Deuteronomy 16:20.

189 Amos 9:7.

190 Psalm 89:14.

191 Pirke Avot 5:8.

192 Attributed to Hillel, Shabbath folio: 31a, Babylonian Talmud.

The words of Martin Luther King, spoken so magnificently in Washington, should serve to remind us as Jews of our own historical involvement in the problem. This reminder was not at all intentional, but when Dr. King spoke of not being satisfied until "justice rolls down like waters and righteousness like a mighty stream," these were the words of our prophet.[193] And when he referred to the ghettos of the northern cities that need to be changed, he was, of course, thinking of Negro ghettos; but this is a term taken from the Jewish experience of segregation in the Middle Ages.[194] How could we possibly retain our integrity as Jews if we did not become involved in this effort to advance the cause of justice for others today, when we have so long pleaded for it and yearned for it so deeply for ourselves in the past?

It must be admitted that in spite of our tradition and experience, we as Jews have been no different than other religious groups with similar ethical values; we have not heretofore done all that might have been done. But today there is a new mood in the land and there are new opportunities to speak up, and we must stand up and be counted. The new mood has come largely because the Negro has increased his own effort. There is truth in the old saying that God helps those who help themselves. Our rabbis expressed this thought all so long ago when they discussed the Exodus from Egypt. The Red Sea parted for the Israelites, they said, only after the Israelites first jumped into the water.[195] Today, the Negro has jumped into the water, and he has therefore earned and is obtaining, more than ever before, the help of others. Today, consequently, our religious groups are confronted by a challenge as never before: to live up to the doctrines that they teach. We are now faced with the acid test of our religious sincerity.

Many wonderful words were spoken in Washington, but perhaps what has been considered by many as the most impressive statement of all was made by Rabbi Joachim Prinz when he spoke of his own experience in Nazi Germany.[196]

> *The most important thing that I learned under those tragic circumstances is that bigotry and hatred are not the most urgent problem. The most urgent,*

---

193 Amos 5:24.

194 The Venetian Ghetto, the first "ghetto," was the area in which Jews were compelled to live under the Venetian Republic, beginning in 1516.

195 Nachshon, according to the Jewish Midrash, initiated the Hebrew's Passage of the Red Sea by walking in head deep until the sea split.

196 "Joachim Prinz (1902–1988) was a German-American rabbi who was outspoken against Nazism and became a Zionist leader. As a young rabbi in Berlin, he was forced to confront the rise of Nazism; he eventually immigrated to the United States in 1937. There, he became vice-chairman of the World Jewish Congress, an active member of the World Zionist Organization, and a participant in the 1963 civil

the most disgraceful, the most shameful, and the most tragic problem is silence.

This is indeed something to think about. We who profess to believe in democracy can no longer be silent. We who preach religion can no longer be silent. And we whose heritage is the Torah must now also join the other religious groups in shouting away the silence.

Of course, it is sometimes difficult to know what to shout. It is easy to come out against sin and indicate a general support of the Negro effort to achieve his just rights. But the problem becomes quite complex when we are confronted with a specific issue on a personal and local basis. While there may be agreement in principle with regard to integration and civil rights, there may also be differences of opinion on what techniques should be used in obtaining them. There will be issues on which even those who are friends of the Negro will disagree with the Negroes, as well as moments when Negroes will differ among themselves, as presently in Lakeview.[197] We are faced with a difficult decision when confronted with the proposals to transport children out of their own neighborhood area in order to avoid *de facto* segregation in schools. We are confronted with a difficult decision when it comes to establishing a quota system for employment or preferential treatment in order to redress some of the past wrongs that have been done to Negro workers. There may be some questioning of sit-ins and boycotts. We as Jews may even be concerned about the anti-Semitism that occasionally shows itself in some parts of the Negro community. I cannot pretend to have the perfect answer to these problems, and even the courts are having difficulty in reaching decisions with regard to some of them. But although these matters may cause much debate and may have to be worked out over a long period of time, and even though the solution may be difficult and not always to our liking, we must not let the difficulty affect our basic attitudes, and we must not abandon the effort to restore racial justice to our American democracy. The Negro may

---

rights March on Washington." Wikipedia contributors. "Joachim Prinz." *Wikipedia, The Free Encyclopedia.* Wikipedia, The Free Encyclopedia, 18 Sep. 2017. Web. 21 Sep. 2017.

197 Lakeview, Long Island, NY is a small, predominantly African-American community adjacent to West Hempstead and Malverne, two predominantly white communities in the 1960s and presently. "In 1963, the New York State Education Commissioner responded to complaints by the NAACP and Black parents living in Lakeview that the Malverne School District was racially segregated. He ordered the reorganization of all of the district's elementary schools to ensure that they were integrated. The proposed plan required that children be bused away from their neighborhood schools... Because of the threat of forced busing, white parents started pulling their children out of public schools and sending them to Catholic or other religious schools. They also protested by electing school board candidates who took their side, and voted down school budgets which included money to fund busing." Joyce Kenny, "Oral History: The Battle Over School Integration in Malverne," Hofstra University, http://studylib.net/doc/14265050/oral-history---the-battle-over-school-integration-in-malv. Accessed 21 Sep. 2017.

often seem impatient with the progress being achieved, but we must understand this impatience that has, after all, taken one hundred years to build up. It is sometimes difficult to convince him that our disagreements are not rationalizations of leftover prejudice and intolerance. Nevertheless, we must not be sidetracked from the major goal. We must not permit our support to be embittered. With constructive effort, imaginative thinking, and genuine goodwill, the obstacles will be overcome.

It is most important, furthermore, that the religious aspect of this Negro struggle for dignity be encouraged and strengthened. The religious character of the Negro revolt is its most important asset. It is because Negro leadership has couched its appeal in religious terms that it has become so difficult for this nation to shrug it off. It is because Martin Luther King speaks of meeting physical force with soul force that his words are so compelling. A nation that professes to be religious cannot in all good conscience turn away from an appeal to its religious sensitivities. It is also because of its religious basis that the protests have been so peaceful. Violence has been resorted to on the part of those who have opposed the Negro effort, but it is significant how little retaliation there has been, even under such a provocation in Alabama.[198] Had there been retaliation, the opposition would have found justification, and chaos would have been the result. In order to avoid chaos and to make it all the more likely that Negro resistance will continue its nonviolent character, it is incumbent upon all religious organizations to encourage and to sustain, by their support, the spiritual quality of the Negro struggle.

Our own Union of American Hebrew Congregations and the CCAR are very definitely committed to the establishment of full equality for all persons in our nation. The Social Action Commission, which is sponsored by both of these organizations jointly, has on a number of occasions joined the Jewish and non-Jewish religious groups in making its feelings known. It has now gone a step further and issued a general call to all our congregations and individual members to take a stand based on our religious precepts in this racial crisis. It has made some very definite proposals that our own social action committee will undoubtedly call to the attention of our membership. These

---

198 This is likely to be a reference to the bombing of the Sixteenth Street Baptist Church in Birmingham "which was used as a meeting place for civil rights leaders such as Martin Luther King, Jr. and Ralph Abernathy. Tensions became high when the Southern Christian Leadership Conference and the Congress on Racial Equality became involved in a campaign to register African Americans to vote in Birmingham. On Sunday, September 15, 1963, a white man was seen... placing a box under the steps of the church. Soon afterwards... a bomb exploded, killing four... girls who had been attending Sunday school classes. Twenty-three other people were also injured in the blast. Civil rights activists blamed George Wallace, the Governor of Alabama, for the killings. Only a week before the bombing, he had told *The New York Times* that to stop integration, Alabama needed a 'few first-class funerals.'" Daryl Lezama, *From the Civil Rights Pioneers to the First African American President and Beyond* (Bloomington, IN: Author House, 2014), 28.

include the insistence on the support of nondiscrimination policies in our own Temple administration, the inculcation of respect for all races and creeds in our teaching, the cooperation of our congregation with other organizations working for racial justice, the practice of nondiscrimination by individual congregational members in their businesses and personal life, the refusal to deal with people who do discriminate, the active support of legislation which protects civil rights, and even the signing of a pledge to work for conditions of equal opportunity for all persons in every phase of American life. It is highly to be desired that Reform Jews will respond to this call in the prophetic spirit that motivated its founders to create the movement.

There is a folk song that I heard played often on the radio during the summer when there was time to listen. It caught my fancy because it seems to come from the hearts of people who are laden and bewildered. In the form of a song were put some of the basic questions that we must contend with in our day, and implicit in the song was the warning that the answer cannot long be delayed. Let me read some of the more pertinent lines to you. They make a fitting conclusion to what we have just been saying.

> *How many roads must a man walk down before he's called a man?*
> *How many times must the cannonballs fly before they're forever banned?*
> *How many years can some people exist before they're allowed to be free?*
> *How many times can a man turn his head and pretend that he just doesn't see?*
> *How many times must a man look up before he can see the sky?*
> *How many ears must one man have before he can hear people cry?*
> *The answer, my friend, is blowin' in the wind, the answer is blowin' in the wind.*[199]

Yes, all about us the winds of change and crisis are blowing; and within the turbulence, an answer is being fashioned to the many questions that disturb us. What kind of an answer will it be? Will it be an answer that brings frustration and destruction as if blown by the winds of the hurricane, or will we have the wisdom to harness the winds so that they will yield an answer that will contribute to the well-being and dignity of all men? At every service throughout the year, we pray that God grant us peace and that he strengthen the bonds of fellowship and friendship among all the inhabitants of our land.[200] May we, indeed, particularly on this Day of Judgment, resolve that this shall also be the spirit of the answer that we shall wrest from the blowing wind.

Amen.

---

199 "Blowin' in the Wind," written by Bob Dylan in 1962, was ranked #14 on *Rolling Stone* magazine's list of the 500 Greatest Songs of All Time.

200 *Union Prayer Book*, 140.

Dad—

The word that comes up for me when I read this sermon is "dignity."

First, I recognize yours. It was almost always present, certainly so in the pulpit. It is with consummate dignity that you present the case for civil rights. It is with full respect for the dignity of African Americans that you do so. Justice and freedom are basic to Judaism, as you point out, and they were long overdue to the descendants of slaves who were so unjustly robbed of their freedom generations ago.

You marched on Washington. I barely remember that you did that, and I can't fathom why I wasn't with you! You remarked on all the young people there. They gave you hope for the future. There has been much progress since 1963. There is integration in virtually all parts of society across the land. We've even elected and reelected an African American President of the United States. Can you believe that?

Sadly, the glass is also half empty. African Americans are among the most disadvantaged people in America. They populate our jails disproportionately. They are victims of police brutality to such a degree that Black communities have taken to the streets in protest—sometimes peacefully, sometimes not. I could go on about the racial injustice in this land.

The question is, "Where, as a nation, will we go from here?" We seem to be at perpetual crossroads. The winds of change continue to blow, and whether we are headed for another storm (yes, there have been quite a few in the years since 1963) or whether we harness those winds peacefully and constructively remains to be seen. The answer is still "blowin' in the wind."

Blessings.
Yesh

JOHN F. KENNEDY MEMORIAL SERVICE
NOVEMBER 24, 1963

We are assembled to voice our prayer to the Almighty on this occasion of national sorrow, to give expression to the emotions which fill us at the sudden loss of our youthful Chief of State. Many words have been spoken in the brief time since he was smitten, but there are no words adequate to the hour, no words that can fully measure the pain we feel.

In our despair, however, we are mindful of the discipline of our tradition that bids us to look beyond our immediate anguish. In the darkness of grief, we take to our hearts the sentiment of the psalmist: "Even though weeping may tarry for the night, yet joy cometh in the morning." Though this is now a time of national calamity, we yet sense in this experience our national strength. Even though this is a moment that brought us the fruit of violence and hate, we are yet aware of the potential in this land of unity and love. In this moment of shared distress, there are yet the seeds of hope and future achievement.

In this hour of confrontation with death, in this moment when God seems to have turned His face away from us, we nevertheless rise to proclaim the ancient meaningful words of our faith, and with them we praise God for the goodness wherewith He has blessed us in the past and for the goodness we know will yet come from His hand. With the loss of our president fresh in our hearts, we all say—

Yisgadal... [beginning The Mourner's *Kaddish*]

24. Joseph and the War on Poverty

December 11, 1964

My father uses the story of Joseph in the weekly Torah portion as a springboard for a sermon that primarily deals with an ageless social problem—that of poverty. Today, a preacher must couch his words so as not to offend congregants of a different political persuasion. But in 1968, my father was not considered blunt; he was seen as forthright, ardent, a man of moral conviction and integrity.

To this end, the poor of our land, whether they be black or white, need a helping hand, and we must do more than dole out the grain or leave the corner of the field. We must provide the ability and the opportunity for every man to maintain himself and to contribute to society with self-respect and dignity.

IN THE TORAH READINGS FOR THIS WEEK[201] AND LAST WEEK,[202] we are told how a bright, young Hebrew boy called Joseph rose to power in ancient Egypt. The ability to interpret dreams and a seeming talent in the field of economics had brought him advancement to the position of second to Pharaoh, and to Joseph had been entrusted the very serious problem of coping with the seven-year famine that was to impoverish the land. It really was not too much of a problem for Joseph. He had filled the granaries of Egypt in the years of plenty, and when the crisis came, he sold this grain to the starving Egyptians. At first, he sold it for money; then, when money and property were gone, he sold it in return for bodies. The Egyptians simply became bondsmen

---

[201] *Vayigash*, Genesis 44:18-47:27.
[202] *Miketz*, Genesis 40:20-44:17.

to Pharaoh. The people did not complain. They even thanked Joseph, because they at least remained alive and survived the famine.

Joseph may have served the interests of his sovereign Pharaoh, but he certainly did not act in the spirit of the Jewish tradition that was later to unfold. The Torah calls for a much more sympathetic attitude toward dealing with the unfortunate poor. It provides that a corner of the field be left untouched so that the poor may come in and help themselves.[203] It provides that what is left on the stalks when the grain is gathered and what is left on the vine when the grapes are harvested shall also be left for the poor, and all the fruit that falls of itself is again left for the poor. The poor are helped without taking advantage of them, and the Talmud elaborates on this spirit by saying, "The life of a man is not a true life, if he does not give aid to his fellow man."

Today, neither the heartless methods of Joseph and the court of Egypt nor the more sympathetic and generous treatment of Jewish tradition is considered acceptable. Today, poverty is recognized not so much as a misfortune to be handled on an individual basis, but more as a significant disease of the social order that needs to be fought on a broad front. Help to individuals in the form of food and clothing and shelter is still desirable, but we recognize that if we are to eliminate poverty, we must go beyond individual relief and fight certain basic social problems. This, of course, is the idea behind President Johnson's *War on Poverty*.[204] Whatever we may say of its adequacy or technique, it recognizes that anti-poverty measures must involve more than immediate aid to individual families in need; rather, it must launch an attack on the problems of the environment which hold great segments of our population in their clutches. Only a politically primitive mind would hold that poverty represents a lack of ambition and/or initiative on the part of those who suffer from it. Rather, poverty is the unhappy byproduct of the way

---

203 "And when ye reap the harvest of your land, thou shalt not wholly reap the corner of thy field, neither shalt thou gather the gleaning of thy harvest. And thou shalt not glean thy vineyard, neither shalt thou gather the fallen fruit of thy vineyard; thou shalt leave them for the poor and for the stranger: I am the Lord your God" (Leviticus 19:9-10). "And when ye reap the harvest of your land, thou shalt not wholly reap the corner of thy field, neither shalt thou gather the gleaning of thy harvest; thou shalt leave them for the poor, and for the stranger: I am the Lord your God" (Leviticus 23:22).

204 "The War on Poverty is the unofficial name for legislation first introduced by President Lyndon B. Johnson during his State of the Union address on January 8, 1964. Johnson proposed this legislation in response to a national poverty rate of around 19%. The speech led the United States Congress to pass the Economic Opportunity Act, establishing the Office of Economic Opportunity to administer the local application of federal funds targeted against poverty... The popularity of a war on poverty waned after the 1960s. Deregulation, growing criticism of the welfare state, and an ideological shift to reducing federal aid to impoverished people in the 1980s and 1990s culminated in the Personal Responsibility and Work Opportunity Act of 1996, which President Bill Clinton claimed 'ended welfare as we know it.'" Wikipedia contributors. "War on Poverty." *Wikipedia, The Free Encyclopedia*. Wikipedia, The Free Encyclopedia, 18 Sep. 2017. Web. 21 Sep. 2017.

in which our society is managed. With few exceptions, the individuals who suffer are not personally to blame and are entitled to the help of society in breaking out of the bonds that hold them.

Until recently, most of us have remained rather oblivious to the serious problem of poverty presently in our midst. Those of us who can remember the early days of Franklin D. Roosevelt will recall that he spoke of the one-third of our nation that was living on a bare minimum subsistence level or less.[205] But World War II drove the problem of poverty into the background. The need for manpower in fighting a war took up the slack and every able-bodied person was busy and could earn a living. Ever since that time, we have assumed that poverty had disappeared as a major social problem.

The civil rights struggle has served to bring it back to our attention. In the effort to give all Americans their equal rights, it has become apparent that there are some who are ill prepared to handle these rights even if they have them. It has become apparent that there are some who could not achieve the kind of dignity a man is entitled to in a democratic society—the mere granting of legal privilege will not ameliorate a lack of job opportunities, education, or housing. And so, there is suddenly a new awareness of poverty—a poverty that exists in spite of the fact that our nation has attained unprecedented economic achievements. In the days of FDR, we were aware of poverty because the entire nation was in a slump. In subsequent years, poverty escaped our attention because the nation was enjoying unparalleled prosperity and extensive poverty did not seem possible. But it has unfortunately been with us in spite of prosperity; even in these good times, if not a third then at least a fifth of this rich nation lives at a marginal level. And by this we mean that a fifth of our nation lives under conditions of want or near want, lives on a family income of $3000 a year or less. And it would perhaps be fair to speak of an even larger number of poor among us, for it certainly takes a good bit more than $3000 a year per family before it can live in any degree of comfort.[206]

There are several interesting aspects of the problem of poverty today that most of us have perhaps failed to realize. First of all, poverty can continue even when the income level of the lowest groups goes up. It was once thought that increasing wealth from rising national productivity would filter down and alleviate the poverty of the lower income groups. This has proved

---

205 "During his first hundred days in office, [which began March 4, 1933 in the depths of the Great Depression,] Roosevelt spearheaded unprecedented major legislation and issued a profusion of executive orders that instituted the New Deal—a variety of programs designed to produce… government jobs for the unemployed." Wikipedia contributors. "Presidency of Franklin D. Roosevelt." *Wikipedia, The Free Encyclopedia*. Wikipedia, The Free Encyclopedia, 8 Sep. 2017. Web. 21 Sep. 2017.

206 The median income of all families in the U.S. in 1964 was about $6,600, which equals $51,568 in 2017 dollars.

not to be true. Wealth does, indeed, filter down, and the income of the lower groups does go a bit higher, but the income of the higher groups goes up even more and poverty is a relative thing. Poverty is not simply a matter of having enough to survive. Professor Galbraith has defined poverty as a condition that exists when a family income that might be adequate for survival is nevertheless far behind that of the community in general. [207] People can have enough to eat, but they are degraded because they cannot measure up to the standard of living that the community in general considers acceptable. Thus, even if the income of the poor goes up, they remain poverty-stricken if their relative position with respect to the rest of the community does not improve. And this is what has happened. In 1947, the lowest fifth of the population received only five percent of the total national income. In 1963, the very same thing was true. The total income of the American people had gone up but the same inequality of distribution prevailed, so no progress in eliminating poverty has been made.

A second interesting aspect of poverty is that although anyone anywhere might possibly become impoverished, there are certain select groups in our country who run the risk of poverty more than others. For these select groups, the risk of poverty has increased in past years in spite of the general prosperity we enjoy. What are these groups? They are the people who are not white; the families where the male head is under 25, over 65, or missing altogether. They are families whose education has been limited, or where there are more than six children under eighteen. They are families who live in rural areas, particularly in the South, and families who live in areas undergoing economic change, like Appalachia. These things, we are now told, are poverty-linked characteristics, and it does not seem to make much difference whether our economy fares well or becomes depressed—people in these categories do not seem to make any progress one way or the other.

Another interesting thing about poverty is that it tends to perpetuate itself. Children born into a poor family tend to remain poor themselves, and sometimes sink even lower than their fathers. Apparently, the reason for this is the lack of parent education, which in turn makes for a lack of aspiration on the part of parents for their children. Fewer children of poor parents go to college or even high school or grade school than the national average, and this

---

207 John Kenneth Galbraith (1908–2006) was a "Canadian-born economist, public official, and diplomat, and a leading proponent of twentieth-century American liberalism. His books on economic topics were bestsellers from the 1950s through the 2000s." He was a professor of economics at Harvard University for half a century. Galbraith was "active in Democratic Party politics, serving in the administrations of Franklin D. Roosevelt, Harry S. Truman, John F. Kennedy, and Lyndon B. Johnson." Wikipedia contributors. "John Kenneth Galbraith." *Wikipedia, The Free Encyclopedia*. Wikipedia, The Free Encyclopedia, 1 Sep. 2017. Web. 21 Sep. 2017.

tends to perpetuate the poverty of the parents. Being born in an impoverished group makes for a barrier which is difficult for anyone to break through.

A final thought to bear in mind is that it is not only the poor themselves who suffer from their poverty. The poverty of a large percentage of our population is something that affects us all. The physical and mental disease it breeds, the moral delinquency and crime that it produces, the waste of manpower that it causes are things we all pay for in the long run. We have been concerned about the large number of young people who fail to pass the standards set for military service. It is estimated that about one third of all the youth of our nation cannot qualify, and poverty is the main reason for their lack of ability to meet the physical and mental requirements.

All of these facts about poverty seem to show that any program that merely tries to alleviate the symptoms is far from adequate. It is a most worthy project to help the distress of Appalachia by sending trucks of food and clothing, but it is far from a final solution to the problem. President Johnson's *War on Poverty* has been a step in the right direction. It is an attempt to break into the vicious cycle that holds the lower groups in its grasp. There are many who consider the initial appropriations that have been made totally inadequate for the gigantic task that lies ahead, but it is at least a beginning. His efforts to better coordinate local projects, expand educational and work opportunities, increase training for adults, and help the aged are the first shots in what the President has called an unconditional war—and it is a war which must be won, even though it is estimated it will take much longer and much more money than the present Economic Opportunity Act of Congress has allowed.[208]

The trouble is that much more than time and money and goodwill are involved in the problem. The President's *War on Poverty* has placed a great deal of emphasis on education, but the educational level needed for good jobs is constantly rising. Even while young people of low income improve their own educational level, the general level is also rising as well, and it will take a tremendous amount of high quality schooling before poor young people can achieve a significant gain. More and more, it appears that even a high school diploma is inadequate for a good job, and what we need perhaps most in this country is to adopt the principle that everyone is entitled to a college

---

[208] "United States Public Law 88-452, the Economic Opportunity Act of 1964, authorized the formation of local Community Action Agencies." These agencies, directly regulated by the federal government, are local private and public non-profit organizations that carry out the Community Action Program (CAP) to fight poverty by empowering the poor as part of the War on Poverty. Wikipedia contributors. "Economic Opportunity Act of 1964." *Wikipedia, The Free Encyclopedia*. Wikipedia, The Free Encyclopedia, 26 Aug. 2017. Web. 21 Sep. 2017.

education at public expense, just as now we have accepted this principle for a high school education.

Another serious difficulty is that even though young people may acquire better education and training for themselves, the number of jobs available for them may decline due to improved work techniques, particularly in the field of automation. This is a problem that has lately aroused great concern, but no good answers have as yet been presented.

But regardless of these kinds of difficulties and the obstacles that lie in the way, we are confronted with a moral problem of great dimensions. In a nation which calls itself religiously motivated, this is a problem that cannot be ignored, and the effort to deal with it must not be opposed. As a democracy, we presumably believe that every man should have the right to develop himself according to his capacity and to realize his full potential as a human being. It is the obligation of a democratic society to remove the stumbling blocks that stand in the way of such achievement.

In the past months and years, many liberal-minded people have been very much aroused over a civil rights bill and the creation of equal political, economic, and educational opportunities for Negroes. But the problem with enforcing democracy does not end with a civil rights bill. This bill was only a much-needed step on the way to achieving an even more necessary goal. There is no point in opening doors to people who cannot step inside them. Now that legal rights have been strengthened, it is even of greater importance to make it possible to use them fully and intelligently. To this end, the poor of our land, whether they be black or white, need a helping hand, and we must do more than dole out the grain or leave the corner of the field. We must provide the ability and the opportunity for every man to maintain himself and to contribute to society with self-respect and dignity. How to do this to perfection is not yet completely clear, even though the first steps have been taken, but a society that can defy the powers of gravity, that can send up a camera to take close-range pictures of Mars, that is planning soon to send men to the moon, such a society should be able to use some of its intellectual and physical resources to deal with these problems of the human spirit as well. It takes a combination of moral will and a sympathy for all people. May we in the future find both of these qualities displayed in abundance.

Amen.

24. Joseph and the War on Poverty—1964

Dad—

There is so much I love about this sermon. It may sound silly, but even your formulaic opening, "In the Torah [reading] for this week..." provides a sense of rhythm and comfort, a familiarity, a reflection of your own quality of reliability. Then, it demonstrates your ability to pick up an ancient Jewish thread and follow it to a current societal conundrum. Through you, the Torah remains alive—in your day, and, as these reflections years later reveal, in succeeding generations as well. Part of that is true because not only were you steeped in ancient history, but you were a bit of a futurist as well. To think that in 1964 you were promoting a free college education for all—a topic very much being debated today. You also foresaw the depletion of jobs "due to improved work techniques, particularly in the field of automation."

But most of all, what I admire is your genuine heart of compassion. Most people admire Joseph's cunning anti-famine measures, but you do not complacently stop there. You question Joseph's "heartless methods," his lack of generosity. You are also dissatisfied by the mere rise in income of our country's poor. You recognize that their dignity is not uplifted if their relative poverty is unchanged. You taught me the Yiddish word *rachmones* (compassion) and you embodied that quality as well.

Blessings.
Yesh

A Precious Heritage

25. Loneliness

October 5, 1965

Kol Nidre

This sermon on loneliness must have really struck a chord with my father's congregation. It is one of the very few sermons that appear in his files not only in roughly typed and hand-edited draft form, but also retyped neatly and reproduced by mimeograph for apparent distribution.[209]

To be human, therefore, is to be lonely with or without people around us. Loneliness is a basic characteristic of man. It is a reality of existence. It challenges us all the days that we live.

ONE OF THE INTERESTING NEWS ITEMS OF THE PAST SUMMER was the story of Robert Manry, who crossed the Atlantic Ocean in a thirteen-and-a-half-foot sailboat.[210] It is almost impossible to believe that a man could succeed in such an undertaking. The boat was seemingly much too fragile for such a journey. It sailed against waves that were sometimes twenty feet high. Manry was washed overboard half a dozen times, but fortunately was able to save himself by a rope that he had tied between himself and the boat. He suffered hallucinations that made him think the ocean was a mountain or that there was a monster in his cabin. But in his column discussing this feat, Max Lerner

---

[209] The mimeograph machine is a low-cost duplicating device that works by forcing ink through a stencil onto paper... Mimeographs were commonly used to print small-quantity jobs until the late 1960s, when they bean to be replaced by photocopiers. Wikipedia contributors. "Mimeograph." Wikipedia, The Free Encyclopedia. Wikipedia, The Free Encyclopedia, 26 Jul. 2017. Web. 19 Oct. 2017

[210] Robert Manry (1918–1971) was a copyeditor for the *Cleveland Plain Dealer.* In 1965, Manry sailed from Falmouth, Massachusetts, to Falmouth, Cornwall, England, in a 13.5-foot sailboat, a voyage lasting 78 days.

tells us that the hardest part of all for Manry was facing and conquering his loneliness.[211] He spent seventy-eight days in the confining area of his small boat with no one to share the work involved, no one to turn to for consultation or guidance, no one for companionship. Robert Manry confronted the vastness of a seething ocean alone and was victorious.

Not a single one of us here tonight, I am sure, would ever think of placing himself in a similar situation. Even if the physical difficulties did not deter us, we certainly would have no desire to subject ourselves to seventy-eight days on the ocean alone. The thought of being completely by ourselves, unable to reach out to another human being either by touch or by sound over so long a time, is enough to make us shudder. And yet, I venture to suggest that Robert Manry is in a sense symbolic of us all. If we stop to think about it, are we not, figuratively speaking, in the same boat after all? Every human being on his journey through life sails alone. Every human being consciously or unconsciously faces the challenge of conquering his loneliness. Indeed, as Norman Cousins wrote, "All of man's history is an endeavor to shatter his loneliness."[212]

Most people think of loneliness only in terms of the feeling that arises when we lose the companionship of those who are very dear to us, when we fail to find friends with whom we can establish a satisfying relationship, or when we are cut off from contact with other human beings. This is, of course, a kind of loneliness. People who are alone and isolated for a long period of time can find it a frightening and painful experience. It can bring depression or anxiety or even anger in its wake. But loneliness is not merely something that has to do with the lack of people around us. We can be lonely even in the midst of our own family circle. We can be lonely even though we pursue a frantic round of social and organizational activities. Dinner parties and card parties do not save us from loneliness. Someone once even described a cocktail party as the personification of loneliness. The mere physical presence of other people is not always sufficient to relieve our loneliness. We can feel most isolated and alone right in the midst of crowds. This was described poignantly in the book *The Lonely Crowd*.[213]

---

[211] "Maxwell "Max" Alan Lerner (1902–1992) was an American journalist and educator known for his controversial syndicated column" in the *New York Post*. Wikipedia contributors. "Max Lerner." *Wikipedia, The Free Encyclopedia*. Wikipedia, The Free Encyclopedia, 3 Sep. 2017. Web. 26 Sep. 2017.

[212] "Norman Cousins (1915–1990) was an American political journalist, author, professor, and world peace advocate." Wikipedia contributors. "Norman Cousins." *Wikipedia, The Free Encyclopedia*. Wikipedia, The Free Encyclopedia, 6 Sep. 2017. Web. 26 Sep. 2017.

[213] "*The Lonely Crowd* is a 1950 sociological analysis by David Riesman, Nathan Glazer, and Reuel Denney. It is considered a landmark study of American character," dealing with extroverts and introverts. Wikipedia contributors. "The Lonely Crowd." *Wikipedia, The Free Encyclopedia*. Wikipedia, The Free Encyclopedia, 26 Aug. 2017. Web. 26 Sep. 2017.

25. Loneliness—1965

Loneliness is not merely the product of special circumstances. The sense of loneliness is inevitable for all of us, whether we are surrounded by people or not. There is a very normal loneliness that any person will feel simply because of the fact that he is human. Thomas Wolfe wrote,

> *The whole conviction of my life now rests on the belief that loneliness, far from being a rare and curious phenomenon peculiar to myself and to a few other solitary men, is the central inevitable fact of human existence.*[214]

Ultimately each man is alone. All human beings are separate from one another, and destined to be separated from each other. Their life's experience is individual. They travel a lone journey through the valley of shadows. Man is alone in his moments of moral decision. He hears the voices all around seeking to counsel him, but he bears his own responsibility. Even in his efforts at communication with others he is alone, for he can never quite succeed. He can never more than approximately express the deepest feelings within him, due to the limitations of language at his disposal. It is always impossible to be certain that the person addressed understands the words that are spoken precisely as they were meant. Man suffers alone in his moments of pain, and he alone feels the full hurts of his bereavements. Who even with deepest possible sympathy, can fight the other man's battle? "At bottom," said Heine, "we live spiritually alone."[215]

To be human, therefore, is to be lonely, with or without people around us. Loneliness is a basic characteristic of man. It is a reality of existence. It challenges us all the days that we live.

How then shall we deal with this loneliness? One thing is certain. We cannot escape it. Therefore, we must accept it. We must have the inner fortitude not to be overwhelmed by it, but rather to face it. We must seek to understand it and thereby transform it into a power that is enriching and ennobling and enables us to be ourselves at our very best. Loneliness is not something to be distressed about; nor is it necessarily an unhealthy condition. Rather, it is something to be treasured and exploited. Dr. Clark Moustakas writes: "Loneliness is a condition of human life, an experience of being human which enables the individual to sustain, extend and deepen his humanity."[216]

---

214 Thomas Clayton Wolfe (1900–1938) was an early-twentieth-century American novelist. Notable works include *Look Homeward, Angel* and *You Can't Go Home Again*

215 German journalist Christian Johann Heinrich Heine (1797–1856) also was a poet, essayist, and literary critic.

216 "Clark E. Moustakas (1923–2012) was an American psychologist and one of the leading experts on humanistic and clinical psychology." Wikipedia contributors. "Clark Moustakas." *Wikipedia, The Free Encyclopedia*. Wikipedia, The Free Encyclopedia, 21 Aug. 2016. Web. 26 Sep. 2017.

Loneliness in itself, therefore, is not an evil. However, sometimes the ways we attempt to escape our experience of loneliness bring us to grief. To fear, evade, or deny the experience of loneliness is to hinder the development of our personal resources, our sensitivity, and our creativity. Not to exercise our loneliness is to impair our capacity for spiritual growth, just as not to exercise our muscles is to impair the development of our physical strength.

This does not mean that the ideal way of life is for every individual to take himself into a corner and remain alone. Not at all. In order to be totally fulfilled, individuals need companionship. But we can be better companions if we are not running away from ourselves. If we have not come to know ourselves, we cannot come to a proper understanding of others. If we have not come to grips with our own pain and suffering, we cannot be duly sensitive to the pain and suffering of others. It is only when we have experienced the pangs of loneliness that we can best appreciate the blessings of friendship. It is only when we have faced our own loneliness that we can relate most meaningfully to others.

Kahlil Gibran has written: "Sing and dance together and be joyous, but let each of you be alone, even as the strings of a lute are alone though they quiver with the same music."[217] Each of us vibrates with his own tone, and it must be clear and true to itself if it is also to blend in concert with others. The experience of loneliness is the bridge that binds all notes together and enables us as individuals to join with others in harmony.

Loneliness not only makes possible deeper friendship, it also generates the power for heightened creativity. We need only to look upon the great spirits of mankind to see what can happen to each of us in smaller measure. In his discussion of gifted people, Dr. Eric P. Mosse claims:

> *The writer, the poet, the novelist, the dancer, the actor, the sculptor or musician—each one is the austere and exclusively devoted servant of his loneliness. Their most spectacular quality is—their intense awareness of their loneliness, an awareness deeper and more poignant than that which most people experience.*[218]

---

217 "Khalil Gibran (1883–1931) was a Lebanese-American writer, poet, and visual artist... chiefly known in the English-speaking world for his 1923 book *The Prophet*. [This] series of philosophical essays... gained popularity in the 1930s and then again in the 1960s counterculture. Gibran is the third best-selling poet of all time, behind Shakespeare and Laozi." This quote is from *The Prophet*'s essay "On Marriage" (15), one of my father's favorite passages that he often incorporated into wedding ceremonies that he performed. Wikipedia contributors. "Kahlil Gibran." *Wikipedia, The Free Encyclopedia*. Wikipedia, The Free Encyclopedia, 26 Sep. 2017. Web. 26 Sep. 2017.

218 Eric P. Mosse is the author of *The Conquest of Loneliness*, 1957.

Dr. Mosse is saying is that without the experience of loneliness, there can be no great creative expression. Loneliness releases the springs of creativity. Loneliness by itself, of course, will not make us creatively great, but it can stimulate whatever powers of creativity do lie within us; it enables us to express our true selves more effectively. Each one of us is born with a certain potential, but it is estimated that most of us use only a small fraction of our true capabilities. Though we may not be destined to reach the level of genius, each of us has greater capacity for achievement than we give ourselves credit for. In our solitude, we are enabled to open the door a bit wider. The artist, writer, or musician does not put himself to work amidst the bustle of a public square. Each one wrestles alone with his own soul and lets his knowledge be distilled in quietness. Then, he moves forward to achievement.

Loneliness is the penalty we often pay if we would be true to conscience, but in turn, it brings the reward of greater self-respect. It is not uncommon for individuals out of fear of loneliness to compromise principles and ideals and conform to the opinions of the crowd. The person who stands by strong convictions is all too often forced to stand alone. The thoughts that he thinks may prove disturbing to others. They may be contrary to general public opinion. To cling to them brings public condemnation and rejection.

Jeremiah cried out to God:

Know for Thy sake I have suffered taunts... I sat not in the assembly of them that make merry nor rejoiced. I sat alone because of Thy hand. For Thou hast filled me with indignation.[219]

John F. Kennedy's book *Profiles in Courage* is but a series of biographies of lonely men.[220] Of Thomas Hart Benton, for example, he wrote:

His biographer believes that "probably no man in history has been more vilified than he was at this time." But Benton pursued his independent and increasingly lonely course.[221]

---

219 Jeremiah 15:15-17.

220 "*Profiles in Courage* is a 1957 Pulitzer Prize-winning volume of short biographies describing acts of bravery and integrity by eight United States Senators throughout the Senate's history... *Profiles* was widely celebrated and became a best seller. John F. Kennedy is credited as the author... although Kennedy's speechwriter Theodore Sorensen [claimed] that while Kennedy provided the theme and supervised its production, Sorensen had written most of the book." Wikipedia contributors. "Profiles in Courage." *Wikipedia, The Free Encyclopedia*. Wikipedia, The Free Encyclopedia, 8 Sep. 2017. Web. 26 Sep. 2017.

221 John F. Kennedy, Profiles in Courage: Decisive Moments in the Lives of Celebrated Americans (NY: Harper and Brothers, 1957), chapter 4. "Thomas Hart Benton (1782–1858) was a U.S. Senator from Missouri, [great-uncle of the painter of the same name,] and an architect and champion of westward expansion of the United States, a cause that became known as Manifest Destiny." Wikipedia contributors. "Thomas Hart Benton (politician)." *Wikipedia, The Free Encyclopedia*. Wikipedia, The Free Encyclopedia, 16 Sep. 2017. Web. 26 Sep. 2017.

Woodrow Wilson also was a target for abuse and invective in his battle for the League of Nations. He described his presidency as "...lonely, very lonely." In the not-too-distant days of McCarthyism, those who stood by their principles were lonely men indeed, as they maintained their integrity. The great man and the common man alike can suffer for conviction, but without accepting the pain of loneliness, there can be no self-respect.

Finally, let us point out that loneliness is also a gateway to faith. "Religion," said the philosopher Alfred N. Whitehead, "is what man does with his solitariness."[222] Modern science has made it difficult for man to be solitary. It is too easy to cover great distances, to be in constant contact with others, either in person or by mechanical means of communication.[223] Perhaps that is why we today are weak in faith. The sense of awe and wonder and mystery that is the root of faith is difficult to grasp amidst the babel and confusion of the modern world. In the Bible, we are told that the prophet Elijah experienced the presence of God not in the wind, and not in the earthquake, and not in the fire, but in the still, small voice.[224]

Admiral Richard Byrd once spent nearly six months alone on an advanced base in Antarctica.[225] It was a terrible experience for him to be completely alone for so long amidst the ice and snow and wind, but he wrote of this experience:

> *Harmony, that was it. That was what came to me out of the silence—a gentle rhythm, the strain of a perfect chord, the music of the spheres, perhaps... The conviction came that that rhythm was too orderly, too harmonious, too perfect, to be a product of blind chance—that, therefore, there must be purpose in the whole and that man was part of the whole and not an accidental offshoot.*

I am not advocating that those of us who might want to bolster our faith should seek to spend six months alone in Antarctica! But Admiral Byrd's experience is in keeping with the thoughts of the theologian Kierkegaard, who wrote:

> *If an Arab in the desert were suddenly to discover a spring in his tent and so would always have water in abundance, how fortunate he would consider*

---

222 English mathematician Alfred North Whitehead (1861–1947) was a philosopher whose work on process philosophy has become very influential.

223 This is a remarkable statement in a time long before personal computers, mobile phones, or social media.

224 1 Kings 19:11-12.

225 "Rear Admiral Richard Evelyn Byrd, Jr (1888–1957) was an American naval officer who specialized in feats of exploration... [He] was a pioneering American aviator and polar explorer." Wikipedia contributors. "Richard E. Byrd." *Wikipedia, The Free Encyclopedia*. Wikipedia, The Free Encyclopedia, 18 Sep. 2017. Web. 26 Sep. 2017.

25. Loneliness—1965

himself—so, too, when a man who as a physical being is always turned toward the outside, thinking that his happiness lies outside him, finally turns inward and discovers that the source is within him, not to mention his discovery that the source is his relationship to God.[226]

It is fitting that we should speak of loneliness as we celebrate tonight the Eve of Yom Kippur. The element of loneliness is very much a part of the symbolism of the day. We dimmed the lights earlier in the service to indicate that we were shutting ourselves off from the world about us and standing alone before the Almighty.[227] We fast this day to signify that we have withdrawn ourselves from every aspect of the material world about us. We sit together *en masse* as a congregation—but nevertheless, we look upon this day as the occasion when we stand individually in judgment. We shall tomorrow have a memorial service that will fill us with lonesomeness for the departed and remind us of our own mortality. But our purpose is to conclude this day, in spite of our loneliness, with a sense of triumph. The quiet meditation of this day is intended to bring us restored faith and new hope, to release untapped spiritual energies. On this Day of Atonement, then, as we briefly face our loneliness, may we indeed find strength to master it. May we go forth to face the New Year in the spirit of David, the psalmist. In his wanderings as a lonely shepherd, David was inspired to exclaim: "*Adonai Ro'ee*," which means not merely, "The Lord is my shepherd," the usual translation, but rather, "The Lord is my companion," which the Hebrew truly implies. In my loneliness, says David, I am not alone. "Though I walk through the valley of the shadow of death, I shall fear no evil, for Thou art with me."[228]

---

226 "Søren Aabye Kierkegaard (1813–1855) was a Danish philosopher, theologian, poet, social critic and religious author who is widely considered to be the first existentialist philosopher." Wikipedia contributors. "Søren Kierkegaard." *Wikipedia, The Free Encyclopedia*. Wikipedia, The Free Encyclopedia, 22 Sep. 2017. Web. 26 Sep. 2017.

227 It was the practice of the Nassau Community Temple to turn off the house lights and stand in the glow of the lighted ark during the recitation of the *Kol Nidre*.

228 Psalm 23.

Dad—

Alone, I sit with your words, as I have now for several years. Alone, I ponder the depths of their meaning. I truly enjoy the solitude. I so appreciate your narrative on loneliness, assuring your congregation that it is nothing to be feared or resisted, but a normal state of the human condition to be embraced and mined for its hidden riches. I am inspired to hear you say, "Not to exercise our loneliness is to impair our capacity for spiritual growth..." Connecting to our isolated selves is the key to such virtues as empathy, creativity, and integrity.

Your words make me wonder about your moments of loneliness even as you served your vast community. I suspect that you might have appreciated having more solitude than was granted to you.

Blessings.
Yesh

26. Faith in God

December 30, 1966

As my father points out, it's difficult to maintain faith in a God that one understands with the mindset of a five-year-old. Here, he provides several "grownup" models of God as a force of nature, an indescribable and indefinable essence of all of creation, and a guide for living a life of righteousness.

Judaism... asks us to stop thinking so much of what God is and who He is. Do not ask for His Name, but know that He is eternally there and is an eternal challenge to you because religion is not a way of thinking, but a way of living.

IN OUR TORAH READING THIS WEEK, WE BEGIN the second book of the Torah, *Sefer Shmot*, the Book of Exodus. Of all the five books of the Torah, Exodus is most important for a proper understanding of our faith. We might get along without the other four, but we couldn't do at all without this one. In the course of reading Exodus, we are told of the period of bondage in Egypt and the redemption from this bondage. We learn of the covenant at Sinai and the giving of the Law. And these thoughts are the foundations on which Judaism rests. *Zecher yetziat mitzrayim* is a phrase that rings out again and again in the Bible.[229] It is given to us as an explanation for the keeping of the Sabbath. It is the justification for commanding the Jew to be generous and just in his dealings with his neighbors and with the underprivileged. The Jew who himself experienced the bitterness and degradation of mistreatment in Egypt is expected to be all the more sensitive to the needs of those in distress and all the more sympathetic to those in danger of being robbed of their human

---

[229] The words *zecher l'yetziat Mitzrayim* ("in remembrance of the Exodus from Egypt") are part of the text of Kiddush for Shabbat and every holiday.

dignity. This story of the bondage in Egypt and the release therefrom planted the seeds of a liberalism that has been predominant in Jewish thinking to this day.

The redemption from Egypt, however, implied more than something physical. There was a spiritual aspect to it as well. Going out of Egypt was but a prelude to the covenant at Sinai that gave meaning to the history of the Jewish people and to the life of each individual Jew. We tend to think of the redemption from Egypt merely in terms of the actual exodus, but Sinai also is an essential part of the redemption. The rabbis made this very clear to us in their Midrashic interpretation of this period of our history, saying that the Israelites could not consider themselves to be completely free of their bondage until they stood at Sinai and accepted the Commandments and the covenant. Then, they had their bodily freedom and had also achieved a *raison d'être*. Henceforth, the purpose of Jewish existence was the commitment to God to live His Commandments.

The pattern of our people in Bible times is the pattern of Judaism today. For modern Judaism, redemption is fundamental. Redemption is found in accepting the ancient covenant of our people, in committing ourselves, even as did our fathers at Sinai, to the service of God and His commandments. For us, redemption means the effort to release our people and all humanity from the bondage of social ills, and to labor for an era of peace and justice and human dignity. Regarding this brief statement about redemption, we might speak the same words that Hillel succinctly used regarding the Golden Rule, "This is all of Judaism. The rest is mere commentary. Go learn it."

It must be admitted that such thoughts of God and covenant are not very popular today. In this scientific age, when anything that is not tested and proved in a laboratory is subject to question and doubt, not everyone respects the words "God" and "covenant." I think that outright atheists are still comparatively few, but surely agnostics abound, even among those who profess to be religious and are members of congregations. It is fashionable today to speak of God as dead or irrelevant, but even the highest-level scientists do not necessarily deny the validity of faith in God.[230] In *Science Ponders Religion*, one of the authors states:

> *A faith in a supreme intelligence can claim no... scientific support, yet I think it must be granted that there are no scientific or philosophical grounds for denying the possibility [of] an "all knower..." that is, of an intelligent*

---

[230] "The cover of the April 8, 1966 edition of *Time* magazine asked the question 'Is God Dead?' and the accompanying article addressed growing atheism in America at the time, as well as the growing popularity of Death of God theology." Wikipedia contributors. "Death of God theology." Wikipedia, The Free Encyclopedia. Wikipedia, The Free Encyclopedia, 19 Apr. 2017. Web. 17 Sep. 2017.

26. Faith in God — 1966

regulating agency of the total cosmos, of which the limited universe known to man is an integral part.[231]

When we speak of God, we are simply out of the realm of science; we are dealing with a question with which science is not concerned. It is an area that surely ought not to be in opposition to science, but which also does not necessarily have to be proved by science or substantiated by science. It is simply and admittedly a faith, but nonetheless reasonable and acceptable to scientific man.

It is admitted also that there are some ideas about God still current that in our scientific age might well be ruled out. Rabbi William B. Silverman (1913–2001), of Nashville's The Temple Congregation Ohabai Sholom, in a book entitled *God Help Me*, has a chapter on "What Not to Believe About God." He points out how often ideas about God that adults have are so much like the ideas that five-year-old children have. Like children, adults often think of God in terms of a divine Superman or a divine magician or as a man of war who can give us victory over our enemies. Joshua Liebman cautioned us against thinking of God as a cosmic bellhop who jumps around heaven carrying out the orders man sends up in his prayers.

However, Judaism at its best fosters an understanding of God that remains relevant even in today's sophisticated mood, and we can find some of these thoughts embedded in the Torah portion of this week. God speaks to Moses at the burning bush and tells him that He wants to send him to Pharaoh to bring his people, the Children of Israel, out of Egypt.[232] Moses is hesitant and says to God, "But when I come to the Children of Israel and say to them that the God of your fathers hath sent me to you, they will ask me, 'What is His Name?'" This is equivalent to asking, "What kind of God is this? Describe Him. Tell us of his attributes and powers." A name was supposed to convey that kind of information. And God tells Moses, "*Ehyeh asher Ehyeh*," usually translated, "I am that I am."[233]

This is one of the most difficult sentences in the Bible, and nobody can be sure if anyone at all has ever really grasped whatever was originally intended. However, several major interpretations of this phrase have emerged, and any one of them does justice to a modern concept of God. Four major possibilities may be found among various commentators.

First of all, it has been suggested that the Hebrew word *Ehyeh* may not be from the root that means *to be*, but rather from a root that means *to fall*

---

231 *Science Ponders Religion*, Harlow Shapley, ed. (Appleton-Century-Crofts, 1960).
232 Exodus 3:2.
233 Exodus 3:14.

or *to cause to fall*, with the implication that He is the God who causes the thunderbolts and the lightning to fall throughout the sky. He is in effect the *Lord of Nature*. This is in the spirit of the story of the burning bush that comes just a bit before. God caused the bush to burn with fire, but it was not consumed, and Moses stopped to wonder at it. We are told that in the wilderness, there are certain bushes with red foliage that seem to be burning; but we may pardon the biblical writer some poetic license even if there are not such bushes. The passage should be read in the spirit of looking on God as the power in nature and the mystery of it all that fills the heart of man with wonder. Einstein said that this sense of mystery is the source of religious feeling, and anyone who could not feel it was a clod. "*Ehyeh asher Ehyeh*" thus connotes the great mysterious unknown power behind the universe and its operation.

A second interpretation of "*Ehyeh asher Ehyeh*" is that it comes from the root meaning *to be*, in the sense of "cause to be." In other words, "*Ehyeh asher Ehyeh*" means, *I am God the Creator*, or perhaps *I am the God of Being, the one through whose eternal existence all else is able to exist*. Some theologians today refer to God as the *ground of being*. This is not too simple a thought, but perhaps we can come close to understanding it if we compare it to grains of sand that are embedded in the ground. Everything that exists is like the grain of sand that has its own individual existence but that is part of the ground in which it is found. God is the totality of existence of which all else is a fragment.

Yet a third interpretation is most interesting if one understands the linguistics. It sees the word *Ehyeh* as an extended form of the Hebrew word *Hu*, which simply means *He*. Tell them "*He* sent you." It is *He* who is God. God is thus referred to without *name*. He cannot be defined by man. He is incomprehensible to man. Man can only see His acts and try to understand His demands; but he cannot describe or define Him beyond speaking of Him merely as *He*.

And lastly, we come to the explanation offered in the Talmud and accepted by many scholars to this day, including the great theologian Martin Buber. The Talmud interprets "*Ehyeh asher Ehyeh*" as "I am the One who will continue to be with you." To justify this, they point to a previous verse that reads, "Certainly I will be with Thee." The implication is that *I am the One* referred to in that verse. Just as I am with you in this present enslavement, I shall always be with you when foreign powers enslave you in the future. God is thus the One who is eternally with Israel, who manifests Himself through Israel's history, who cares for Israel, and who fulfills His promise to Israel. He is thus the God who takes seriously the covenant made with the Patriarchs and with Israel in which He promised to be concerned with Israel; and if so, there is a further implication that Israel in return also owes allegiance to the covenant. This, as we noted before, gives meaning and purpose to Israel's existence.

We must all recognize today that we cannot test the validity of our concept of God by means of science. We cannot aspire to a full understanding of God who is beyond comprehension by our human senses. But it is not inconsistent with modern thinking to look upon God in the terms of these interpretations of *Ehyeh asher Ehyeh*. He is the indescribable and indefinable Creator who is eternally present; He eternally stands before us as a challenge to live up to our covenants, and as a challenge to redeem our lives by accepting as Israel's purpose and man's purpose the duty to exemplify godliness and to live a life of righteousness that contributes to the welfare of humanity. In a sense, this chapter of Exodus and Judaism in general asks us to stop thinking so much of what God is and who He is. Do not ask for His Name, but know that He is eternally there and is an eternal challenge to you—because religion is not a way of thinking, but a way of living. And more important in Judaism than theological understanding is living the Commandments that are part of our covenant.

Moses says to God, "Who am I that I should go to Pharaoh and demand justice?"[234] But God reassures Moses and says that He will be with him and He will give him his brother as a spokesman. We all feel small in this world and do not know how to wrest justice from it and create a better world. But let us all be reassured, as was Moses, by the thought that the unseen God is with us, and let us all join our brothers in accepting this eternal challenge to make of ourselves something better than what we are.

---

234 Exodus 3:11.

Dad—

Wow! Let's talk theology! I'm sure I've heard your postulates about God's existence, but saying "God is" doesn't really help me get past the natural resistance that I, like so many others, have to the G-word.

I love that these words speak to the mystery, the unknowing. All of us who think we know something—even those who know quite a lot (you mention Einstein)—eventually come up to the limits of human knowledge. What's next?

I love that you posit the everything-ness of God—very Hasidic! There is nothing devoid of God. That makes it easy to substitute easier language, such as energy, or cosmic vibration, or love.

I love that if nothing else, God is the bedrock of right action, that being Jewish does not rely on believing, but in doing.

These all help. They help in my conversations with nonbelievers, with seekers, and with myself.

Blessings.
Yesh

27. The Aftermath of a Miracle

October 5, 1967

Rosh Hashanah Morning

My father spoke passionately about the Jewish homeland before and after statehood. In the aftermath of the Six-Day War, he was no less passionate. He saw it not merely as a great military victory, and not just as the modern miracle that it was. For him, it demonstrated that, in this crisis, both Israeli and American Jews were awakened to a hidden truth of how deeply they were connected to one another and committed to another. This was one of his other favorite themes: Jewish survival.

We cannot wait only for a moment of great crisis for our Jewish feelings to be shaken up. Jewish life is always in crisis... We must be Jewishly aware and Jewishly alert even in time of comparative calm.

AS WE GATHER NOW ON THIS DAY OF ROSH HASHANAH, there is one subject above any other that clamors for attention. To borrow a phrase from Rashi, that some of you may remember from our adult education course, "*Ain zeh omair ela darshayni*—this matter begs for comment."[235] It is impossible not to make mention on this day, as we look back upon the past year, of one of

---

[235] "Shlomo Yitzchaki (1040–1105), generally known by the acronym Rashi (Rabbi Shlomo Itzhaki), was a medieval French rabbi and the author of a comprehensive commentary on the Talmud and the Tanakh (Hebrew Bible). Acclaimed for his ability to present the basic meaning of the text in a concise and lucid fashion, Rashi appeals to both learned scholars and beginner students, and his works remain a centerpiece of contemporary Jewish study. He is considered the "father" of all commentaries that followed on the Talmud and the Tanakh." Wikipedia contributors. "Rashi." *Wikipedia, The Free Encyclopedia*. Wikipedia, The Free Encyclopedia, 11 Sep. 2017. Web. 19 Sep. 2017.

the most significant happenings in centuries of Jewish history: the crushing defeat by Israel of the Arab nations who were posed to destroy it.

Don't you still recall with amazement the events of that week in June![236] Here was a tiny nation of approximately two million, confronted by hostile Arabs totaling over two hundred million! These Arabs were inflamed by venomous words poured into the airwaves by the president of Egypt.[237] Soviet Russia, who was very outspoken about her pro-Arab sympathies, had furnished these Arabs with two billion dollars' worth of military supplies and equipment. Israel presumably also had friends, but they were hesitant and embarrassed. They did not want to offend the Arabs or provoke the Russians. The picture was dark, indeed, as Nasser blustered, U Thant capitulated, and Israel's big-power allies vacillated or deserted her.[238]

But when the showdown came, it was all over in less than a week. Some call it a six-day war, some a four-day war, and some even just a two-day war. But whatever it was, it was already obvious within only a few hours what the result would be. The Arab defeat was total and disastrous. Their armies were thrown into reverse. The desert was strewn with their equipment. Their territory was overrun. Their fortifications destroyed. The Straits of Tiran were opened.[239] Jerusalem was reunited.

The Israelis had had a great deal of confidence in their own ability to defend themselves, but even they were surprised; and the world referred to their achievements not as military victories but as the enactment of a miracle.

---

[236] "The Six-Day War, fought from June 5-10, 1967, was a conflict between Israel and the neighboring states of Egypt (known at the time as the United Arab Republic), Jordan, and Syria. After a period of high tension, the war began... with Israel launching surprise bombing raids against Egyptian air-fields. Within six days, Israel had won a decisive land war." Israeli forces had taken control of the Gaza Strip and the Sinai Peninsula from Egypt, the West Bank and East Jerusalem from Jordan, and the Golan Heights from Syria. *Just the Facts 101*, 1st edition (Content Technologies: 2017).

[237] Gamal Abdel Nasser.

[238] "U Thant (1909–1974) was a Burmese diplomat who served as the third Secretary-General of the United Nations from 1961 to 1971... He was criticized in the U.S. and Israel for agreeing to pull UN troops out of Sinai in 1967, in response to a request from Egyptian president Nasser... Thant tried to persuade Nasser not to go to war with Israel by flying to Cairo in a last-minute peace effort." Wikipedia contributors. "U Thant." *Wikipedia, The Free Encyclopedia*. Wikipedia, The Free Encyclopedia, 17 Sep. 2017. Web. 19 Sep. 2017.

[239] "The Straits of Tiran are the narrow sea passages between the Sinai and Arabian peninsulas which separate the Gulf of Aqaba from the Red Sea... Access to Jordan's only seaport of Aqaba and to Israel's only Indian Ocean seaport of Eilat is contingent upon passage through the Gulf of Aqaba, giving the Straits of Tiran strategic importance...." Egypt's blockade of the Straits to Israeli ships and ships bound for Israel in 1956 and again in 1967 was a catalyst to the Suez Crisis in 1956 and the Six-Day War in 1967. "Straits of Tiran," *Marine Encyclopedia*, https://www.wikimarine.net/index.php?title=Straits_of_Tiran&oldid=13356. Accessed 24 Sep. 2017.

27. The Aftermath of a Miracle—1967

There are those who will argue that to speak of miracles in connection with this brief war against the Arabs is to belittle the courage and ingenuity of the Israel Defense Forces—it implies that the Israelis merely sat back and let Heaven do the rest. But the Israeli army itself speaks in terms of miracles. Elie Weisel reports that the Chief of Staff, General Yitzhak Rabin, admitted without embarrassment that he no longer understands what he and his men had accomplished.[240] From Rabin down through the lowest grade soldier in the ranks, we are told that they feel they are alive today because of a miracle.

But what is a miracle? Martin Buber once described a miracle as something that leaves us with abiding astonishment.[241] The natural and rational explanation of what happens is not the issue. It is not that something seems to happen due to supernatural cause that makes a miracle. It is rather that the event is experienced as a miracle—as an act of God—by those involved. Thus, he says, the crossing of the Red Sea may have its scientific explanation, but what is important and what makes it a miracle is that the very natural process involved was so unexpected and surprising that it was understood by the Israelites only as an act of God. It was experienced as a miracle and filled them with an abiding astonishment.

Israel's victory over the Arabs this past year has left the modern Hebrews also with an abiding astonishment. Even the religiously indifferent among them now wonder whether they have not beheld an act of God. A professor at Bar Ilan University writes that "the attitude of miracle is uppermost. The vivid experience of God's unbelievable power prevails in the minds of religious and nonreligious alike."[242] Elie Weisel says that even the freethinkers interpret the recent experience as fundamentally a religious one—it has compelled each Jew to confront his people, his past, and his God. Thus, the war has had an interesting and profound effect upon the Jews of Israel. Stories have

---

240 "Eliezer "Elie" Wiesel (1928–2016) was a Romanian-born Jewish-American writer, professor, political activist, Nobel Laureate, and Holocaust survivor. He was the author of 57 books... including *Night*, a work based on his experiences as a prisoner in the Auschwitz and Buchenwald concentration camps." "Elie Wiesel." *Wikipedia, The Free Encyclopedia*. Wikipedia, The Free Encyclopedia, 7 Sep. 2017. Web. 19 Sep. 2017. "Yitzhak Rabin (1922–1995) was an Israeli politician, statesman and general. He was the fifth Prime Minister of Israel, serving two terms in office, 1974 to 1977 and 1992 until his assassination in 1995." Wikipedia contributors. Wikipedia contributors. "Yitzhak Rabin." *Wikipedia, The Free Encyclopedia*. Wikipedia, The Free Encyclopedia, 21 Sep. 2017. Web. 24 Sep. 2017.

241 Martin Buber (1878–1965) was an Austrian-born Israeli philosopher best known for his philosophy of dialogue, a form of existentialism centered on the distinction between the I-Thou relationship and the I-It relationship. Wikipedia contributors. "Martin Buber." *Wikipedia, The Free Encyclopedia*. Wikipedia, The Free Encyclopedia, 4 Sep. 2017. Web. 19 Sep. 2017.

242 Bar-Ilan University, established in 1955, is Israel's second-largest academic institution. It is in Ramat Gan, located east of Tel Aviv. Wikipedia contributors. "Bar-Ilan University." *Wikipedia, The Free Encyclopedia*. Wikipedia, The Free Encyclopedia, 27 Aug. 2017. Web. 19 Sep. 2017.

been told of how in the excitement of the war, some Israeli soldiers turned to their religious comrades and begged to be taught how to pray and put on the *tefillin* because they had never done either before.[243] Other nations would have rejoiced on such an occasion with great victory parades that boasted of military prowess. Israel's military heroes gathered at the Western Wall and wept as they responded to the mystique of Jewish history.[244] Religious emotion that many people had long thought they were incapable of feeling swept the land.

One hopes that these emotions that have been aroused will not be transient. One hopes that there will be some lasting effect. The Jews of Israel have experienced the revelation that some religious feeling lies dormant in all of us, after all. This revelation is both a challenge and an opportunity. One hopes that they will be moved to accept this as a challenge to re-explore the Jewish faith, and as an opportunity to find their way back not to religious uniformity, but rather to the common recognition that the religious aspect of Jewish peoplehood is essential, that in the religious dimension we find our common bond as people.

The element of the miraculous was not confined to Israel alone. What happened amongst ourselves in this country was almost as great a miracle as what happened to the Jews of Israel. What happened here was also a cause of abiding astonishment.[245] The deep anxiety that took hold of the Jewish community, the cries of protest, the outpouring of funds for the UJA and Israel bonds were unbelievable. Young people clamored at the doors of the Israeli Consulate to be permitted to go to Israel and help. Children went around ringing doorbells and making a collection. The normally faithful, of course, extended themselves far more than ever in the light of the emergency; but now, many a Jew who had been aloof and indifferent to Jewish life suddenly experienced a deep concern and was drawn into the orbit once more. Jews whose sense of identification with the Jewish community had heretofore been

---

243 *Tefillin*, also called phylacteries, are a set of small black leather boxes containing scrolls of parchment inscribed with verses from the Torah. They are worn by observant Jews during weekday morning prayers. Wikipedia contributors. "Tefillin." *Wikipedia, The Free Encyclopedia*. Wikipedia, The Free Encyclopedia, 4 Sep. 2017. Web. 19 Sep. 2017.

244 "The Western Wall, Wailing Wall, or *Kotel* (Hebrew) is an ancient limestone wall in the Old City of Jerusalem. The Wall is the holiest place where Jews are permitted to pray, though it is not the holiest site in the Jewish faith, which lies behind it." Wikipedia contributors. "Western Wall." *Wikipedia, The Free Encyclopedia*. Wikipedia, The Free Encyclopedia, 18 Sep. 2017. Web. 19 Sep. 2017.

245 "The response of American Jewry to the Six-Day War surprised even those most sanguine about the depth of American Jewish identity. In June 1967 alone, more than 7,500 American Jews volunteered to take over the civilian jobs of Israelis serving in the armed forces... In 1966, over $136 million had been pledged to the various community fund drives, and an article in *Fortune* magazine discussed 'the miracle of Jewish giving.' In 1967, the figure was $317 million." Edward Shapiro, "American Jews and Israel in the Post-War Period," *My Jewish Learning*, http://www.myjewishlearning.com/article/american-jews-and-israel-in-the-post-war-period/. Accessed 24 Sep. 2017.

most tenuous now were aroused by emotions they never knew they could feel. It was an amazing performance as money poured in from rallies and mass meetings held everywhere. New York City had its million-dollars-a-minute meetings.[246] Numerous individuals emptied their savings accounts. Congregations gave away funds accumulated for the building of new synagogues. It is, of course, always easier to raise money in a time of emergency, but never in their wildest dreams had any fundraisers expected the kind of response that took place, even under the most provocative of circumstances. Our own congregation contributed more than six times its normal amount to the United Jewish Appeal, and that, you know, has to be put into the category of a miracle. Like the Jews of Israel, we Jews in America surprised even ourselves by the spontaneity and the extent of our concern.

It is not too difficult to analyze why such an overwhelming response took place. Back in our minds was first of all the memory of the six million. It seemed to every one of us that in a somewhat different manner, a similar catastrophe might be in the making. It was not too far-fetched to think that if the Arabs were to continue successfully on their way, mass destruction of our people in Israel would be the consequence. Genocide was again the objective. The Arab masses were being incited not merely to wage war against a government, but to annihilate a people. This was the tone of Arab propaganda before the war; and this is what had been spelled out in detail in actual written battle orders that were captured by the Israelis during the war and are now available for all the world to see.

Secondly, there was a sudden realization that the continued existence of the State of Israel was of no little significance to every Jew, and the thought of Israel disappearing from the world proved to be all too terrifying. We experienced a feeling of personal involvement as never before. It became not merely an Israeli war, but a Jewish war. How could you think of the blood, sweat, and tears of the past nineteen years going down the drain, of the idealism and self-sacrifice of pioneers for decades before that going for naught? What would happen to Jewish morale everywhere? What would happen to the Jewish image that in recent times had acquired so much more respect and self-respect? When and how would we again be enabled to emerge from a new lamentation over the destruction of our people? Consciously or unconsciously, these were the questions that troubled us.

And again, there was the realization that if Jews the world over did not stand by Israel, who would? We were stirred by a deep sense of brotherhood and commitment to our people, all the more because of the very fact that to

---

246 $15 million was raised in fifteen minutes at one New York City luncheon, and over $100 million was raised in a month. *Ibid.*

the rest of the world, the emergency was just another political problem to be carefully weighed from many angles. It was only the Jews who were passionately concerned with the fate of their people. The rest of the world temporized and debated and worried only about oil and Cold War politics.

And it was not only the political leadership that disappointed us, but the religious leadership as well. Official Christian circles were comparatively silent in the face of the threat to Israel. There were some individuals who rose to our defense, but official Christian leadership held back. Some of them now plead with Israel to be generous in dealing with the Arabs, but we did not hear any outcry when the Arabs seemed to have the upper hand and threatened annihilation of Jews. Christian concerns have been more with Holy Places than with Jews, more with currying the favor of Arab Christians than with the preservation of Jewish lives. Whatever excuse the Christian world may now offer, or whatever their explanation may be, in the moments of emergency there was a great reluctance to speak forth. Their reaction was painfully slow. It was almost as if they might have been happy to see the whole political and theological problem of Palestine solved by Jewish defeat.

These are the elements, I believe, that contributed to the miraculous response of American Jewry. And even though we know this and understand this, I think that like the Israelis, we nevertheless surprised ourselves. For us, too, there was a revelation in the midst of the miracle—the revelation that for so many of us, our Jewish ties were stronger than we thought, that beneath the mask of indifference to Jewish life that so many of us wear, there was a residue of feeling that could on occasion churn its way to the surface. There was the revelation that our Jewishness may, after all, be the number one loyalty in our life, that we are more deeply involved in it emotionally that we might have imagined.

And again, as with respect to the Israelis, one hopes the emotions stirred by this emergency will not be transient among us, either. The shock of circumstances aroused our innermost feelings and revealed to ourselves our true identity. We also are faced with a challenge to act accordingly, to seize the opportunity to strengthen our Jewishness and make the most of it at all times instead of stifling it between emergencies. An individual is at his best when he is himself. When he tries to be something other than his true self, he fails as a person and lives a lie. The Israel crisis has revealed to us who we really are. Let us fulfill ourselves meaningfully.

According to Emil Fackenheim, a well-known theologian, the one significant principle by which an authentic Jew must live today is that he is forbidden to do anything that shall hand Hitler yet another posthumous victory.[247] He must not contribute in any way to the dissolution of the Jewish people, but must rather so act always as to build it and preserve it. This means we must all continue to be interested in Israel. We must all be concerned with the vitality of our synagogues and with the Jewish education of our children. We must all be generous in our material support of whatever is meaningful to Jewish survival and fulfills Jewish ideals. We cannot wait for a moment of great crisis for our Jewish feelings to be shaken up. Sometimes the crisis is more dramatic than at other times, but Jewish life is always in crisis. The dangers of acculturation and assimilation are always with us and we must be permanently on guard against them. It is senseless to act only when there is a knife at our back. We must be Jewishly aware and Jewishly alert, even in times of comparative calm.

On this occasion of the New Year, let us give thanks to the Almighty for the great deliverance we have experienced. Let us also pray for our understanding to appreciate the revelation of our inner selves that it has brought us. May we always remember who we are and what our responsibilities must be, and may we respond authentically to the appeal of Jewish emotions that stir us. And let us remind ourselves and all the world that we justify our existence as a people and our faith as Jews by holding constantly before us a vision not only of Jerusalem restored and Zion at ease, but also of an entire world at peace, when all nations shall dwell unafraid together, Jews and Arabs and all the rest.

In the words of the prophets:

...the Lord has comforted His people, He has redeemed Jerusalem. The Lord has made bare His holy arm in the eyes of all the nations; and let all the ends of the earth see the salvation of our God.[248]

Amen

---

247 "Emil Ludwig Fackenheim, Ph.D. (1916–2003) was a noted Jewish philosopher and Reform rabbi. He was born in Halle, Germany, arrested by Nazis on the night of November 9, 1938, known as *Kristallnacht*... He researched the relationship of the Jews with God, and is noted for his belief that the Holocaust must be understood as an imperative requiring Jews to carry on Jewish existence and the survival of the State of Israel. Fackenheim argued that continuing Jewish life and denying Hitler a posthumous victory was the "614th law," referring to the 613 *mitzvot* given to the Jews in the Torah." Wikipedia contributors. "Emil Fackenheim." *Wikipedia, The Free Encyclopedia.* Wikipedia, The Free Encyclopedia, 9 Sep. 2017. Web. 25 Sep. 2017.

248 Isaiah 52:9-10.

Dad—

You've touched on some of your favorite themes here. Ostensibly a sermon about Israel, you've captured the theology of miracles, something about the threat of our external enemies as well as a caveat about our internal sabotage. I don't doubt the feeling of euphoria you had at the swift military victory by the outnumbered and unsupported Jewish nation. (I know how excited you got when merely the Giants or the Mets pulled out a victory.) This historical event grabbed everyone's attention, as it should have. The residual messages are important:

- Pay attention to moments of "abiding astonishment"—they just might be miracles.
- Feel the depth of our commitment and love for the State of Israel, and stand up for her.
- Last, and of greatest importance, act always to build and preserve the Jewish people.

I get all three of these. They are part of my life that I inherited from you. More than anything, I pray and act to keep not just the values of Judaism but Judaism itself alive as a vital part of the community of the world.

Blessings.
Yesh

28. The Missing Al Chet

October 13, 1967

Kol Nidre

When my father speaks about spousal relationships, it seems not only theological and philosophical, but also deeply personal. I picture the tenderness as well as the friction between two strong, vulnerable, and very loving partners.

This is a prime example of prose that is of its era. Had he written this today, it is likely that my father would show sensitivity about fertility issues and assumptions about bearing children. He would be more inclusive when referring to gender and sexual orientation, and to the sanctity of marriage, more broadly defined in the twenty-first century than in his time. With that disclaimer in mind, this is a heartfelt and moving description of Jewish values as they apply to committed spousal relationships.

A happy, successful marriage is not something acquired by chance or good fortune. It is rather something into which we have poured the proper ingredients.

ONE OF THE DISTINCTIVE PRAYERS of the Yom Kippur service with which we are all familiar is the *Al Chet*. It is a kind of confessional; in the course of it, we make mention of a number of human shortcomings we might have been guilty of during the past year, and we pray for forgiveness. In our Reform prayer book, this list of sins that we have sinned is a comparatively short one. It is a good bit longer in the traditional prayer book, and the worshiper makes mention of many more of his possible shortcomings. But even the longer traditional list, it seems to me, is not quite complete, and something of importance has been left out that might have been included. We read of the sin that we have sinned by disrespecting parents and teachers. We read of the sin that we have sinned by exploiting or dealing treacherously with our neighbor. But strangely enough, no mention is made in this prayer of a human relationship more important than the ones between neighbors or teachers or even parents. This is the relationship between husband and wife.

In all probability, no great significance should be attached to this omission, but it is nevertheless surprising. The editor of the prayer may have thought the list of sins as given was already inclusive enough to cover any problems between husband and wife; but if this is so, the same thing could also be said about parents and teachers and neighbors. It may, perhaps, be that the author had such an exalted opinion of Jewish family life that it was inconceivable to him that any wrong could be committed between a husband and a wife. The fact is that we Jews collectively do have a reputation for having achieved an exceptionally high quality of family life. A director of the Catholic Conference on Family Welfare once wrote, "Any student of social history will recognize that the world owes much to the Jewish family."

I remember that once when I had occasion to speak to a college sociology class, the professor asked me to comment on the strength of Jewish family life. He said the Jewish family had a reputation for more stable and closer ties; he felt that in these days, when family life is so shaky and divorce rates so high, it would be worthwhile to listen to the secret of success of the Jewish family. To be realistic, however, it must be admitted that even in the most blessed of marriages there may be moments of tension and irritation, and that as human beings none of us do or can attain perfection in any respect. And even though the reputation of the Jewish family is high, surely even as husbands and wives, as well as children, pupils, or neighbors, we may pause on this solemn day and at least think to ourselves an *Al Chet* for the sin that we have sinned by falling short in some way, in word or deed or attitude, in our family relationships. We can say in our hearts a prayer for forgiveness from God and from one another.

It would not be amiss on this day when we look to self-improvement in all aspects of our life to ask ourselves why it is that the Jewish family has indeed acquired such renown. What are the basic principles of family life that Judaism has set before us that have helped us achieve such a reputation? There are four Hebrew words or phrases we ought to know around which these principles revolve. And just in case you may not already know them, let us make a bit of a Hebrew lesson out of this sermon.

The first of these terms is *Kiddushin*. Very often when performing a marriage ceremony, I center my remarks upon this word, the traditional name by which the marriage ceremony is known. The literal meaning of *Kiddushin* is "sanctification," meaning investment with holiness. *Kiddushin* comes from the same root as *Kadosh*, a word that you will remember from one of the more important congregational responses in the service—*Kadosh, Kadosh, Kadosh,* Holy, Holy, Holy. It is from the same root as *Kiddush*, the prayer over wine by which we sanctify the Sabbath and the festivals. It is also the same root as *Kaddish*, the prayer by which we sanctify God's name in memory of the dead.

There is an important implication in the use of this term. We know that the institution of marriage rests upon a biological basis—it meets a human physical need and assures continuation of the race. We know that marriage rests upon an economic basis—it makes it much more convenient for men and women to care adequately for the requirements of food, shelter, and other necessities of life. We know that marriage rests also upon a psychological basis—men and women escape their loneliness and satisfy their desire for companionship more easily through marriage. But by the title *Kiddushin*, Judaism suggests that there is yet another, much more significant dimension to marriage than those we have just mentioned. This is the element of holiness. Marriage is a sacred covenant. It is a union involving ethical responsibility and religious principle. Leo Baeck, noted theologian, describes marriage as "the experience by two people of a divine mystery which commands them to realize and fashion their whole life through each other."[249] It is a relationship so significant that the prophets in the Bible often used the terminology of marriage to describe the covenant that binds together God and Israel. God's love for Israel is compared to that of a husband for his wife. And perhaps more beautifully than anywhere else, this figure is used by Hosea when he proclaims in the name of God,

> I will betroth thee unto Me forever, yea, I will betroth thee unto Me in righteousness and in justice, and in loving-kindness and in compassion. And I will betroth thee unto Me in faithfulness, and thou shalt know the Lord.[250]

Out of this concept of *Kiddushin* there follows quite naturally the second basic principle upon which the Jewish idea of the family is based. This is *Taharat Hamishpacha*, the Purity of the Family, by which is meant sexual discipline and fidelity to marriage vows. One of the most significant factors in making for the health and well-being of the Jewish family and the Jewish community has been its very strong emphasis on the laws against

---

[249] "Leo Baeck (1873–1956) was a twentieth-century German rabbi, scholar, and theologian. He served as a leader of Liberal Judaism in his native country and internationally, and later represented all German Jews during the Nazi era. After the war, he settled in London, U.K., where he served as the chairman of the World Union for Progressive Judaism." Wikipedia contributors. "Leo Baeck." *Wikipedia, The Free Encyclopedia*. Wikipedia, The Free Encyclopedia, 19 Jul. 2017. Web. 25 Sep. 2017.

[250] Hosea 2:19-20.

sexual promiscuity. It is interesting to note that just as the Bible compares the marriage covenant to the relationship between God and Israel, so also is adultery used as the figure of speech to describe the betrayal of God and the violation of His commandments. We hear a great deal today about the New Morality.[251] The New Morality does not consider it necessary to limit the sex relationship to marriage. It has other criteria that Judaism, however [sic], *cannot accept* because Jewish tradition calls for discipline, fidelity, and responsibility in the sexual relationship.[252]

The third important phrase in Jewish family life is *Shalom Bayit*, literally "peaceful household." This, too, is but a secondary aspect of *Kiddushin*, for how can marriage be sanctified if the household is contentious? To avoid contention, there must be truth, respect, and understanding. Truth, the rabbis said, is the beginning and end of all things, and this is especially so in the circle of family life. Deception even in little things contributes to the erection of barriers, the diminishing of sanctity. Husband and wife may differ on many questions, but they cannot afford to conceal the truth; the lines of honest communication must remain open. Nor is telling the truth merely a matter of refraining from deception. It is also a matter of not holding back one's true feelings when they should be made known. It is not necessarily good to avoid debate by seeking refuge in silence. It is important to be able to bring into the light the truth of our feelings, to bring into the light whatever it is that disturbs us. Otherwise, what we repress may remain within us and continue to disturb us until it surprises us by breaking out at some time in an unfortunate and undesirable manner. The knowledge of husband and wife, that one can have complete faith in the other, that there is honest spoken and unspoken communication between them, is a cement that strengthens their bond.

Furthermore, lines of communication must operate not only when there are grievances that need to be aired, but also for the expression of appreciation and tenderness. What may sometimes seem to be a problem can melt away in the warmth of an affectionate word or an appreciative caress.

---

251 The New Morality is linked to the term "Situation Ethics," coined by Harvard professor Joseph Fletcher whose 1966 book on the topic described "a system of ethics that evaluates acts in light of their situational context rather than by the application of moral absolutes." The sexual revolution and the free love movement of the Sixties, spawned by the new technology of oral contraception, were primary instances of Situation Ethics and the New Morality—"if it feels good, do it, as long as it doesn't hurt anybody." *The American Heritage Dictionary of the English Language*, 5th ed., (Houghton Mifflin Harcourt Publishing Company, 2016).

252 Editor's Note: I've left this sentence as written despite what seems like a possible inadvertent contradiction. My father's use of the word "however" seems to imply that Judaism accepts sexual relationships outside marriage, that it's only certain unnamed "other criteria" of the New Morality that Judaism rejects. He is leaving open the possibility of pre-marital sexual relationships that by definition are outside the limits of marriage but may still demonstrate "discipline, fidelity, and responsibility."

28. The Missing Al Chet—1967

Everyone needs to be loved and appreciated, and we respond to those who express such love and appreciation to us. It is not a sign of weakness or maudlin sentimentality when we speak such words. It is rather the stuff by which homes are brightened.

The last Hebrew term I would mention this morning is *Gidul Banim* or "the raising of children"—the readiness to assume a responsibility for the future. The sanctification of the marriage bond is not complete without such a sense of purpose and meaning. It is most unfortunate that altogether too many young people look upon marriage only as the fulfillment of a personal desire for romance and happiness. There is no doubt that romance in marriage is desirable and that happiness is not to be disparaged. In the marriage ceremony, we even recite a benediction that praises God who maketh bride and bridegroom to rejoice together. But Hollywood notions of romance are not realistic and married couples do not remain forever on cloud nine. Happiness is not something we can go out and acquire merely because we selfishly want it. It is, rather, a byproduct of a more stable and meaningful way of life. Marriage implies not only the satisfaction of our own personal desires, but a social responsibility.

The purpose of Jewish marriage is to create a Jewish home, to raise a new Jewish generation. A child not only is the fulfillment of the love of husband and wife, but is the link with the future of our people and the vehicle for the transmission of our heritage. Husband and wife are thus responsible for the development of their child. They have the responsibility of giving him a sense of security and self-esteem so that he may be an adequate human being. They are to provide him with the benefit of a good example and to inculcate him with an appreciation of Jewish values. The rabbis even said that the biological parent is not the true parent of a child, but rather his teacher is the true parent. To fulfill the highest ideal of parenthood is to be mindful of the responsibility of being, in the best sense, the teacher of one's child. When husbands and wives lift themselves above a selfish concern for themselves and look upon themselves as partners in the fulfillment of some higher Jewish purpose—as partners with God in the creation and perpetuation of life, when they join wholeheartedly in the responsibility of creating a pleasant and meaningful Jewish home, and when they express a mutual interest in the wholesome Jewish development of the child, their marriage is sanctified and approaches the Jewish ideal.

To repeat the Hebrew phrases I would have you remember: *Kiddushin, Taharat Hamishpacha, Shalom Bayit,* and *Gidul Banim*—sanctification, purity of the family, a peaceful household, and the responsible raising of children. These are the most important traditional ideals of the Jewish life. Taken all together, they imply that a happy, successful marriage is not something acquired by chance or good fortune. Rather, it is something into which we have poured the proper ingredients. It is something to which we must give our best effort. It is something that resides upon a meaningful philosophy, upon appropriate objectives. It requires that we build upon a sound ethical and moral foundation.

The rabbis of the *Midrash* once pointed out that the Hebrew word for man, which is "*Ish*," and the Hebrew word for woman, which is "*Isha*," have two letters in common and a third wherein they differ. The two letters that differ are *yod* and *hay*, which taken together spell "*Yah*," a Hebrew word for God. The two letters they have in common are *alef* and *shin* which taken together spell "*Aish*," the Hebrew word for fire. Thus, they pointed out, if you take away God from man and woman you are left with fire. Only when God is present can there be a peaceful and a meaningful union. May we, on this Holy Day, always resolve to have God as our partner in our households. May His Divine presence bring peace into our hearts. May we forgive and be forgiven our faults and resolve that they shall be no more. May we all know the joy that comes from a happy home and a devoted family. May we be gladdened by our children, and may God's blessings ever be with us.

Amen.

Dad—

These beautiful words should be read by every couple entering into matrimony. Oh, I suppose there could be some pushback about the necessity of having children. There are some who do not wish to do so, and perhaps for that reason alone they should not. And there are some for whom conception does not readily occur, and they should be relieved of the burden of guilt heaped upon any disappointment they may already feel. Nonetheless, the value of passing on our heritage to succeeding generations is to be held high, along with the values of holiness, fidelity, peace, and truth, to which you also refer. My prayer for my children and their children is that they live lives filled with the blessing of these traits.

Blessings.
Yesh

29. The Sins of a Nation

October 14, 1967

Yom Kippur Morning

My father held nothing back in his opposition to the Vietnam War.

What is it that should trouble us with regard to the war in Vietnam? We should be troubled by the immorality of what we are doing, the futility of our course of action, the lack of forthrightness on the part of our government, and the diversion of our attention and resources from our social needs here at home.

ON ROSH HASHANAH MORNING, I SAID that there was one subject in particular which during these High Holy Days demands our attention.[253] There is also a second topic that I feel makes a similar demand. Thinking specifically of the Jewish people and Jewish history, we felt the necessity of some comment about the recent war between Israel and the Arabs. But turning our attention to ourselves as Americans and thinking about the welfare of the world in general, we feel an equal compulsion to say something about the war in Vietnam.

Yom Kippur is a most appropriate time for such consideration. In this afternoon's service, we shall read of the procedures of the High Priest as he officiated over the rites in the ancient Temple in Jerusalem. We shall note that he first made atonement for himself personally, and then for the whole House of Aaron, and then for the entire Jewish people. Thus, in ancient Israel the principle was apparently accepted that not only as individuals do we sin and have reason to seek forgiveness and make atonement, but also as a nation, as an entire society. I do not know of any other people or religion that makes

---

[253] Chapter 27, *The Aftermath of a Miracle*, concerning the Six-Day War.

this point as strongly as Judaism. Nonetheless, there is certainly a need for modern nations to sponsor a similar moment of national introspection, a period of national confession of error, of national repentance of sin. And it certainly would not be out of order in these times for our own United States of America to observe its own such national Day of Atonement. We have, indeed, much sin to confess with respect to the manner in which we handle many of the problems of our society, and ranking first perhaps on this list of sins is the war in Vietnam.

I must confess at the outset that for quite some time I myself was ambivalent about our action in Vietnam. The arguments of the hawks as well as the doves seemed to have some merit. But the more time that elapses, the more we see the effect of the policies we pursue, the more we are able to read and learn about what has been going on in Vietnam, the more we must be convinced that we are embarked upon a venture that is morally wrong and politically foolish. If our nation is as great and worthy as we like to think it is, it will indeed confess its errors and seek to mend its ways.

I must confess also, though it is hardly necessary, that I am not a political scientist. I have no access to the State Department and I certainly have not been to Vietnam, but by this time there has been much public debate. There are those who have studied the situation carefully. We have accumulated literature about Vietnam, and it becomes possible to gain insight into some of the political developments and form some moral judgments. In this connection, I should like to call your attention to two books in particular that summarize the problem in an excellent manner. Both are available in paperback. They are *Vietnam: Crisis of Conscience*, written by Brown, Heschel, and Novak,[254] and a volume just recently reviewed in the *New York Times* entitled *The Abuse of Power*, by Theodore Draper.[255] Reading these, it seems that we have stumbled into war unintentionally through political mistakes and miscalculations, and are trying to cover up our embarrassment through a sheer display of power.

What is it that should trouble us with regard to the war in Vietnam? We should be troubled by the immorality of what we are doing, the futility of our course of action, the lack of forthrightness on the part of our government,

---

254 *Vietnam: Crisis of Conscience* (1967) was notably a joint Catholic, Jewish, and Protestant book questioning the U.S. purpose in Vietnam. It was authored by Robert McAfee Brown (1920–2001), an American Presbyterian minister and anti-Vietnam War activist, Michael Novak (born in 1933), an American Catholic philosopher, journalist, novelist, and diplomat, and Abraham Joshua Heschel (See Chapter 16, Note 6). "Heschel believed the teachings of the Hebrew prophets were a clarion call for social action in the United States and worked in the American Civil Rights movement as well as in opposition to the Vietnam War." Wikipedia contributors. "Abraham Joshua Heschel." *Wikipedia, The Free Encyclopedia*. Wikipedia, The Free Encyclopedia, 22 Jul. 2017. Web. 25 Sep. 2017.

255 American Theodore H. "Ted" Draper (1912–2006) was a Communist political writer before becoming an award-winning historian.

and the diversion of our attention and resources from our social needs here at home.

First of all, we ought to realize that we are fighting in this small area one of the most destructive wars in all of history. As we sit comfortably in our own living rooms, it is hard to believe that by the end of 1966 we had already dropped more tonnage in bombs than Germany had received in the whole period of World War II. Our policy of fighting a guerrilla war with bombers has been compared to weeding a garden with a bulldozer. The result of this tactic has been that the chief casualties in the war are not military but civilian; and we have been developing an ever more indifferent attitude to the suffering we cause these non-combatants. It has been reported that out of every 100 casualties only about 10 will be Viet Cong, and that we Americans, who pride ourselves on our humanitarianism, wound or kill 3 to 4 times as many people as the Viet Cong.[256] Of all the civilians who have been killed, at least half are children. In the effort to drive out Viet Cong infiltrators, an entire area may be taken over by our troops, the residents uprooted and sent to relocation centers, their homes destroyed, and the ground scorched. Close to a million South Vietnamese have thus been uprooted. We have used the agonizing napalm which has often found the wrong target, and we have laid waste fertile countryside and destroyed its capacity to produce.[257] There are many in South Vietnam who are wondering what it is that will be left when we are finished. Not long ago, the *New York Times* ran a story on a Buddhist girl who said,

> Most of us in Vietnam hate from the bottom of our hearts the Americans who have brought the sufferings of this war... The tons of bombs and money you have poured on our people have shattered our bodies and nationalist sentiments... If the war continues, we will lose not only thousands of lives but all of the cultural and human values of our country. [258]

The frustration our military men have encountered in Vietnam has apparently left them callous to moral principles.

---

256 The Viet Cong was the name given by Western sources to the National Liberation Front (1959–1975) that fought the United States and South Vietnamese governments, eventually emerging on the winning side.

257 "Napalm is an inflammable liquid, a mixture of a gelling agent and petroleum or a similar fuel, used in warfare. It was initially used as an incendiary device against buildings; later, it was primarily used as an anti-personnel weapon, as it sticks to skin and causes severe burns. The United States used napalm extensively in incendiary attacks on Japanese cities in World War II, as well as during the Korean War and Vietnam War." Wikipedia contributors. "Napalm." *Wikipedia, The Free Encyclopedia*. Wikipedia, The Free Encyclopedia, 19 Sep. 2017. Web. 25 Sep. 2017.

258 In his book *The Nonviolent Alternative*, Thomas Merton (1915–1968), an American Catholic writer, Trappist monk, and social activist, attributed this quote to a Buddhist nun on the eve of her self-immolation.

Secondly, we should be disturbed by the utter inconsistency between our stated aims and the way we go about trying to achieve them. We defend our presence in Vietnam with the argument that it is necessary to stem the Communist tide, which will otherwise envelop Asia and threaten freedom throughout the world. But this is a prime example of political nonsense. Communism is no longer a single, united movement controlled by Moscow. It has been breaking up into a number of nationalistic groups, each desiring its own independence. The wise thing to do would be to take advantage of this split in the communist world and to nourish a sense of independence in each group where its existence is inevitable. By proclaiming a crusade against communism in general and committing our power to destroy it in a place such as North Vietnam, we are merely inviting all communist groups to unite in self-defense rather than drift apart. We are forcing them to make common cause against us instead of playing them off one against the other. We are on the way to accomplishing the very opposite of our stated purpose.

We have also been told again and again by the military minds that one more step in escalating the war will bring the other side to its knees and then we can go home. We are told that one more step in escalating the war is needed to protect our men and save the lives of our boys. But the results of escalation have only been higher casualty rates and more American lives lost, while the enemy develops an ever-more intense determination to resist. Escalation has brought us closer to the Chinese border and threatens to involve China. It has brought both sides closer to the frustration of a kind that might tempt one side or the other to introduce nuclear weapons, with all the danger of mutual destruction that this implies.

Because we are a nation of enormous power, we think that the use of such power is the answer to all problems. However, the enemy in Vietnam is not communism but the poverty and disease and ignorance that have given rise to it. It takes political wisdom rather than military power to deal with such enemies. Our reliance on brute force is an exercise in futility.

Furthermore, we ought to be deeply disturbed by the discrepancy between what we are told by the administration is taking place and what we learn afterwards has actually happened.[259] It is interesting to note that it is not merely the starry-eyed pacifists who accuse the government of misleading the public, but staid, conservative newspapers and columnists and politicians as well. There may be some who accuse the critics of the Vietnam War of being unpatriotic and crackpot leftists, but the list of critics whose credentials show them to be anything but unpatriotic and leftist is too great. And the lack of

---

259 President Lyndon Johnson was in office.

candor on the part of government officials is being carefully documented and can no longer be denied.

We were led to believe, for example, that the presence of ground troops in Vietnam and the bombing of North Vietnam were initiated in response to an armed invasion of South Vietnam by a division of North Vietnam troops. In his book, Theodore Draper reveals that it has now been admitted that our forces were brought in prior to the presence of North Vietnamese troops, and that even when our intelligence first discovered an invasion from the north, only about four or five hundred men were involved. Later, as we continued to increase the number of our men, the number of North Vietnamese also understandably increased in response to us. Draper, furthermore, lists the many occasions when it seemed as though negotiations for peace with Hanoi were possible. According to our State Department, Hanoi never responded favorably—but Draper accuses our officials of either ineptitude or lack of sincerity and of doing the very thing that would cause Hanoi to back off rather than to develop the confidence that meaningful discussions might be possible. Even reports on casualties and bombings are not always to be trusted; frequently, one version is given out to the public only to be changed later on as newspapermen on the scene report what had been suppressed. I cannot think of any other time when the American people have been so confused and skeptical with regard to official information emanating from Washington.

And we cannot help but also be disturbed not only by what the war is doing to Vietnam, but by the effect it is having upon our own country and our own people. It is not only the military effort that continues to escalate; it is the financial burden. And this financial burden is being born at the expense of needed reforms and improvement here at home. At a time when our cities find themselves in the midst of revolution due to rat-infested slums, inadequate opportunities for employment, and the need to raise our educational standards, we are squandering millions of dollars in a war most Americans do not want, the nations of the world frown on, and the South Vietnamese themselves are failing to support. Our loss is not only financial. If we have hippies and other rebellious young people to contend with, it is at least partly due to the fact that they do not want to be involved in a senseless war and give their lives for an incomprehensible cause.[260]

---

[260] "A hippie is a member of a liberal counterculture, originally a youth movement that started in the United States and United Kingdom during the mid-1960s and spread to other countries around the world... Hippies created their own communities, listened to psychedelic music, embraced the sexual revolution, and used drugs such as cannabis, LSD, peyote, and psilocybin mushrooms to explore altered states of consciousness... Hippie fashion and values had a major effect on culture, influencing popular music, television, film, literature, and the arts. Since the 1960s, many aspects of hippie culture have been assimilated by mainstream society. The religious and cultural diversity espoused by the hippies has

We have also been dangerously close to slipping into another era of McCarthyism. Fortunately, dissent from our government policy has grown to such an extent among businessmen and politicians, let alone clergy, educators, and students, that it is difficult to apply the label of "communist" or "unpatriotic" to everyone who opposes the war in Vietnam. Nevertheless, there are those who try. They would like to silence those who are critical, and we are compelled to maintain a careful vigil if we are to protect freedom of expression and the right of dissent for every citizen of our nation.

Our dissent from what has been going on in Vietnam does not imply that we must immediately arrange a full-scale withdrawal. Having gotten ourselves into this situation, we cannot suddenly change our course without serious complications. But the continued escalation must be stopped before we complete the destruction of the entire land and its people, and before we draw other nations into the struggle and perhaps bring on nuclear war. Moreover, we must embark on what is admittedly a most difficult task of trying to effect a negotiated peace. It will not be easy to win the confidence of the other side after so long a struggle and after so many mistakes in judgment have been made. Perhaps they really do not want to negotiate peace. But if we can escalate a military offensive, we can also try to escalate a peace offensive. It may take time and it may require the help of others, but the risks involved in trying to achieve some kind of negotiation are nowhere near as great as the risk involved in mounting an ever-increasing military offensive, and they are definitely preferable to spending the next ten or fifteen years fighting in Vietnam, as many experts predict will be the case.

It is to such a thought that a movement called *Negotiation Now* has dedicated itself and is seeking a mass of signatures with which to impress official Washington. I ask you to take some opportunity to read the petition that I have placed on the bulletin board and sign it if you can possibly agree. It simply asks for cessation of bombing and an honest effort at negotiation for peace. The only alternative would seem to be to continue to escalate the bombing to an even more vindictive degree and to launch a full-scale invasion on the impossible terrain of Vietnam. I would hope that no one is really so naïve as to think that we can ourselves come out unscathed if we do this, or that we can achieve anything but a Pyrrhic victory at best.

There will be no disgrace attached to us if we seem to reverse our policy in this war. If we have made mistakes in the past, it would be foolish to continue

---

gained widespread acceptance, and Eastern philosophy and spiritual concepts have reached a larger audience." The cultural revolution of the Sixties was still in its ascendency at the time of this sermon. Wikipedia contributors. "Hippie." *Wikipedia, The Free Encyclopedia*. Wikipedia, The Free Encyclopedia, 15 Sep. 2017. Web. 25 Sep. 2017.

them and a sign of greatness to correct them. We often disparage the Oriental need to save face, and we ought not ourselves to be obsessed with such a concern. This is a time for our nation to emulate the procedure of the Temple in ancient days. This is a time for national repentance. Let us conclude with a Hasidic parable.

Our Master, Rabbi Chaim of Sanz, told the following parable:

A man had been wandering about in a forest for several days, not knowing which was the right way out. Suddenly, he saw a man approach him. His heart was filled with joy.

"Now I shall certainly find out which is the right way," he thought to himself.

When they neared one another, he asked the man, "Brother, tell me which is the right way. I have been wandering about in this forest for several days."

Said the other to him, "Brother, I do not know the way out either. I, too, have been wandering about here for many, many days. But this I can tell you: do not take the way I have been taking, for that will lead you astray. And now let us look for a new way out together."

Our Master added,

So it is with us. One thing I can tell you: the way we have been following thus far we ought to follow no further, for that way leads one astray. But now let us look for a new way.

Dad—

Once again, I'm proud of you and your willingness to speak your unvarnished truth. As I recall, 1967 was still a bit early to speak out so forcefully in opposition to the war. The Chicago riots outside the Democratic convention were almost a year away. Also, I'm sure you had plenty of hawks among your congregants. I wonder what their reaction was.

Now as for your intolerance of hippies, I'll have to take exception to that! Sure, in '67 I was still a straight-laced Ivy Leaguer, but it wouldn't be long before I tuned in, turned on, and dropped out myself—not at all a bad thing! Although I wouldn't characterize myself as a hippie, I suspect it may have crossed your mind when I returned from art school in '68 unshaven, with long (for me) hair, sandals, and torn jeans. It was the beginning of a long journey of self-discovery that I might never have made cooped up inside Brown University's ivy-covered walls. I know; this has little to do with the antiwar movement per se, but you brought it up! Moreover, I would be remiss if I didn't add how Debbie and I met on a peace march—the Moratorium to End the War in Vietnam, November 15, 1969!

Blessings.
Yesh

30. Remarks on the Death of Robert F. Kennedy

June 7, 1968

The following is not a sermon, but some poignant remarks offered just before the congregation rose to recite *Kaddish* two days after the assassination of Robert F. Kennedy. These words of grief, outrage, hope, and ultimately faith continue to resonate.

The need of today is... the prophetic prescription of a laiv chadash, *a new heart, a change of attitude, a genuine willingness to deal with the basic causes of unrest and unhappiness among our people, to discipline our prejudices, to convince all Americans we are genuinely concerned about each other.*[261]

WE CANNOT LET THIS EVENING GO BY without a reference to the tragic loss this week of Robert F. Kennedy, senator of our state and presidential candidate. [262] Perhaps this moment before we rise to recite the *Kaddish* is the appropriate time to make it. It is, however, most difficult to know what to say at this moment that truly makes sense. Once again, our nation has been robbed of a great personality. Once again, we find ourselves gripped in a deep national sorrow. In the face of the new tragedy which has taken place, certain people are expected to say things, to make statements which will express grief,

---

261 *Laiv chadash* may be taken from Ezekiel 36: 26: "A new heart also will I give you, and a new spirit will I put within you; and I will take away the stony heart out of your flesh, and I will give you a heart of flesh."

262 "Following his brother John's assassination on November 22, 1963, Kennedy continued to serve as Attorney General under President Lyndon B. Johnson for nine months. In September 1964, Kennedy resigned to seek New York's U.S. Senate seat, which he won in November. In March 1968, Kennedy began a campaign for the presidency and was a front-running candidate of the Democratic Party. In the California presidential primary on June 4, Kennedy defeated Eugene McCarthy, a U.S. Senator from Minnesota." Rick Kearns, *Step Inside the Truth* (Bloomington, IN: AuthorHouse UK Ltd., 2014), 48-9.

which will offer some explanation, which will attempt to lift our spirits. Newspapermen are writing, politicians are eulogizing, sociologists are explaining, and the clergy is expected to give comfort. I have listened, as have you, to many words in the past couple of days, but the situation is so depressing, the reawakened memories of similar terrible episodes of the recent past are so disturbing. What is happening in our country today is so unbelievable that very few of the multitude of words that have poured forth are really meaningful, and I do not profess be able to do much better.

What is being said today is very much like what was said when the life of John Kennedy was taken; the thoughts of today are very much like what they were when the life of Martin Luther King, Jr. was snuffed out.[263] The same words, to a large extent, are being repeated, but now they have become trite; they have lost their comforting effect. They only add to our despair. I feel a sense of total frustration and can only agree with James Reston when he writes:

> *The problems of our society are too big for the words we have at our disposal to deal with, too complex for us to be able to communicate with each other. We need to find new ways to say new things.*[264]

A terrible state of affairs has come to pass in our land. The lives of leaders who have courage and imagination, who have a charismatic effect on numbers of people, who impart youthful enthusiasm and offer a sense of purpose and hope in confronting difficult problems—these lives are being snuffed out, and we seem powerless to protect them. Is it always going to be only at the peril of assassination that men are willing to speak out (and whether we agree with them altogether or not is irrelevant), but is it always only at the peril of assassination that forthright and forceful men are to speak prophetic words to America? Is there to be safety only for mediocrities and men who use bland words that will offend no one and therefore mean nothing to anyone? Are we going to be able to maintain law and order in our land? Shall we be unable, henceforth, to solve our political problems in a peaceful, democratic manner? Are we unable to prevent not only personal assassination, but public rioting and looting and violent disregard for duly constituted authorities?

I am afraid I cannot go along with the rationalization that it is unfair to blame all America for the assassinations that have been committed, that it was, after all, just the violent deed of a single mad personality or even a plot concocted by groups of sinister people. It is happening too often, and

---

263 King was assassinated on April 4, 1968, in Memphis, Tennessee.

264 James Barrett Reston (1909–1995), nicknamed "Scotty," was a journalist for many years with *The New York Times*. Wikipedia contributors. "James Reston." *Wikipedia, The Free Encyclopedia*. Wikipedia, The Free Encyclopedia, 4 Sep. 2017. Web. 25 Sep. 2017.

30. Remarks on the Death of Robert F. Kennedy—1968

these individual mad personalities and these groups of extremists, if such be responsible, express their madness and this extremism in the context of their environment. It is because we are becoming a desensitized nation, a nation that verbally protests violence but, unhappily, is becoming used to it and condones it and has not really done enough to come to grips with its causes and to try sincerely to end it, that these mad people and extremists increasingly express themselves in such violent deeds.

We have become a nation that stands out as a symbol of violence throughout the world—because of what we have done in Vietnam, and because of what we have not done at home to solve the problems of human rights and degrading poverty in our own country. One or two more political assassinations and we may not even react against them; we will have been emotionally drained and lost our capacity altogether even to grieve and to mourn and to feel for our fellowman at all. This is the tragedy of America today, and is evident in the official reaction of President Johnson to the assassination of Robert Kennedy. With all due respect to the President, he reminds me of the presidents of the average lodge or congregation or some other local organization. He had a problem and so he formed a committee. We are now going to have another commission to study the causes of violence, and what, may we ask Mr. Johnson, did he do with the report of the Kerner Commission that studied the causes of rioting in our urban centers?[265] And now, what will this new commission find out that the other did not? We cannot improve America by filing reports! We do indeed need to find new ways not only to say new things, but, more significantly, to do new things!

The need of today is not another commission, but truly rather the prophetic prescription of a *laiv chadash*, a new heart, a change of attitude, a genuine willingness to deal with the basic causes of unrest and unhappiness among our people, to discipline our prejudices, to convince all Americans we are genuinely concerned about each other. We need a willingness to spend for peace what we are spending for war. We need to clean our own house before we try to tell others how they should live. We need to reestablish our nation as a true symbol of democracy. Then, mad people, living in a more healthful

---

[265] "The National Advisory Commission on Civil Disorders, known as the Kerner Commission after its chair, Governor Otto Kerner, Jr. of Illinois, was an 11-member commission established by President Lyndon B. Johnson to investigate the causes of the 1967 race riots in the United States and to provide recommendations for the future... Johnson appointed the commission on July 28, 1967, while rioting was still underway in Detroit, Michigan. Mounting civil unrest since 1965 had stemmed riots in the Black neighborhoods of major U.S. cities, including Los Angeles (1965), Chicago (1966), and Newark (1967)." Wikipedia contributors. "Kerner Commission." *Wikipedia, The Free Encyclopedia*. Wikipedia, The Free Encyclopedia, 23 Sep. 2017. Web. 25 Sep. 2017.

environment, will not be so mad and will not be moved to such irrational and violent behavior.

Robert Kennedy has joined his brother John on the list of American martyrs. His energy, his forthrightness, his enthusiasm, and even his ambition—which some have criticized—will be missed. Again, a youthful spark that aroused the passions of so many in the interest of social causes has been extinguished. Again, a distinguished family that has devoted itself so wholeheartedly to public life is smitten with deep anguish and pain, is so ill-repaid for the public service it has sought to render. Whatever our political convictions, we share the pain of this bereaved family. We pray that they will find comfort in some form of good that may perhaps ultimately result either from the life of this public servant or from his tragic loss. We pray that God will grant healing unto our nation and that the rule of reason will be reasserted. And in the spirit of our Jewish tradition, even in a moment when things seem so irrational and unreasonable, even in a moment of great sorrow and despair, we can but declare our faith; and thus, as we remember our own dear ones who have passed away and at the same time think of the national tragedy of this week, let us all rise to recite the *Kaddish* together.

30. Remarks on the Death of Robert F. Kennedy—1968

Dad—

I wept when I read these words. They took me back to a period of great national mourning—a very different time than these days. Today, tragedies continue to abound—violence and inexplicable deaths, although not of the famous and powerful, but typically of the anonymous and powerless. What concerned you—that repetitive events of this nature might cause us to become numb almost to indifference—may have come to pass. We've gotten to a state where even the rhetoric is caustic and hateful.

The need today continues to be for a *laiv chadash*. We need a new heart that is open and vulnerable, empathetic and embracing. We need that as a nation and as individuals. The people for whom Bobby Kennedy fought are still desperately in need of a change in heart among themselves and all Americans. The people of the world, in all corners of the earth, likewise need a *laiv chadash*.

You chose to speak of Kennedy in conjunction with the recitation of the *Kaddish*. Now, in an era of repeated sorrow and despair, we need the whole world to take comfort and to rise with a declaration of faith and love.

Blessings.
Yesh

31. Understanding Our Youth

September 23, 1968

Rosh Hashanah Morning

The turbulent late 1960s were notable for campus unrest and civil disobedience among the nation's youth. In this sermon, my father takes one of the most famous and problematic Biblical father-son relationships, that of Abraham and Isaac, and uses it as a foundation for commentary on the so-called generation gap. Despite his discomfort with much of their behavior, he was willing to hear the message of the younger generation and to acknowledge the principles that they sought to uphold.

One additional note—from a twenty-first century perspective almost fifty years later, it is ironic to hear how the youth of that era may have been influenced by rapid social and technological changes that may seem trivial by today's standards.

Young people... are challenging our unrecognized hypocrisies and have the daring to insist that societies and individuals live by the values they preach, that they wipe out the gap between principle and practice, between national creed and policy. Thus, it may well be... [they] have indeed followed the preachment of their elders only too well.

WE HAVE JUST READ FROM THE TORAH THIS MORNING, as we do every year on Rosh Hashanah, the story of the *Akeda*—the binding of Isaac.[266] Our tradition attaches a great deal of significance to this chapter. It is considered to be an awesome illustration of the deep commitment of our ancestor Abraham, and a convincing demonstration of God's goodness in that Isaac ultimately was spared.

---

266 Genesis 22:1-19.

Despite the importance, however, that tradition places upon this tale, it is one that often troubles the modern reader. The idea of God commanding Abraham to sacrifice his son is a disturbing one. The idea of a father being willing to sacrifice his own son, even at God's command, is even more disturbing. And our distress is not relieved even though we know beforehand that Isaac will survive and a ram will be offered in his stead.

Several explanations have been offered. We are asked, first of all, to remember that the sensibilities of people in biblical times were not quite as delicate as ours today. We are told that the early Hebrew people also abhorred child sacrifice, but that the idea was not altogether devoid of plausibility for them because it was practiced by their neighbors. There are many, indeed, who interpret this story of the *Akeda* as a Hebrew protest against this practice of child sacrifice. They consider it a subtle way of proclaiming that God did not really want that kind of sacrifice after all.

It has also been pointed out that the telling of the story takes for granted that God's demand is something extraordinary, something no man would think of doing on his own. But precisely therein, it is said, is its value as a test of faith. The very unreasonableness of God's demand and Abraham's readiness to do something one might ordinarily find repulsive and inhuman was only greater proof to the storyteller of Abraham's worthiness, and this is the point of it all.

The modern reader, however, may still be left unsatisfied by either of these explanations. He may still be disturbed by the fact that God gave such an order to a father concerning his son, whatever the reason may be.

Because of this theological difficulty, Edmond Cahn, an eminent professor of law, decided to evaluate this story from a lawyer's point of view.[267] He came to the conclusion that we really have not been given the true facts of the case. In a typical legal manner, his first question is, "Who were the witnesses that could have reported this event and given us the facts?" Only two, obviously, were possible—Abraham and Isaac themselves, who were alone on the mountaintop. He then decides that the witness could not have been Abraham, because everything we know about the character of Abraham is inconsistent with his actions as reported in this passage. Abraham was not a passive personality. The Bible tells us that he was a fighter. He did not fear to argue even with God himself. When Sodom was about to be destroyed, Abraham bargained with God in an effort to save it. He challenged God with the words,

---

[267] Edmond Nathaniel Cahn (1906–1964) taught at New York University, and lectured on the philosophy of law at the Hebrew University in Jerusalem and on ethics at the Jewish Theological Seminary of America in New York City.

"Shall not the judge of all the earth act justly?"[268] It is unlikely, then, that Abraham, when his own son was involved, would be so submissive and not argue with God against the idea of taking his life.

Therefore, the conclusion is that our report of the *Akeda* has come from Isaac, who must have embellished the incident to suit his own purposes. Isaac, from the little we hear of him, was not as strong a personality as Abraham. He was quieter, more submissive. And one day, possibly when he was in despair about the behavior of his twins Jacob and Esau, he must have cried out to them, "Why can't you obey me as I obeyed my father, and as my father obeyed God?" And he probably tried to impress them by telling them the story of his trip to Moriah—with some conscious or unconscious variations. Thus, we do not know what really happened on Moriah. We know only what Isaac told his sons to demonstrate to them how obedient he was to his father Abraham.

Whether this theory is correct or not, Jewish tradition has already accepted the idea of Isaac's exemplary obedience to his father. When Rashi comments on the phrase *"Vayailchu shnaihem yachdav*—And the two of them walked together," he says, "Isaac knew he was to be sacrificed and yet he did not rebel."[269] It has become very common even for modern rabbis to overlook the more disturbing aspects of the *Akeda* and to focus rather on this beautifully worded phrase, "And the two of them walked together." Many a congregation on many a Rosh Hashanah has heard a sermon using this text and expatiating on how wonderful it would be if contemporary fathers and sons would emulate Abraham and Isaac, walking together and avoiding a clash between the generations. How wonderful it would be if children followed quietly in the footsteps of their fathers.

Apparently, these sermons have not been altogether successful. Regardless of how many of them may have been preached, it is obvious that today, the problem of walking together, the problem of establishing rapport with our young people, is greater than ever before. This is the age of the generation gap,[270] of hippies, and of campus rebellions.[271] We are deeply disturbed by the

---

268 Genesis 18:23-25.

269 "And Abraham took the wood of the burnt-offering, and laid it upon Isaac his son; and he took in his hand the fire and the knife; and they went both of them together." (Genesis 22:6)

270 "The sociological theory of a generation gap first came to light in the 1960s, when the younger generation (later known as Baby Boomers) seemed to go against everything their parents had previously believed in terms of music, values, and governmental and political views." Wikipedia contributors. "Generation gap." *Wikipedia, The Free Encyclopedia*. Wikipedia, The Free Encyclopedia, 24 Sep. 2017. Web. 25 Sep. 2017.

271 Protests raging throughout 1968 included a large number of students. Worldwide, campuses became battle grounds for social change. While opposition to the Vietnam War dominated the protests (at least in the United States), students also protested for civil liberties, against racism, and

restlessness of so many of our young people, by their defiance of convention, by the violence that has sometimes come to pass. We are perplexed as to the wisest way of responding, and we vacillate between trying to reason with them and cracking down on them, between exhortation and condemnation.

The thought that I am leading to this morning is that before we altogether condemn, perhaps we should seek to understand. To be sure, we cannot condone or justify every extreme act that students or other young people have engaged in to make their point, but there may be a silver lining in the cloud. They may even be walking together with us more closely than we realize. A recent book entitled *The Young Radicals* by Kenneth Keniston tries to give us insight into the nature of our thinking young people today.[272] It is worth reading. It is a study of a limited number of college students who have been exceedingly active in the protest movements, but through this study of a few we do gain some understanding of the mood of young people in general. Keniston concludes that it is easy to find good grounds to criticize these young radicals—they seem "unrealistic, anarchistic and romantic." But however we judge them, he suggests that:

> ...to describe their search is to enumerate the problems of our changing, affluent and violent society, a society that has barely begun to catch up with the dilemmas it has created... The new radicals are at least confronting the central issues of our time, and confronting them more directly than we can afford to. They are asking the basic questions, making the mistakes, and perhaps moving towards some of the answers we all desperately need.

The adjectives "changing, affluent, and violent" seem to be key to understanding our young people. The major factors in the rebellion of youth today seem to be that they live in a society which has undergone the most rapid change that the world has ever known; they live in a society that is the most affluent the world has ever known; and they live in a society that has suffered the greatest violence the world has ever known, and is capable of even more.

Since World War I, social, technological, and political change has proceeded with unprecedented and ever-increasing rapidity. Space has been contracted. Communications are instant. Technological skills have increased. Our young people have not only benefited from these changes personally, but have also grown more open and receptive to change than any other generation has been. They are accustomed to the idea of constant readjustment, and

---

for feminism; and the beginnings of the ecological movement can be traced to the protests against biological and nuclear weapons.

272 Kenneth Keniston (1930-), psychologist, taught at Harvard University, Yale University, and the Massachusetts Institute of Technology.

they do not fear even greater readjustment when they feel that their elders are lagging behind the times.

Not all the young people of our nation, of course, have been free from the shackles of poverty. We still have our vast number of deprived, but the rebels among our college youth are not usually among them. They have grown up in middle and upper class families that have taken for granted American prosperity and the luxuries it provides. This has not only made them physically comfortable, but also has provided the opportunity to be independent, to acquire a higher education, to have the leisure to think for themselves. They begin to seek new values in living that will fill the spiritual emptiness created by such material affluence. These young people are freed from the concern for providing for their own immediate needs, and are thus also free to concern themselves with the welfare of others and the wider society. Their own security makes it possible for them to give thought to the insecurity of others, and they do not hesitate to express their outrage and indignation at the social evils that they see.

Our young people today are also part of the first generation to grow up in the shadow of possible worldwide atomic destruction. They are aware of Hiroshima, and they are aware of Auschwitz. They are mindful of the many violent struggles that have taken place in many parts of the world in the past quarter-century—and of our own involvement this very day in faraway places, justifiable or not. Such a background of violence has had two opposite consequences. On the one hand, it has stimulated further violence among young people. On the other, it has convinced particularly the more highly intellectual of the futility of conflict, and created a determination to oppose all war and to bring all violence as much as possible under control.

The study of our young people, however, seems to show that in spite of their seeming desire to change things, they do not really want a change in the basic values that they have learned from their family groups. Our young people often seem to reject the philosophy and politics of their elders, but they still act in accord with a basic set of moral principles that adults also profess to embrace. They are concerned with justice and decency, equality and nonviolence, honesty and kindness. They are profoundly faithful to many of the fundamental values of American democracy. What makes these young people different is that they take these values more seriously than their parents, and they propose that American society and the world set about implementing them. They may seem to be revolutionary and disruptive, but they are merely trying to apply more completely a great variety of political, personal, and social principles that no one before seemed to think of extending to things like dealing with strangers, relations between the races, or international politics. When we talked about peace and love, we somehow managed to exclude foreigners and Negroes from our thinking. Young people, however, are challenging our unrecognized hypocrisies and have the daring to insist that societies and individuals live by the values they preach, that they wipe out the gap between principle and practice, between national creed and policy. Thus, it may well be, as was previously suggested, that young people have indeed followed the preachment of their elders only too well.

It should be noted that even Isaac, the exemplar of obedience, dared to question a little bit. Intuitively, he sensed that something was not quite right; as he walked with his father, you will remember, he turned to him and said, "But where is the lamb for the offering?"[273] It is true that Isaac did not resist or protest too loudly, but his question is not too different, basically, from what is troubling our young people today. They, too, are being led by their fathers to a remote place under circumstances that they cannot comprehend, and so they, too, ask, "Where are we going and who will be the sacrifice?" The big difference is that today, young people refuse to wait for an angel to stretch forth his hand to save them, and so they cry out for themselves:

> *Do not put forth thy hand unto the youth! Do not offer us as a sacrifice in Vietnam! Do not let us die in hate-infested cities! Do not carry on your business as before, in betrayal of all you have taught us!* [274]

We may not necessarily excuse all that young people do today in the name of justice. Sometimes they seem to pervert the very justice they crave. But neither should we be too quick to condemn. Like William S. Paley, member of the Board of Trustees of Columbia University, we must recognize that they do have legitimate complaints.[275] He deplored the student violence on the campus, but he cautioned that "we should not lose sight of the... widespread feeling of sincere discontent, not only about the university but about the entire world." [276]

---

273 Genesis 22:7.

274 "And the angel of the Lord called unto him out of heaven, and said: 'Abraham, Abraham.' And he said: 'Here am I.' And he said: 'Lay not thy hand upon the lad, neither do thou any thing unto him...'" Genesis 22:11-12.

275 "William S. Paley (1901–1990) was the chief executive who built Columbia Broadcasting System (CBS) from a small radio network into one of the foremost radio and television network operations in the United States." Wikipedia contributors. "William S. Paley." *Wikipedia, The Free Encyclopedia*. Wikipedia, The Free Encyclopedia, 18 Sep. 2017. Web. 25 Sep. 2017.

276 "The Columbia University protests of 1968 were among the many student demonstrations that occurred around the world that year. The Columbia protests erupted in the spring after students discovered links between the university and the institutional apparatus supporting the United States' involvement in the Vietnam War. They also were concerned about an allegedly segregatory gymnasium to be constructed in the nearby Morningside Park. The protests resulted in the student occupation of

Students may challenge and question, but perhaps in this very fact lies our best hope for the future. There must be some good and promise in young people who risk their careers for a social ideal. If we could only combine the honesty and energy of youth with the judgment and discipline of age. With such a pooling of natural resources, we could move much faster toward the objectives we desire in common, and achieve more easily the walking together we so fervently desire. May the year to come bring us closer to this goal.

Amen.

---

many university buildings and their eventual violent removal by the New York City Police Department." Wikipedia contributors. "Columbia University protests of 1968." *Wikipedia, The Free Encyclopedia*. Wikipedia, The Free Encyclopedia, 11 Aug. 2017. Web. 25 Sep. 2017.

Dad—

On the day you delivered this sermon about the breach between our generations, I was sounding shofar in a temple in Portland, Oregon. On the one hand, I had absented myself at as great a distance from you as I could possibly achieve. On the other hand—literally with my right hand—I pressed to my lips the ram's horn that you entrusted to me—to make the very intonations our ancestors made across the generations to recall that moment of conflict and resolution, that moment of Divine providence of which you spoke. How distant and how connected were we in that moment! How distant and how connected are we today!

Somehow, with the perspective of time, the connections seem stronger than the disconnections. I look back and wonder, had I been in your congregation that morning, would I have heard all you had to say? Would my youthful discomfort and contrariness have caused me to fixate on the injustice of the proposed sacrifice of Isaac? Would I have heard your deeply empathetic recognition of the legitimate concerns of my generation, or would I have only bristled at your characterization of hippies and rebels?

Time has made that question moot. Time has demonstrated that, in my own way, I am living your words:

> *They begin to seek new values in living that will fill the spiritual emptiness created by such material affluence.*

I look back with great appreciation for your forbearance and vision that I, in all likelihood, was unable to recognize in those days. Would that I measure up to the challenges of my own generation and of today's youth, to bridge the gap between principle and practice.

Blessings.
Yesh

32. The Sense of Prayer

October 1, 1968

Kol Nidre

Here, my father makes an impassioned case for the power and the meaning of prayer, even in a post-modern society.

Does prayer… make sense? Does it serve a purpose? Should we indulge in prayer… with any sort of regularity? The answer on all counts is yes. Prayer makes sense. Prayer has a purpose. We should engage in regular prayer.

RABBI LEVI YITSCHAK OF BERDITCHEV was a saintly eighteenth-century Hasidic rabbi.[277] The story is told that one day, just after the morning services in the synagogue had been concluded, he shook hands with several of the participants, saying, "*Shalom Aleichem, Shalom Aleichem.*"[278] He greeted each one of them as though he had returned from far away. Of course, they looked at him with questioning eyes. He said to them:

> *Why are you so surprised? Anyone could see just now that you were far away. You, my friend, were on a vacation, and you, my friend, were in the marketplace. And when the prayers ended, you all were back again. You had returned from your journeys, so naturally, I welcome you back with a Shalom Aleichem.*

---

277 Rabbi Levi Yitzchak of Berditchev (1740–1809) was "one of the most beloved leaders of Eastern European Jewry… and considered by some to be the founder of Hasidism in central Poland." Wikipedia contributors. "Levi Yitzchok of Berditchev." *Wikipedia, The Free Encyclopedia*. Wikipedia, The Free Encyclopedia, 10 Sep. 2017. Web. 25 Sep. 2017.

278 *Shalom aleikhem* is a greeting in Hebrew meaning "peace be upon you." The appropriate response is "*aleikhem shalom*," "upon you be peace." This form of greeting is traditional among Jews throughout the world.

If Rabbi Levi Yitschak were here with us this evening, it is quite possible that his searching eyes might find some of us to whom he might want to say, "*Shalom Aleichem.* Welcome back from your mental wanderings and your reveries." Human nature being what it is and the size of our congregation this evening being what it is, chances are that here, too, not everyone was concentrating in full on the service. There are surely some among us also who consciously or unconsciously let their minds wander and indulged in thoughts unrelated to the purpose of the evening.

Nevertheless, we would be happy indeed if this were the only problem that we faced with respect to prayer. We may envy Rabbi Levi Yitschak. He faced a congregation whose problem with prayer was a comparatively simple one. It was a problem merely of how to pray so that prayer would not be mechanical, so that the service would be carried on with *kavana*, with concentration, with feeling.[279] The Hasidim were able to offer rather simple solutions to their problem. Come to the synagogue early and recite Psalms to get into the proper mood before the regular service begins. Close your eyes so that it will be easier to concentrate. Maintain strictly the separation of the sexes.

But we have a more difficult problem, for in our congregations today are many people who question the value of prayer altogether. If we have gathered here in large numbers on this sacred night, for many—not for all to be sure—it may be because of the weight of tradition or as a bow to convention. It may be as an expression of Jewish identity or because of an emotional tie to the past that we come, rather than out of a deep-seated conviction that we need to pray for forgiveness, that God will somehow respond to the words we utter. At other times during the year, it is not necessary to make the same elaborate preparations to seat our worshipers that we make on the High Holy Days. The call to worship is poor competition to the activities of the secular world. Indeed, for the rest of the year, most Jews find little compelling force to bring them into the synagogue even with a wandering mind, let alone to pray with *kavana*.

The main reason our fathers were more zealous in prayer than we are, it must be confessed, is that their concept of the God to whom they addressed their prayers was better defined and their faith in Him much stronger. It was much easier for people to pray when they thought of God literally in terms of a King who governed the earth in His wisdom and who could dispense

---

279 *Kavana* or *kavanah* (Hebrew), meaning intention or "direction of the heart," is the "mindset often described as necessary for Jewish rituals (*mitzvot*)... Traditional Jewish sources [consider] that fulfilling *mitzvot* without at least minimal *kavana* is insufficient... *Kavana* in prayer may require understanding of the words of prayer, not merely reciting the sounds. Some perceive this as especially difficult to achieve when they pray using liturgical Hebrew, which many Jews outside of Israel do not understand." Wikipedia contributors. "Kavanah." *Wikipedia, The Free Encyclopedia*. Wikipedia, The Free Encyclopedia, 2 Sep. 2017. Web. 25 Sep. 2017.

His favor, if He so chose, to obedient subjects who offered Him their supplications. If someone were seriously ill, one's prayers were offered to God; hopefully the Healer of Israel would grant healing. If one had an eligible daughter, he prayed like Tevye to the Almighty, and hopefully He would send a worthy suitor.[280] If one found himself in any kind of dire circumstances, he prayed and hopefully the Redeemer of Israel would improve his lot.

Of course, in our Jewish tradition the ways of God were beyond understanding, and one could not always be absolutely certain of delivery, even if the order were properly filed. Sometimes, the sick were not healed. Sometimes, the daughter remained a spinster or made a match that was not so desirable. Sometimes, the distressed were not rescued. Think of the six million!! Even in the Bible, the prophet Habakkuk complained, "How long, O Lord, shall I cry, and Thou wilt not hear?"[281] But still there remained a fundamental confidence in a God who listened and answered, and even when He seemed not to grant petitions, the Jewish faith was not disturbed: it must be for good reasons known to Him. The Jew could always say with Job, "Even though He slay me, yet will I trust in Him."[282]

This faith prevails even today among a goodly number of our people, and where it thus prevails, we would not question it or disturb it. But what happens to prayer if we can no longer accept this understanding of our faith? If we fancy ourselves to be more sophisticated or modern, and do not think of God as literally a Father and King who listens to us carefully and rewards our goodness with His favors, does prayer then make sense? Does it serve a purpose? Should we indulge in prayer, nevertheless, with any sort of regularity? The answer on all counts is *yes*. Prayer makes sense. Prayer has a purpose. We should engage in regular prayer.

Before we can come to accept this conclusion, however, there are two prerequisites. First of these is that we must have a totally different understanding of what prayer is supposed to achieve for us. This different understanding of prayer, I would suggest, is really not so new. It is already actually a part of our tradition and needs only to be underscored. We can find it embedded in the very word the Hebrew language uses for prayer. In Hebrew, to pray is *L'hitpalel*. If we look closely at the root of the word, we find it is related to the

---

280 "Tevye the Dairyman is the fictional narrator and protagonist of a series of short stories by Sholem Aleichem, the pen name of Sholem Rabinovitsh (1859–1916). "The popular author and humorist was noted for his stories of life in the *shtetl*, originally written in Yiddish and first published in 1894. Tevye is best known as the main character in *Fiddler on the Roof*, the Broadway musical adaptation of Aleichem's stories." Wikipedia contributors. "Tevye." *Wikipedia, The Free Encyclopedia*. Wikipedia, The Free Encyclopedia, 15 Sep. 2017. Web. 25 Sep. 2017.

281 Habakkuk 1:2.

282 Job 13:15.

Hebrew word *nafal*, meaning "to fall." Thus, prayer is quite naturally connected with prostration and bowing and kneeling. It is also related to another Hebrew word, *palal*, meaning "to judge." But what is most interesting of all is that the verb "to pray" in Hebrew is expressed in a grammatical form peculiar to Semitic languages, a form which ordinarily signifies a reflexive action. Thus, the root *palal* means "judge," but *hitpalel*, "to judge oneself." The implication is that when one prays, he is bowed down in self-judgment. It is as though every time you pray, a touch of the High Holyday spirit is involved. In prayer, one articulates goals and ideals and measures himself against their standard. He compares himself as he is to what his conscience tells him he ought to be. He speaks to himself as much as to God, and the answer to his prayer comes in the extent to which he betters himself and comes closer to the ideal.

Samuel S. Cohon, for many years professor of theology at the Hebrew Union College, writes:

> *Prayer... makes our shadowy ideals shine forth like radiant stars upon our horizon, and shows us the role that we are to play in life. We learn to judge ourselves in the light of these ideals.*[283]

Even a person such as Dr. Immanuel Jakobovits, who is the Chief Rabbi of Great Britain and an outstanding protagonist of orthodoxy, has written:

> *God does not change His mind. Prayer changes us, not God. When we say that prayer averts the stern decree (words which are in our High Holyday liturgy), what we really mean is that prayer transforms us from being deserving of such a decree into more meritorious people who are no longer deserving of that decree.*[284]

To quote yet another theologian, Sherwood Eddy, a Christian leader of great repute, has similarly written:

> *Prayer is not to... change God, but our own ignorant and sinful hearts. It is like the pull of a rope from a small boat upon a great ship at anchor; it is not the ship that moves but the little boat.*[285]

---

283 Samuel Solomon Cohon (1888–1959), a Russian born, American Reform congregational rabbi, was then Chair of Theology at Hebrew Union College.

284 "Immanuel Jakobovits, Baron Jakobovits (1921–1999), was the Chief Rabbi of the United Hebrew Congregations of the Commonwealth from 1967 to 1991. Prior to this, he had served as Chief Rabbi of Ireland and as rabbi of the Fifth Avenue Synagogue in New York City. In addition to his official duties, he was regarded as an authority in medical ethics from a Jewish standpoint. He was knighted in 1981 and became the first Chief Rabbi to enter the House of Lords in 1988 as Baron Jakobovits." Wikipedia contributors. "Immanuel Jakobovits, Baron Jakobovits." *Wikipedia, The Free Encyclopedia*. Wikipedia, The Free Encyclopedia, 22 Jul. 2017. Web. 25 Sep. 2017.

285 Sherwood Eddy (1871–1963) was a American Protestant missionary and a member of Niebuhr's Fellowship of Socialist Christians.

What all these men of varying religious traditions mean to say is that prayer is not to be considered as a request for supernatural intervention in or on behalf of our personal wants, but rather, the effort to link our thoughts and our lives with what we believe to be worthy goals and ideals. In prayer, we should be moved to lift ourselves above ordinary and self-centered concerns and to think in nobler and more altruistic terms. In prayer, we devote ourselves to meditating upon that which we conceive to be the highest and the finest, and we reach forth out of what we really are to what we yearn to be.

The second prerequisite for finding sense in prayer is that even though we do not think of God in conventional terms, we must believe God is not dead and that religion has not lost its relevance for modern man. We live in the age of science and many of us have been misled by its miraculous accomplishments. Some people have been so enamored by scientific progress that they believe there is no longer any need for religion or religious exercises at all, that science, either right now or in the near future, will be able to answer any question of man and account for all his problems. I hear this often from children in our religious school, whose minds are captivated by the science they learn in our schools and from innumerable adults as well. But responsible scientists know that for whatever answers science has given us about the universe we live in, it has raised multitudes of additional questions. The more we come to know, the more remains unknown. Foremost scientists admit that science helps us in our effort to control nature, but does not give us any final or absolute knowledge of nature's real character. Even if science could penetrate the infinity of space or the infinitesimal parts of an atom, we human beings are limited in the power of our observation to the capabilities of our five senses.

Scientists and psychologists today recognize that there may be a reality that the five senses of man are unable to apprehend. There is the superhuman or divine dimension, which our senses do not penetrate but which only occasionally do some men, through intuition or mystic experience, barely touch upon. This, too, is part of reality. Joseph B. Fabry of the University of California writes:

> *Science, which was expected to disprove the existence of a divine dimension, has on the contrary brought into focus the limits of human reach... Today the logic of the scientists has joined the vision of the prophets in indicating the existence of a reality which goes beyond the human grasp. Scientific discovery can go only as far as the limits of the human dimension. To reach the reality that lies beyond requires a leap.*[286]

---

286 "Joseph B. Fabry (1909–1999) was an Austrian-born author and longtime editor and translator at the University of California at Berkeley. He retired in 1972 to devote his life to his second career as the

Religion helps us make this leap, and whether as a result of this leap we are moved to think of God in terms of a Father/King, or in terms of a creative force, or as a power that makes for righteousness, or as the essence of existence itself, we must take this reality into consideration in order to find meaning for our own existence. The failure to do so, the failure to see reality beyond the merely human dimension, will result in feelings of emptiness, meaninglessness, and frustration, which are, indeed, the hallmarks of modern society.

Freud, unfortunately, gave aid and comfort to pseudo scientists by labeling religion a neurosis of mankind. For him, religious concepts were the projections of man's own wishful thinking and intimations of divinity were illusions of his own mind. But Freud is already out of date. Contradicting Freud, Abraham Maslow writes:

> *Contemporary existential and humanist psychologists would probably consider a person sick or abnormal... if he were not concerned with the religious questions. Man has a need to find meaning for himself as a pinpoint in an infinite universe. He has a need to find his place in the mysterious universe and feel himself part of the divine plan.*[287]

Man fulfills this need through his religion, and his religion must express itself in prayer.

For Jews, the process of prayer carries with it yet another significant purpose. When we join the congregation in speaking words in the synagogue that have their roots in generations past, we are joining with our fellow Jews, both of the past and of the present, in a symbolical declaration of our unity and concern for each other. Judaism has always preferred public prayer to private prayer. Our prayer book speaks mostly in the plural rather than in the singular because it has tried to guide the Jew away from thoughts about himself and his own selfish concerns and toward thoughts of the well-being of the Jewish people as a whole and also of all mankind. It has tried to impress the Jew with a reminder of his collective responsibility, of a collective Jewish destiny to create and work for a better world, of a covenant of the people to

---

founder, executive director, and president of the Institute of Logotherapy... a practice of existential therapy that provides tools for people to handle life's vicissitudes by asking the question: 'How can I deal with this?' as opposed to 'Why is this happening to me?'" J.L. Pimsleur, "Joseph Fabry," *San Francisco Chronicle*, 12 May 1999, SFGate.com. Web. 24 Sep. 2017.

287 "Abraham Harold Maslow (1908–1970) was an American psychologist best known for articulating the concept of the hierarchy of needs, a theory of psychological health predicated on fulfilling innate human needs in priority, culminating in self-actualization. He stressed the importance of focusing on the positive qualities in people, as opposed to treating them as a 'bag of symptoms.'" Wikipedia contributors. "Abraham Maslow." *Wikipedia, The Free Encyclopedia*. Wikipedia, The Free Encyclopedia, 20 Sep. 2017. Web. 25 Sep. 2017.

be a co-worker with God in so doing. The Jew who withdraws himself from the prayer of the congregation cuts himself off from his roots and permits his Jewish spirit to wither. He loses his unique quality as a Jew, and he has surrendered his Judaism to the forces of the environment that may even annihilate it.

Let us, therefore, on this occasion of Yom Kippur in particular, not treat lightly the prayers we offer. May they help us remember our human weaknesses and shortcomings, and in so doing, bring us peace and forgiveness. May they represent a sincere reaching out for the divine presence in the universe, and help to link us meaningfully with it. May they remind us of the past and future hopes of our people and strengthen our loyalty to them. And above all, may they help us grow as worthy human beings toward the fulfillment of the highest and the best that is within us.

Amen.

Dad—

You say we don't pray to a cosmic bellhop, that prayer is not for God to fulfill our requests, but for us to turn inward and search for our own answers, for inspiration to be worthy human beings. We pray to connect to the Divine, even when we have no comprehension of that Divinity. We pray to connect to *Klal Yisrael*—the entire Jewish community past, present, and future. This makes more sense to me than placing an order with an e-God and expecting 2-day delivery.

Blessings.
Yesh

33. Footsteps on the Moon

September 13, 1969

Rosh Hashanah Morning

My father witnessed extraordinary advancements in aerospace travel during his lifetime. He was a teen when Charles Lindbergh completed the first solo transatlantic flight. He was a young rabbi when the Soviets launched Sputnik. And twelve years later, he watched as Neil Armstrong walked on the Moon. Dad looked at the lunar landing through his rabbinical glasses and saw the theological and moral concerns regarding the onset of space travel.

If only we would turn the intelligence and power we used to achieve a landing on the Moon in other directions as well! If only we had the will, seemingly impossible goals here on Earth also could be attained.

IN THE BOOK OF PSALMS, IT IS WRITTEN, "The heavens, the heavens are the Lord's, but the Earth is given to man."[288] If the psalmist were alive today, he might want to revise these words. Man is leaving the sphere to which he has thus far been limited and is invading that which was thought to be the exclusive domain of the Lord. To borrow a phrase from another psalm, "There is no speech, there are no words…" that can adequately describe the phenomenal achievement of man a short time ago in planting his footsteps on the Moon.[289] There cannot possibly be anyone on Earth, whether friend or foe, who would not concede the brilliance in planning, the daring in execution, the magnitude of accomplishment of this long perilous journey through space. There can be no one of the millions who went along with the astronauts by

---

288 Psalm 115:16.

289 Psalm 19:4.

television or radio who was not thrilled—and relieved— by Neil Armstrong's terse announcement, "The Eagle has landed."[290]

Yet man must never be so arrogant as to look uncritically upon any of his achievements. On this day of Rosh Hashanah, which is a day of examination of the deeds of man and a day also with cosmic significance as the traditional birthday of the world—this day would seem to call for some comment on this most remarkable event in the history of mankind. Whatever comment we may be moved to offer will, of course, not pertain to the technical aspects of the Moon flight. This is very obviously the prerogative of qualified scientists alone. But there remain some judgments of a moral or religious nature that may appropriately be expressed.

The first item that invites our attention is the plaque that the astronauts placed on the Moon as a token of their visit. Its words read beautifully, "We came in peace for all mankind." But somehow, the phrase has a hollow ring. It seems to me a bit incongruous to proclaim peace for all mankind on the Moon, where the United States alone has touched down, while we have for the past several years been engaged in a process of irrational destruction on Earth, where we face the challenge of dealing with other people. The president has stated that the Moon landing has brought the world together as never before, but our skepticism is pardonable when we note the "togetherness" of battle, with its daily casualty lists, or our "togetherness" with a government in South Vietnam renowned for its corruption and high-handedness.[291] It was narrow-minded chauvinism, not togetherness, that moved Congress to direct the astronauts to plant the flag of the United States upon the Moon, rather than all the flags of the United Nations as the astronauts, with far greater sensitivity, had proposed. It was not togetherness that prompted presidential and congressional approval of a missile program, which many have warned will only intensify the arms race rather than help slow it down.

It is not only international togetherness that we failed to perceive, but even togetherness within the bounds of our own country. This was symbolized by a quiet demonstration staged near the launch site just before the liftoff of the space capsule that went to the Moon. The demonstration was

---

290 *Apollo 11* was the first spaceflight that landed humans on the Moon on July 20, 1969. "After being sent toward the Moon by a Saturn V rocket, astronauts Neil Armstrong, Buzz Aldrin, and Michael Collins separated their spacecraft from it until they entered into lunar orbit. Armstrong and Aldrin then moved into the Lunar Module (LEM), which the crew had named Eagle, and landed in the Sea of Tranquility... Collins piloted the command spacecraft alone in lunar orbit [until Armstrong and Aldrin returned]." After the LEM landed on the lunar surface, Armstrong radioed to NASA Support, "Houston, Tranquility Base here. The Eagle has landed." Wikipedia contributors. "Apollo 11." *Wikipedia, The Free Encyclopedia.* Wikipedia, The Free Encyclopedia, 24 Sep. 2017. Web. 25 Sep. 2017.

291 Richard Milhous Nixon (1913–1994) was the 37th President of the United States. He was elected in 1968; in 1974, he became the only U.S. president to resign from office.

created by a group of poor people led by the Rev. Ralph D. Abernathy, who wanted to make the point that even while we paid the price of $30 billion to land on the Moon, there was a serious problem of poverty here on Earth. The Rev. Mr. Abernathy was not unmindful of the grandeur of the flight, but he could not help but feel for the distressed whose problems also need our most intelligent attention. He said: "It is really holy ground. And it will be more holy once we feed the hungry and care for the sick and provide for those who do not have houses."[292]

This unfulfilled need in our affluent society somewhat dims the glory we have attained by reaching the Moon. Our political leaders were naïvely and self-righteously deluding themselves with their pretty phrases—or perhaps they were even deliberately taking advantage of the Moon flight to delude us and divert our attention from the war and other social ills by offering us pie-in-the-sky. It surely was very sobering to read the comment of Lewis Mumford, noted historian, as reported in *The New York Times*.[293] He points out that the most conspicuous scientific and technical achievement of our age—nuclear bombs, rockets, computers—all are direct products of war and are still being promoted under the guise of "Research and Development" for military and political ends that would shrivel under rational examination and candid moral appraisal. Mumford says,

> The Moon landing is no exception. It is a symbolic act of war... In order to achieve both military power and economic prosperity... every other human enterprise must either be trimmed to meet their needs or abandoned. It is no accident that the climactic Moon landing coincides with cutbacks in education, the bankruptcy of hospital services, the closing of libraries and museums, and the mounting defilement of the urban and natural environment, to say nothing of many other evidences of gross social failure and human deterioration... Thanks to the very triumphs of technology, the human race hovers on the edge of catastrophe.

---

[292] "Ralph David Abernathy, Sr. (1926–1990) was a leader of the African American Civil Rights Movement, a minister, and a close friend of Martin Luther King Jr. ... Abernathy co-founded and was an executive board member of the Southern Christian Leadership Conference (SCLC). Following the assassination of King, Abernathy became president of the SCLC. As president, he led the Poor People's Campaign March on Washington, D.C. in 1968." Together with a few families, Abernathy had watched the launching from the VIP area, after making a request of NASA for special badges. He spoke these words after the launch. Wikipedia contributors. "Ralph Abernathy." *Wikipedia, The Free Encyclopedia*. Wikipedia, The Free Encyclopedia, 22 Sep. 2017. Web. 25 Sep. 2017. Norman Mailer "A Fire on the Moon," *Life* 67:9, August 12, 1969, 40.

[293] "Lewis Mumford (1895–1990) was an American historian, sociologist, philosopher of technology, and literary critic... particularly noted for his study of cities and urban architecture." Wikipedia contributors. "Lewis Mumford." *Wikipedia, The Free Encyclopedia*. Wikipedia, The Free Encyclopedia, 15 Sep. 2017. Web. 25 Sep. 2017.

This dark view, however, need not be the last word. If only we would turn the intelligence and power we used to achieve a landing on the Moon in other directions as well! If only we had the will, seemingly impossible goals here on Earth also could be attained. Balanced against the not so hopeful words of Lewis Mumford is the opinion of Kenneth Clark, psychologist, who wrote:

> *But our triumph on the Moon need not be an occasion for despair. This latest conquest may be an omen that we are on the threshold of returning to the unfinished business of Earth—that the power of human intelligence which was mobilized to accomplish this feat can also be mobilized to address itself to the ultimate acts of human compassion.*[294]

Thus, the Moon landing is a source of pride in the abilities of the human race. It is a source of satisfaction that it was America that was able to reach the Moon first. It is a stimulus to dreams of reaching out still further to other planets. But at the same time, it is a challenge to us to be honest with ourselves. It is a challenge to apply our skills to the human needs we see about us. It is a challenge to come in peace for all mankind, not only on the Moon but on the Earth as well.

Another comment that suggests itself is of an entirely different nature. Just after the Moon landing, I attended the service club meeting at which the scheduled speaker had failed to appear. The chairman suggested that in its place we have a discussion amongst ourselves pertaining to the impact of this great event. Hardly had the suggestion been approved, however, when to my surprise, he turned to me and said, "A good first question would be what is the impact of man's lunar flight on religion? Rabbi, what do you think?" The question has also been raised by others. There is the sometimes uneasy and sometimes gleeful feeling that believers will find trouble with man's exploration of space.

I believe, however, that each person will find what he wants to find. You may remember that when the first Russian astronaut made his flight into space, he returned to tell us that he had searched the heavens diligently but had found no sign of God.[295] For him, the exploration of space was a

---

[294] "Kenneth Bancroft Clark (1914–2005) was an African-American psychologist who [along with his wife, Mamie Phipps Clark] conducted important research among children and was active in the Civil Rights Movement. Clark also was an educator and professor at City College of New York, and the first Black president of the American Psychological Association." Wikipedia contributors. "Kenneth and Mamie Clark." *Wikipedia, The Free Encyclopedia*. Wikipedia, The Free Encyclopedia, 3 Sep. 2017. Web. 25 Sep. 2017.

[295] "Yuri Alekseyevich Gagarin (1934–1968), Russian Soviet pilot and cosmonaut, was the first human to journey into outer space when his Vostok spacecraft completed an orbit of the Earth on April 12, 1961." Wikipedia contributors. "Yuri Gagarin." *Wikipedia, The Free Encyclopedia*. Wikipedia, The Free Encyclopedia, 24 Sep. 2017. Web. 25 Sep. 2017.

confirmation of the official communist doctrine that God does not exist. Our astronauts, however, who first circled the Moon, were moved by their experience to read aloud the opening verses of Genesis: "In the beginning, God created the heavens and the Earth."[296] For them, man's exploration of space served only to underscore the great mystery of existence, the grandeur of the universe, and the improbability of its being all a meaningless accident. If the psalmist, with his limited understanding, could be moved to exclaim, "The heavens declare the glory of God and the firmament showeth His handiwork!" how much more impressive is that glory when our awareness not only encompasses the Earth and the solar system, but penetrates also into the infinity of space beyond them.[297]

If anything, the trip to the Moon only confirms the fact that man can rely on a certain basic orderliness of nature. There are established rules. There are principles and laws that govern. It is only because we have learned to take advantage of some of these basic principles and because these principles do not deceive us that we were able to get to the Moon. Thus, our faith can only be strengthened in what the scientist Alfred North Whitehead, long before the Moon flight, referred to as the Divine Orderer.[298] As a matter of fact, it was his contention that all scientific endeavor is really based on religious faith, because without the conviction that there is such a thing as an order of nature, there would have been no scientific enterprise throughout the ages.

The fact is that religion had more problems years ago in the times of Copernicus or Darwin than it has today with the exploration of space. When religion first faced the idea that the Earth, rather than being the center of the universe, instead revolves around the sun, and when it first faced the idea that man and the Earth were not the products of instant creation but rather of an evolutionary process, these were indeed moments of great crisis. But modern religious thinkers soon learned how to distinguish between matters that properly belong to religion and those which do not, between physical questions that must be left to science to investigate and metaphysical questions

---

296 *Apollo 8*, launched on December 21, 1968, was the "first crewed spacecraft to leave Earth orbit, reach the Moon, orbit it, and return safely to Earth. The three-astronaut crew—Frank Borman, James Lovell, and William Anders—were the first humans to directly see the far side of the Moon... and the first to see Earth as a whole planet... The crew made a Christmas Eve television broadcast where they read the first 10 verses from the Book of Genesis." Wikipedia contributors. "Apollo 8." *Wikipedia, The Free Encyclopedia*. Wikipedia, The Free Encyclopedia, 21 Sep. 2017. Web. 25 Sep. 2017.

297 Psalm 19:2.

298 "Alfred North Whitehead (1861–1947) was an English mathematician and philosopher. He is best known as the defining figure of the philosophical school known as process philosophy, which today has found application to a wide variety of disciplines, including ecology, theology, education, physics, biology, economics, and psychology." Wikipedia contributors. "Alfred North Whitehead." *Wikipedia, The Free Encyclopedia*. Wikipedia, The Free Encyclopedia, 19 Sep. 2017. Web. 25 Sep. 2017.

dealing with God and man, life and death, moral values. Religion, except for the diehard fundamentalists, has long ago adjusted to science; and science, it may be noted, has also adjusted to religion.

The more science has discovered, the more it has realized what there is that remains unknown, and the more it has conceded that it cannot penetrate the innermost secrets of creation, and the more it has become aware of an all-pervading cosmic intelligence which transcends human understanding. In this spirit, Albert Einstein once wrote:

> *The human mind, no matter how highly trained, is not capable of grasping the universe. We are like a little child entering a huge library. The walls are covered to the ceiling with books in so many different tongues. The child knows that someone must have written those books. It does not know who or how. It does not understand the languages they are written in. The child notes a definite plan in the arrangement of the books—a mysterious order that it does not comprehend, but only dimly suspects. That, it seems to me, is the attitude of the human mind toward God. And because I believe this, I am not an atheist.*[299]

To the extent that space exploration has given religion any problems to think about, I believe that it is Christianity more than Judaism that is affected. Much of Christian theology in the past has emphasized man's sin and helplessness, but how can we speak of man's helplessness when he has accomplished so much! In a recent article on technology and religion, *The New York Times* reports:

> *Most theologians have begun to emphasize man's strength, creativity, and capacity to shape the world on which God placed him... For theologians, this shift has meant an emphasis on a God who is involved in a quest for justice in the world rather than... one who is distant and aloof. It has produced speculation about how man can act as a "co-creator" with God in the continuing evolution of the world.*

Judaism has had no such problem. Judaism has always had great respect for man and his powers. The rabbis long ago spoke of man as *shutaf l'hakodesh baruch hu*—a partner and co-creator with God. They did not overlook the

---

[299] "Albert Einstein (1879–1955) was a German-born theoretical physicist who developed the theory of relativity, one of the two pillars of modern physics." Einstein is best known by the general public for his mass–energy equivalence formula $E = mc^2$. He received the 1921 Nobel Prize in Physics. Einstein's intellectual achievements and originality have made the word "Einstein" synonymous with "genius." "Albert Einstein." *Wikipedia, The Free Encyclopedia*. 22 Sep 2017. Web. 25 Sep 2017.

humility of the psalmist when he asked, "What is man that Thou art mindful of him?" But neither did they forget his conclusion:

> Yet Thou hast made him but little lower than the angels and hast crowned him with glory and honor. Thou hast made him to have dominion over the works of Thy hands.[300]

The Moon flight has now served to re-emphasize for all people man's great capabilities and potentialities, and this may, indeed, in the long run strengthen the religious faith of man and direct it into more constructive channels rather than weaken it, as some may have supposed.

It has been our great fortune to live through one of the greatest moments in the history of man. This age we live in is a difficult age, but a wondrous one. When man put his footprints on the Moon for the first time, we might well have pronounced a blessing of "*Shehechiyanu*—Praised be Thou, O Lord, who has given us life and enabled us to witness such a time as this." And to this we might add also the blessing, probably less familiar to you, "*Oseh maaseh veraishit*—Praise be Thou, O Lord, King of the universe, who is responsible for the workings of creation." And together with these blessings, which reflect reverence for the presence of God manifest in all His works, there must also sincerely go the prayer we have read this morning—"May all the children of men come before Thee in humility and unite to do Thy will with perfect heart."[301]

Amen.

---

300 Psalm 8:5-7.

301 *Union Prayer Book II*, p. 54.

Dad—

I love that you see a sermon —or, shall I say, a Jewish learning opportunity—in so many aspects of the secular world. The world celebrates this colossal feat and what is your first impulse? To note the moral lapse that this accomplishment harbored. Not to say you didn't marvel at this colossal achievement, but even then, you used that awe to support your theology. I hope I'm not sounding critical or cynical. I am truly amazed and inspired that your Jewish and moral antennae that were always operating, discerning a deep message in so many unlikely places. This is a form of God-consciousness to which I aspire.

Sh'viti Adonai l'negded tamid.
I will place God before me always.

Blessings.
Yesh

BIRKAT HAGOMEL
A PRAYER OF GRATITUDE FOR THE SAFE RETURN
OF THE *APOLLO 13* ASTRONAUTS
APRIL 17, 1970

Our Heavenly Father, we join this day with myriads of people throughout the world in giving thanks for the safe return to earth of brave men suddenly confronted in outer space with uncertainty and danger.

We pray that the unity of spirit of all nations concerned about these astronauts shall impress itself upon our hearts and lead us toward the establishment of a permanent unity of man. We pray that we be moved to remember that man has potential for great achievements, but is, nevertheless, beset by human frailty, that man may be but little lower than the angels, but is dependent upon Thy providence and grace.

May the spirit of man continue to soar and to explore, but may it do so with humility, with awareness of our need for our fellowman, with appreciation of the great mystery of the universe that is comprehensible to God alone. *Baruch atta adonai hagomel l'chayavim tovot.*

Praised art Thou, O Lord, who bestows His care upon men.

Apollo 13 was to be the third mission to land on the Moon. An explosion in one of the oxygen tanks crippled the spacecraft during the flight, and the crew were forced to orbit the Moon and return to the Earth without landing.

MEMORIAL SERVICE FOR STUDENTS KILLED AT KENT STATE UNIVERSITY
MAY 5, 1970

Our Heavenly Father, with anguished hearts we think now of those young people whose lives were taken on their college campus as they joined fellow students expressing hatred of war and desire for peace. They are unknown to us, and yet they are a part of us. They shared our hopes and longings for a better world. They shared our fears that these hopes and longings were being frustrated.

Their voices are now silenced. We cannot bring them back to us, but we pray that in their silence they will achieve eloquence. We pray that this tragic occurrence will arouse our nation to the dangers that lurk ahead of us on the path we are moving. We pray that those who lead us will sit down in self-judgment and find the wisdom to restore harmony in our midst. May they be moved not to belittle the pain of our youth, not to disparage those who speak with courage and sincerity. Our young people see visions. May our old men know how to dream dreams along with them. Our nation has in the past been confident of its humaneness and has believed in its goodness. These students cherished the democratic ideals of its founders. May we not lose sight of this original vision. May we not have reason to lose faith and our capacity to achieve it.

In this trying moment, O Lord, give us all patience and understanding. Help us to find the right way that will heal our wounds and restore our health. May the sun of righteousness arise with healing on its wings. May the moment come when the hearts of the fathers shall be turned again to the children and the children to the hearts of the fathers. May we find the way to peace for all of us, for all races, for all faiths, for all nations.
Amen.

On May 4, 1970 unarmed college students at Kent State University in Kent, Ohio were protesting the Vietnam War when twenty-nine members of the Ohio National Guard fired approximately 67 rounds over a period of 13 seconds, killing four students and wounding nine others, one of whom suffered permanent paralysis.

A Precious Heritage

34. Is American Jewry Secure?

September 19, 1971

Erev Rosh Hashanah

My father spoke frequently of the enemies of the Jewish people throughout history—from biblical times through the twentieth century. It's that history that caused him to never feel settled, even in the benign environment of American democracy. In this sermon, he gently touches on his other frequent concern—that of Jewish ignorance and apathy—by suggesting we "assert and enhance our Jewishness" as a defense to possible rising anti-Semitism. Regardless of the listener's commitment to Judaism, one might well receive this as a compelling and passionate argument for protecting our democracy for the benefit of all.

The civil rights and freedom of all groups in our country must be our concern, not only because our religious ideals tell us to be concerned with the welfare of our neighbors, but also for the very selfish reason that if other groups are made to suffer abuse and indignities, if other groups are oppressed and treated unjustly, we shall become the targets of their frustration.

WHENEVER WE COME TO THE BEGINNING OF A NEW YEAR, it has been usual to think of the problems which confront society as a whole or the Jewish people in particular. For a number of years now, we Jews have been fairly relaxed about one of these problems that has troubled us in the past, but the question of anti-Semitism and the Jewish position in this country seems to be once again pressing upon our consciousness. In recent times, a number of reliable observers of the Jewish scene have expressed concern with regard to the future position of the Jew in America. Following World War II, under the impact of the Holocaust and the birth of the State of Israel, anti-Semitism in this country reached its lowest ebb. A smitten conscience, a new respect for the Jew because of his accomplishments in Israel, and economic well-being all combined to create an attitude toward the Jew more favorable than ever before. But today there is the feeling among some that our gains have been eroding, and that the future could bring us problems.

At the last biennial of the Union of American Hebrew Congregations, Morris Abram, formerly president of the American Jewish Committee and also of Brandeis University, said that peace in Vietnam without an American victory might generate a wave of conservative-rightist resentment and thus trigger a resurgence of anti-Semitism.[302] He warned: "When a major power cannot justify its war losses, it then begins the search for a scapegoat, and Western history has a favorite scapegoat at hand—the Jews." There may be as many non-Jewish doves as Jewish ones, but it is the Jews who would be singled out for blame. And in any case, it actually makes no difference if Jews are doves or not. They can just as easily be blamed for being hawks as doves.[303]

In the August issue of *Commentary* magazine, editor Norman Podhoretz writes that he and some of his intellectual friends have begun to feel "A Certain Anxiety."[304] Two major events have contributed to this anxiety. One is the reaction to Jewish victory in the Six-Day War. We all know how much concern Jews suddenly showed for their fellow Jews during the war. It was a revelation, even to Jews, to note how closely identified they were with one another, regardless of how dormant their Jewishness may have been up to that moment. But Jews also discovered how difficult it was for many people to accept the thought of a Jewish victory. There was deep sympathy for the Jews while they were the underdogs, but they were not supposed to win. When they prevailed over the enemy that threatened to push the Israelis into the sea, then the Jews became the imperialists and aggressors, the oppressor of

---

302 Morris Berthold Abram (1918–2000) was a civil rights activist and lawyer, and the president of Brandeis University from 1968-1970. The American Jewish Committee (AJC), established in 1906, is one of the oldest Jewish ethnic advocacy organizations. "Besides working for civil liberties for Jews, the organization has a history of fighting against forms of discrimination in the United States and working on behalf of social equality. For example, the AJC filed a friend-of-the-court brief in the May 1954 case of *Brown v. Board of Education*, and participated in other events in the Civil Rights Movement." Wikipedia contributors. "American Jewish Committee." *Wikipedia, The Free Encyclopedia*. Wikipedia, The Free Encyclopedia, 20 Sep. 2017. Web. 25 Sep. 2017.

303 "A dove is someone who opposes the use of military pressure to resolve a dispute; a hawk favors entry into war. The terms came into widespread use during the Vietnam War, but their roots are much older than that conflict." "Doves and Hawks," *Dictionary of American History*, The Gale Group, 2003.

304 "*Commentary* is a monthly American magazine on religion, Judaism, and politics, as well as social and cultural issues… [As its editor,] Norman Podhoretz, originally a liberal Democrat turned neoconservative, moved the magazine to the right and toward the Republican Party in the 1970s and 1980s." Wikipedia contributors. "Commentary (magazine)." *Wikipedia, The Free Encyclopedia*. Wikipedia, The Free Encyclopedia, 15 Sep. 2017. Web. 25 Sep. 2017.

the Arabs, unreasonable in their desire to protect themselves, unjust because they would not return the gains and enable the Arabs to start their threatening actions all over again. A wave of anti-Zionism swept over the intellectual community, and a long-time taboo against expressing open hostility toward Jews was broken.

Podhoretz speaks of intellectuals, but he might also have referred specifically to churchmen as well. The Protestant clergy, in particular, resented the Jewish victory because they simply could not abide the thought of a completely Jewish Jerusalem. When the Arabs desecrated synagogues and cemeteries of the Old City, there was silence. When the Arabs violated the agreement in 1948 to internationalize Jerusalem, there was silence. When Jordan violated the truce agreement to permit Jews to visit their holy places, there was silence. But when the Jews gained control and made it possible for everyone to visit the holy places without restriction, there was an uproar and a clamor for internationalization.

The second cause of anxiety mentioned in the *Commentary* article was the 1968 teachers' strike.[305] This strike brought to the surface a disturbing picture of Black anti-Semitism; and what was even more disturbing was the apparent willingness of what is called the "white power structure" to sacrifice Jewish interests for the sake of buying peace with the Blacks. The anti-Semitism of the Blacks may not have been any more prevalent than anti-Semitism among whites, but it seems to have been explained more and excused more, and it has brought sympathy for Blacks rather than condemnation of anti-Semitism. Whatever the problem, whether it be Israel, the teachers, or anything else, there would seem to be an insensitivity to Jewish needs and Jewish accomplishments. It is the Jew from whom sacrifice is demanded, the Jew who is wrong and unreasonable. Hence the anxiety.

We can, of course, make a good case for the fact that these fears for the future are exaggerated and unfounded. There have always been anti-Semitic irritants in this country, and it is unrealistic to expect that they will completely disappear. In spite of them, we can say that American Jewry has become the largest Jewish community the world has ever known. Whatever

---

305 "The New York City teachers' strike of 1968 was a months-long confrontation between the new community-controlled school board in the largely Black Ocean Hill–Brownsville neighborhoods of Brooklyn, and New York City's United Federation of Teachers. The strike dragged on from May 1968 to November 1968, shutting down the public schools for a total of 36 days and increasing racial tensions between African Americans and Jews. Thousands of New York City teachers went on strike when the neighborhood school board (which is now two separate neighborhoods) abruptly dismissed a set of teachers and administrators. The newly created school district, encompassing a mostly Black neighborhood, was an experiment in community control over schools; and the dismissed workers were almost all white and Jewish." Wikipedia contributors. "New York City teachers' strike of 1968." *Wikipedia, The Free Encyclopedia*. Wikipedia, The Free Encyclopedia, 11 Sep. 2017. Web. 25 Sep. 2017.

economic handicaps may have existed have not prevented us from becoming also the most affluent Jewish community there has ever been. The separation of church and state has worked to our advantage, and the government guarantees Jewish rights to the same extent that it does the rights of all of its citizens. We live here without legal restrictions or anti-Jewish legislation. There is no record of pogroms or physical violence, as in many places in Europe. Our young people are among the best educated. We attain high political positions, and there is complete freedom of the ballot. We build our synagogues and institutions as we will. Our government has been a mainstay for the State of Israel from its very beginning. Certainly, the position of the Jew is safeguarded here better than it has been anywhere else. What is there to fear?

It would seem, then, that American Jews should have full confidence as we face the future, that there is nothing of a serious nature to disturb us. And yet history bids us to stop and think. History teaches us never to forget that the seemingly impossible may nevertheless come to pass. Unfortunately, there is the example of history to keep us watchful.

We read in our history books of the Golden Age of Spain, but it ended in tragic expulsion.[306] The French Jews were the first to be emancipated in modern times, but this did not prevent Jews being denounced as traitors after defeat in the Franco-Prussian War, nor the suggestion by DeGaulle, in more recent times, that Jews were disloyal to the state.[307] German Jews attain the highest degree of acculturation and many consider themselves Germans of the Mosaic persuasion, but they were blamed for World War I and Hitler was encouraged in his efforts to make European *Judenrein*.[308]

The record in America is surely not so dismal, but the dividing line between the rational and irrational in man is very thin, and the history and laws of our country might not be enough of a barrier in a time of national

---

[306] "The Golden Age of Jewish culture in Spain coincided with the Middle Ages in Europe, a period of Muslim rule throughout much of the Iberian Peninsula. During intermittent periods, Jews were generally accepted in society and Jewish religious, cultural, and economic life blossomed." Wikipedia contributors. "Golden age of Jewish culture in Spain." *Wikipedia, The Free Encyclopedia*. Wikipedia, The Free Encyclopedia, 29 Aug. 2017. Web. 25 Sep. 2017.

[307] "Charles de Gaulle (1890–1970) was a French general and statesman, and President of France... He was the dominant French figure during the Cold War era." Wikipedia contributors. "Charles de Gaulle." *Wikipedia, The Free Encyclopedia*. Wikipedia, The Free Encyclopedia, 21 Sep. 2017. Web. 25 Sep. 2017.

[308] "The German words *judenrein* (lit: "clean of Jews") and *judenfrei* (lit: "free of Jews") are Nazi terms to designate an area that was "cleansed" of Jews during The Holocaust. While *judenfrei* referred merely to "freeing" an area of all of its Jewish inhabitants, the term *judenrein* (literally "clean of Jews") was also used. This had the stronger connotation that any trace of Jewish blood had been removed as an impurity." Wikipedia contributors. "Judenfrei." *Wikipedia, The Free Encyclopedia*. Wikipedia, The Free Encyclopedia, 1 Jul. 2017. Web. 25 Sep. 2017.

adversity and despair. The fact is that in spite of our full citizenship in a democratic country, in spite of our feeling of "at-homeness," there is an "otherness" to the Jewish people, which leaves us forever vulnerable. Those Jews who may have lost their awareness of otherness had it revived for them during the crisis of the Six-Day War. They found themselves passionately concerned with the survival of their people. As for non-Jews, they have been conditioned to feel this otherness of the Jews by centuries of Christian history. Christians have looked upon Jews as rebels against truth, a wandering people punished for its rejection of the truth. We Jews live in two communities. We will not permit anyone to tell us that we are not part of the American community, but at the same time, we are involved in a worldwide Jewish community. This makes the Jew different from the rest of the population. The rest of the population ignores this difference when times are good, but reacts to it irrationally when there is discontent in the land or social problems to disturb the peace.

We need not be embarrassed by this otherness. Its presence is a lesson to the world. It acts as a barometer of the world's condition. The Jew affords an example of a people living on its own soil and being part of the world as a whole. Only when the world can accept this without complaint, only when the world can rise above its tribal nationalisms and do likewise, will the world be at peace. This factor in the makeup of the Jew, however, makes it impossible to predict a totally secure future for us, whether it be in America or any other place.

This is not to say that the Jews of this country need be pessimistic about the future—far from it. But it does mean that we ought not take that future for granted. We may well have faith in America, but at the same time, the Jew, as an American, must ever be vigilant with regard to the protection of democratic principles. The civil rights and freedom of all groups in our country must be our concern, not only because our religious ideals tell us to be concerned with the welfare of our neighbors, but also for the very selfish reason that if other groups are made to suffer abuse and indignities, if other groups are oppressed and treated unjustly, we shall become the targets of their frustration. The Jew thrives best in democracy, and we must be actively concerned with the preservation and advancement of democracy in America.

On the other hand, we must not be so concerned with the welfare of others that we neglect our own well-being in the process. For example, today we face the phenomenon of the radical left, which has attracted a great deal of support from Jews because of the unusual Jewish concern for liberal principles.[309] A peculiar feature of the radical left, however, is that it is concerned

---

309 It is unclear if Ballon is referring to left-wing domestic terrorist groups such as the Weather Underground, the Black Panther Party, the Black Liberation Army, and the Symbionese Liberation Army.

with everyone's problem except the Jew's. The Jew is always expendable. If it is teachers we deal with, the Jew must give up seniority and positions earned by merit to make way for a quota system that would drive them out of the profession. If it is Israel we speak of, the Jew must yield to the Arabs even if it means that Israel would thereby be destroyed. If it is Black-Jewish relationships we speak about, the Jews must accept the left's condemnation of any prejudice on their part, but swallow the left's justification for any Black anti-Semitism. If a Jew expresses some concern with regard to a Jewish problem, he is advised that it is more important to think in universal terms and that it is petty and selfish to have any special concern for fellow Jews.

Our young people who become enamored of the radical left need to be reminded that history shows that ultimately these so-called universalistic movements consume the Jews that support them. There may be some pretense that Jewish problems also will be solved by them, but the usual method of solving a Jewish problem is to eliminate the Jews. These movements soon expel from their ranks even those Jews who supported them most faithfully, as witness what has happened in Russia and Poland. There were once Jews in Germany who supported Hitler in his early days and were reputed to have shouted, "Down with us!" Jews who partake of the radical left do the same; they also in effect are shouting, "Down with us!"

But it is not only outside factors that need to be considered in securing the American Jewish future. To do so, we need also to build an authentic Jewish life in America. That is, we must create a Jewish community with the self-knowledge and self-respect that will keep it from doing harm to itself. It must be a community that does not neglect any factor of its existence that has a survival value: its synagogues, its educational system, its religious faith, its cultural institutions, its charities, and especially its link with Israel. To neglect any of these is to make the task of the anti-Semite easier and to do his work for him, to let ourselves dissolve as a community into nothingness. We must make a conscious effort to assert and enhance our Jewishness, and not let it wither away by default. If we thus contribute to the establishment of justice in the world at large, if we speak up in our own behalf for justice to ourselves as Jews, if we nourish and sustain a Jewish spirit in our own ranks, then our faith in the future of American Jewry will be warranted.

On this day of Rosh Hashanah, we take stock of ourselves and our Jewishness. Let this self-searching not be routine. Let us resolve earnestly to fulfill the duty that is ours by virtue of the covenant of Abraham, our Father, and Moses, our teacher. Let us so live as individuals that the Jewish people as a whole also will live, that Judaism will survive. Let us say with deep conviction and resolution, *"Am Yisrael chai*—the Jewish people shall live!"

Amen.

34. Is American Jewry Secure?—1970

Dad—

That's a powerful message. That's a message for all time, isn't it? It makes me sad—sad to think that there in the mid-twentieth century, with all the growth and expansion of Jewish life in the United States and Israel, that the long shadow of oppression never left our doorstep. It makes me sad, especially today, to watch how the current administration has built its platform on creating feelings of otherness, not only within this country, but around the world.

I've noticed that many of your sermons come from a well of sadness and grief, if not fear. And I've noticed that you typically rise up and embrace your congregation, and urge them to rise up as well with a clear notion of what they can do and who they can be to transcend that grief and sadness, and to build a life on Jewish values that will sustain the Jewish people and bring peace to the world.

Thank you and bless you for your evenhanded assessment of what is real and true in both the darkness and the light.

Blessings.
Yesh

A Precious Heritage

35. Mission of Israel

September 26, 1974

Yom Kippur Morning

In this, my father's first (and last) Yom Kippur with Temple Beth Tefilloh in Brunswick, Georgia, he reiterated that he was not content that Jewish values alone be part of society. He absolutely felt that Judaism itself must be maintained to ever be a light unto the nations.

We Jews have been a unique people with a unique history... It is our obligation not only to use what we have learned from the ages, but to preserve it and transmit it. We have received a precious heritage. It is our duty to know it, enlarge upon it, and pass it on to the future.

LATE THIS AFTERNOON, AS PART OF THE *NE'ILA* SERVICE with which we end the Day of Atonement, we shall recite the prayer known in Hebrew as *El Nora Alila*, freely translated in our prayer book as, "O Lord, we stand in awe before Thy deeds." [310] As part of this prayer, we also read the words, "We, who are few in number, lift our eyes in worship." I can remember that years ago I used to think how prophetic was the writer of this line. For what used to happen very often in some congregations was that the majority of the people would leave the synagogue on Yom Kippur before the *Ne'ila* service began, and

---

[310] *Ne'ila* (lit. locking, as the "gates of prayer are closing"), the concluding service, is a special Jewish prayer service that is held only on Yom Kippur. It is the time when final prayers of repentance are recited at the closing of Yom Kippur. In Sephardic practice, it begins with the hymn *El Nora Alila*; this has been adopted into Ashkenazic Yom Kippur services as well. The shofar is blown at the end of *Ne'ila*. During the leader's repetition of the *Ne'ila Amidah*, the ark remains open, and it is traditional to stand throughout the service. A more literal translation makes the title and recurring line *El Nora Alila*, "God of awesome deeds."

we would really be "few in number" by the time this prayer was recited. In most congregations, this is no longer the case, and I hope it is not so here. I have been told that it isn't. In my Long Island congregation, it was rare that anyone walked out before *Ne'ila*. It was an established custom to end Yom Kippur service with a full congregation, and it was an inspiring conclusion to the day. Nevertheless, I would always smile to myself as we read these words, and I thought of how they lent themselves to misinterpretation.

I am sure you realize that the real meaning of these words is something altogether different. "We, who are few in number" did not refer to the attendance of the congregation at *Ne'ila*. It was rather a reference to the entire Jewish people, who in comparison to the other peoples of the earth were, indeed, few in number. This prayer was written by Moses ibn Ezra in medieval times, when Jews everywhere could not help but feeling overwhelmed by the world around them.[311] Scattered as they were throughout the world, subject to all kinds of uncertainties in life, buffeted from place to place, they undoubtedly felt weak, forlorn, and few in number.

Today, unfortunately, the phrase is still a poignant one. Under the best of conditions, we still would remain comparatively few in number, always a small minority compared to the millions of other peoples in the world. But conditions have not been at their "best." Even in our own generation, we have lost six million to Hitler. We are losing almost three more million, if not physically, then spiritually, in the Soviet Union. And so the comparison with others is far more unfavorable even than it should have been. The world in general is concerned about a population explosion, but Jewish numbers have been sadly reduced. And so when we say "few in number," it has again the overtones of distress, because not only is the Jewish people small to begin with, but so much of it has been brutally and unnaturally cut off. And as an aside, we might also point out that in addition to the problems just mentioned, there is yet another factor that we contend with. The more highly educated groups in modern society, and we Jews are among them, do not see eye to eye with the Pope on the subject of birth control, and this, too, profoundly affects our total number.[312]

---

[311] "Rabbi Moses ben Jacob ibn Ezra (c. 1055–1138) was a Jewish-Spanish philosopher, linguist, and poet. Although Jewish by religion, ibn Ezra also considered had great influence in the Arabic literary world. He is considered one of Spain's greatest poets." Wikipedia contributors. "Moses ibn Ezra." *Wikipedia, The Free Encyclopedia*. Wikipedia, The Free Encyclopedia, 12 Apr. 2017. Web. 25 Sep. 2017.

[312] On July 25, 1968, Pope Paul VI issued an encyclical *Humanae vitae (Of Human Life)*, subtitled *On the Regulation of Birth*, that "reaffirmed the orthodox teaching of the Catholic Church regarding married love, responsible parenthood, and the continued rejection of most forms of birth control." Robert Young, *Urgent Advice from Your Catholic Grandpa* (Bloomington, IN: iUniverse, 2017).

In view of all of this, we are all the more concerned about what is happening today within the Jewish community of the United States. We are all the more distressed by the phenomenon we behold of Jews who are not threatened by persecution or pogrom, but who by their own free choice or indifference contribute to the decline in number of our people. The Jewish people today suffers not only the effect of hostility, but is further seriously threatened by the drifting away that takes place in a democratic way of life and an open society. The Jewish people is threatened today even by those who do profess their Jewish attachment and perhaps even belong to synagogues, but who do not take seriously the obligation of Judaism. We are threatened by those who remain nominally Jewish but do not live their Jewishness, whose Judaism is of secondary importance in their life as they succumb to the materialism and false values and seductive anti-Jewish influences of our environment.

We cannot bring back the six million. The effort to save the Jews of Russia for Judaism is a battle against almost overwhelming odds and does not depend altogether on our own wishes and our own decisions. But in this country, it is still possible to determine our own fate and fashion our own destiny, and our greatest challenge is what to do about it. How shall we convince ourselves to hold the line? How shall we reason with ourselves effectively that Judaism may be preserved and Jewish numbers not dwindle?

A Jewish poet once wrote, "A man must not be born with no yesterdays in his heart." One of the great problems we face is that too many of us have no appreciation or understanding of our Jewish yesterdays. It is unfortunately considered a sign of maturity and sophistication by altogether too many that they have no interest or knowledge of our religious traditions or the history of our past. Modern educated individuals who would be ashamed to admit knowing nothing about economics or literature have been indifferent to—and sometimes even proud of—their total illiteracy in the field of Judaism. Fair-minded and objective individuals who would never think of passing judgment on some political issue or scientific problem without some examination of the background have no hesitation belittling the values of their Jewish heritage on the basis of nothing at all, or perhaps based on no more than the bits of childish learning that stem from a nearly instant bar mitzvah.[313] It is true that there are some aspects of religious tradition with which a modern intellectual might quarrel, but Judaism is essentially a rational faith that enables the Jew to find meaning for his life, and it is also responsive to challenge and change. The kind of religion that does not permit its tradition

---

313 Ballon is referring to the practice among some families of cramming Jewish study into a short time before a child's coming of age at thirteen, rather than providing years of preparation.

to be questioned and debated might well be repudiated in frustration, but Judaism is not that kind of religion. Judaism has grown through the centuries. Out of the roots of its past, new shoots are continually springing forth. Today, also, new growth takes place. It should not be uprooted, but rather carefully nurtured, pruned, preserved, and possessed. The poet Goethe wrote, "What thou hast inherited from thy fathers, acquire to make it thine."[314] In the same spirit, eminent psychologist Rollo May says that we need to relate in a healthy way to our inherited traditions. When we do not do so, we shut ourselves off from a potentially creative relationship; this contributes to the feelings of rootlessness so many individuals have in our day.[315]

Because they have no yesterdays in their hearts, there are some amongst us today, and especially amongst our young people, who often do certain things which are very much in keeping with our tradition—even things that are the products of our tradition—but without seeming to be aware of that connection. There are those who are deeply committed to the building of the good society and to the fight for social reform, but seem to be unmindful that such activity is the very essence of Jewish teaching. We just read in the *haftarah*[316] for this morning:

> *Is not this the fast that I have chosen? To loose the fetters of wickedness, to undo the bands of the yoke and to let the oppressed go free, and that ye break every yoke? Is it not to deal the bread to the hungry and that thou bring the poor that are cast out to thy house?*[317]

This is Jewish tradition! "Seek peace and pursue it" is Jewish tradition.[318] It is not merely by chance that we Jews have such a disproportionately high percentage of our people in liberal causes in our country today. Professor

---

314 Johann Wolfgang von Goethe (1749–1832) was a German writer and statesman. *Faust*, Part I, Scene 1.

315 American Rollo Reece May (1909–1994) was an author and an existential psychologist.

316 "The *haftarah* (lit. "parting," "taking leave"—despite resemblances, it is not related to the word *Torah*) is a series of selections from the books of Prophets of the Hebrew Bible. They are publicly read in synagogue as part of Jewish religious practice. The *Haftarah* reading follows the Torah reading on each Sabbath and on Jewish festivals and fast days. Typically, the *haftarah* is thematically linked to the Torah portion that precedes it." Wikipedia contributors. "Haftarah." *Wikipedia, The Free Encyclopedia*. Wikipedia, The Free Encyclopedia, 24 Sep. 2017. Web. 25 Sep. 2017.

317 Isaiah 58:6-7.

318 "Depart from evil, and do good; seek peace, and pursue it." Psalm 34:15.

William F. Albright, a non-Jew, acknowledged this fact when he said that in some ways he felt

> more at home in Jewish circles than anywhere else, because Jews tend to have a more intelligent attitude toward education and culture and also to have a keener feeling for moral and social problems. [319]

This is not merely because we ourselves have been a persecuted minority. It is because a sense of justice is deeply ingrained in our religious heritage. Other religious groups have placed a major emphasis on the salvation of individual souls in the future life, but the major emphasis for the Jew is the concern for right relationships between man and his fellow man in this world. This is salvation. The overwhelming interest of the Jew in law and all its details is because this is a means by which to regulate the life of society here and now. The contemporary concern for civil liberties, racial equality, and peace has its roots in the Bible. The liberal slogans about the dignity of man, equality, and brotherhood have grown out of biblical teaching. It is our Bible that proclaims we must know the heart of the stranger.[320] It is hard to understand, therefore, why so many modern Jews who like to be considered liberal either ignore the wellsprings of their liberalism or are altogether hostile to it. It is not a question of either/or. Judaism and liberalism do not contradict each other—they complement each other. The eminent Jewish sociologist Manheim Shapiro has written:

> Participation in society and social reform does not require a choice between our Jewish commitment and an equal society. Quite the contrary, the closer we come to knowing and living the meaning of Judaism, the more surely can we combine the maintenance of group identity and the sharing with other Americans in the making of a good society. [321]

We can carry this a step further. Not only does our concern for society *not* require a choice between Jewish commitment and liberal ideas, but we may say even more positively that for the sake of society, it is better that Jewish identity be maintained and strengthened. We Jews have been a people who

---

[319] "William Foxwell Albright (1891–1971) was an American archaeologist, biblical scholar, philologist, and expert on ceramics... From the early twentieth century until his death, he was dean of biblical archaeologists and the acknowledged founder of the Biblical archaeology movement." Wikipedia contributors. "William F. Albright." *Wikipedia, The Free Encyclopedia*. Wikipedia, The Free Encyclopedia, 18 Sep. 2017. Web. 25 Sep. 2017.

[320] "And a stranger shalt thou not oppress; for ye know the heart of a stranger, seeing ye were strangers in the land of Egypt." Exodus 23:9.

[321] Manheim Shapiro (1913–1981), "a social psychologist, was long active in Jewish communal work." "Manheim Shapiro Dead at 67," *Jewish Telegraphic Agency*, March 24, 1981. http://www.jta.org/1981/03/24/archive/manheim-shapiro-dead-at-67. Accessed 25 Sep. 2017.

conceive of ourselves as having a special mission in this world. This mission was first expressed in the biblical account of Abraham, who was charged by God to go forth and be a blessing, and who was promised as a reward for his faith that in him all the nations of the earth would be blessed.[322] This mission is reflected in the story of Sinai, where the Hebrew people were told to become a kingdom of priests and a holy nation.[323] It is proclaimed perhaps best of all by the prophet Isaiah, who says in God's name, "I, the Lord, have called thee in righteousness to be a light of the nations."[324]

The world still needs our mission and us. To some, the idea of a nation thinking that it has a special mission in the world seems to be arrogant and out of step with modern times. But many peoples think of themselves in terms of having a special purpose, and whether this is good or bad depends only on what this purpose is. Hitler proclaimed it to be Germany's mission to conquer the world. Russia's mission is to communize the world. Our Jewish mission is to liberate the world. It may be a bit ambitious, but it is a worthy purpose that is yet far from fulfillment, and we need not feel embarrassed by it. We need only to measure up to the challenge.

That Judaism does fulfill a special purpose and continues to have special relevance in the world today is recognized even by non-Jews. Roman Catholic scholar Father Flannery has written:

> *From Judaism comes a concept of worldliness which is better developed than in Christianity, and a sense of social justice that can restrain the selfish individualism that has often marked much of modern Catholic life.* [325]

And Protestant leader Franklin Littell states:

> *For the Christians, Jewry serves another vital function... highlighted by the tragic events of our times... the Jew... is by his very existence a witness to the God of the Bible... and is frequently called upon to suffer for what the Christians would suffer if they remained Christians.*[326]

---

322 Genesis 12:1-3.

323 Exodus 19:6.

324 Isaiah 42:6.

325 "Edward H. Flannery (1912–1998) was a priest in the Roman Catholic Diocese of Providence... Throughout his career, he fought against anti-Semitism and defended the State of Israel and the Jewish people against attacks on the local, national and international levels. Through his work, he displayed great sensitivity to issues of the Holocaust; and he strongly promoted education in the history of anti-Semitism, both for the Jewish and Catholic communities." Wikipedia contributors. "Edward Flannery." *Wikipedia, The Free Encyclopedia*. Wikipedia, The Free Encyclopedia, 17 Mar. 2017. Web. 25 Sep. 2017.

326 "Franklin Hamlin Littell (1917–2009) was an American Protestant scholar. He is known for his writings rejecting supersessionism [a Christian theological view that holds that the Christian Church has succeeded the Israelites as the definitive people of God or that the New Covenant has replaced or superseded the Mosaic covenant. After the Holocaust, Littell] advocated educational programs to

The Western world may already have adopted many Jewish ideas and ideals, but the God of the Bible still needs His Jewish witness. Our task is not yet finished and the mission is not yet fulfilled. Its fulfillment will come probably only in the Messianic era.[327] Until then, there is no reason to surrender our identity, and it is important to the world that we do not do so.

We Jews are a unique people with a unique history. Our experience through the centuries has brought us much wisdom. With experience and wisdom come responsibility. It is our obligation not only to use what we have learned from the ages, but to preserve it and transmit it. We have received a precious heritage. It is our duty to know it, enlarge upon it, and pass it on to the future. It has been said that the greatest sin of our time would be to give Hitler and Stalin a posthumous victory. We must be dedicated to forestalling such disaster. We must learn to cherish our yesterdays by adding to our Jewish knowledge. We must maintain the institutions that serve Judaism in the present, and we must try to exemplify in our own lives the spirit advocated by Judaism. We shall pray this afternoon, "Endow us, Our Guardian, with strength and patience for our holy mission." May we indeed have an appreciation of that mission and the will to pursue it. May we always proclaim with certainty and pride, *Am Yisroel Chai*—the people of Israel lives.

Amen.

Dad—

Indifference to the traditions of Judaism was continually a sore point for you, and hence a frequent sermon topic. This sermon may state your case as well as any other. I am publishing this collection to support your fervent desire—to provide our family, at the very least, with a piece of its own Jewish history and values.

Blessings.
Yesh

---

improve relations between Christians and Jews." Wikipedia contributors. "Franklin Littell." *Wikipedia, The Free Encyclopedia*. Wikipedia, The Free Encyclopedia, 28 Aug. 2017. Web. 25 Sep. 2017.

327 "The Messianic Era or Messianic Age is a theological term referring to a future time of universal peace and brotherhood on the earth, without crime, war, or poverty. Many Abrahamic religions believe that there will be such an age; some refer to it as the consummate 'kingdom of God,' 'paradise,' or the 'world to come.'" Wikipedia contributors. "Messianic Age." *Wikipedia, The Free Encyclopedia*. Wikipedia, The Free Encyclopedia, 20 Sep. 2017. Web. 25 Sep. 2017.

Sidney and Jean Ballon, HUC Campus, Jerusalem, c. 1972

36. Chaim Weizmann

November 8, 1974

This biographical sketch of Chaim Weizmann is included less for its style or substance than for the notable fact that it was the final sermon that my father delivered from the pulpit. In it he honors the memory of a man of faith, vision, and courage—qualities that Sidney Ballon also possessed in good measure.

Moses did not see the Promised Land. Herzl died long before the coming of the Jewish State. But Weizmann not only witnessed its achievement, he enjoyed the honors heaped upon him as a result.

TOMORROW, NOVEMBER 9, IS THE 100TH ANNIVERSARY of the birth of one of the great Jews of modern times, Chaim Weizmann. He has been gone since 1952. And enough time has elapsed to indicate that his inspiration and his influence are lasting, that he will be for years to come the symbol of faith and self-confidence for the Jewish people.

Chaim Weizmann was the first president of Israel, and, of course, this in itself would be enough to ensure him lasting remembrance. But more significant than the fact that he became the first president is that no other choice was logical. There was no contest for the office. There was no political opposition. When it became necessary to choose a president for Israel, he was the natural for the position. And this was because if Israel was in position to choose a president, it was because Weizmann's vision and effort, more than that of any other man living at the time, had made it possible.

What is it that Chaim Weizmann contributed that others did not? What made Weizmann unique? Apparently, it was the ability to combine within himself divergent ways of life and thought. He was a visionary, but he did not lose himself in dreams. He insisted upon practical action. He was the product of the intense Jewishness of Eastern Europe, but he was completely at home in the culture of Western Europe as well. He felt the importance of gaining some political recognition for the rights of the Jews in the Holy Land, but he insisted that practical deeds were more significant than political victories. He is known for his lifetime devotion to the cause of Zionism; yet his achievements in the field of science also were sufficient in themselves to bring him honor. In all these respects, Weizmann was unique.

He was born in November 1874 in the town of Motol in Russia. The influence of this East European town was never forgotten. Here, he acquired a sensitivity to the feelings of the Jewish masses, who labored under social, political, and economic hardships but who maintained a passion for Jewish learning and a faith in the messianic promise of return to the ancient homeland. Whatever else may have contributed to the creation of a Jewish homeland, and whatever the needs of the Jewish people, certainly the driving spiritual force, the motivation for self-sacrifice, the compulsion to achieve miracles came from this East European attachment to an ancient dream. And Weizmann shared in this attachment.

Weizmann was fortunate, however, that his father, a lumber merchant, saw the need of a secular education as well as a religious one and could afford to give it to his son. Chaim studied in Russia, Germany, and Switzerland, where he obtained his doctorate. His field was chemistry, and he became a research expert. His early Jewish background gave him the Zionist dream. His scientific background taught him that one cannot build on dreams but must deal with facts and reality, and this dual background influenced his Zionist philosophy. Other Zionist leaders were one-sided. Herzl, the founder of the Zionist movement and organization, concentrated all his efforts on the attainment of a political charter that would give the Jewish people legal right to settle on the land.[328] Achad Haam, another important figure in the Zionist world, preached that spiritual awakening among the Jews must precede the founding of a Jewish homeland.[329] Weizmann disagreed with neither of them,

---

328 "Theodor Herzl (1860–1904), born Benjamin Ze'ev Herzl, was an Austro-Hungarian journalist, playwright, political activist, and writer, and one of the fathers of modern political Zionism. Herzl formed the World Zionist Organization and promoted Jewish migration to Palestine in an effort to form a Jewish state. Though he died long before its establishment, he is generally considered a father of the State of Israel, formed in 1948." Wikipedia contributors. "Theodor Herzl." *Wikipedia, The Free Encyclopedia.* Wikipedia, The Free Encyclopedia, 16 Sep. 2017. Web. 25 Sep. 2017.

329 "Asher Zvi Hirsch Ginsberg (1856–1927), primarily known by his Hebrew pen name Ahad Ha'am (*lit.* "one of the people"), was a Hebrew essayist and one of the foremost pre-state Zionist thinkers. He is known as the founder of cultural Zionism. [His was a] secular vision of a Jewish 'spiritual center' in Israel... Unlike Herzl, the founder of political Zionism, Ha'am strived for 'a Jewish state and not merely a state of Jews.'" Wikipedia contributors. "Ahad Ha'am." *Wikipedia, The Free Encyclopedia.* Wikipedia, The Free Encyclopedia, 3 Sep. 2017. Web. 25 Sep. 2017.

but his view was that whatever else might be of value, the Jewish homeland would never be won except by building the land step-by-step—even before legal rights were assured, and even before the spiritual renaissance among the masses was complete. History proved him right. When the state finally came into being, its lines were primarily drawn according to the places of settlement. Where Jews had built became Jewish soil, and if only in the early years of Zionist activity more funds had been available and more building had been accomplished, the original partition would have resulted in a larger state at the time, and possibly the subsequent wars would have been easier to fight.

In 1904, Weizmann was invited to become a lecturer at the University of Manchester in England. It was in Manchester that he first became acquainted with James Balfour, whose friendship later proved to be so helpful to the Jewish cause.[330] Balfour issued the 1917 declaration stating that His Majesty's government looked with favor upon the establishment of a Jewish national home in Palestine. This declaration was the first step toward giving the Jewish people formal legal rights in Palestine. There is a dramatic legend as to how this came about. At the outbreak of World War I, Weizmann placed his talents as chemist at the disposal of the British government and was able to render valuable service. In 1916, there was a shortage of acetone, an essential ingredient in the manufacture of a certain type of explosive necessary in carrying on the war. Weizmann discovered a solution to the problem. The story is that he was then asked what reward he wanted for this great contribution. He is supposed to have said that he wanted nothing for himself but he did want Palestine for his people, and this was granted to him. Like many other legends, this is somewhat true in spirit, but not in fact. In fact, his war effort quite naturally won for him a great deal of goodwill and sympathy in government circles; therefore, he had the opportunity to cultivate interest in the Zionist cause. This made it possible for the Balfour Declaration to be issued.[331]

---

330 "Arthur James Balfour, 1st Earl of Balfour (1848–1930), a British Conservative politician, was the Prime Minister of the United Kingdom from July 1902 to December 1905, and later Foreign Secretary." Wikipedia contributors. "Arthur Balfour." *Wikipedia, The Free Encyclopedia*. Wikipedia, The Free Encyclopedia, 3 Sep. 2017. Web. 25 Sep. 2017.

331 The Balfour Declaration was "contained in a letter dated 2 November 1917 from the United Kingdom's Foreign Secretary, Arthur James Balfour, to Walter Rothschild, 2nd Baron Rothschild, a leader of the British Jewish community, for transmission to the Zionist Federation of Great Britain and Ireland... It read: 'His Majesty's government view with favour the establishment in Palestine of a national home for the Jewish people, and will use their best endeavours to facilitate the achievement of this object, it being clearly understood that nothing shall be done which may prejudice the civil and religious rights of existing non-Jewish communities in Palestine, or the rights and political status enjoyed by Jews in any other country.'" Wikipedia contributors. "Balfour Declaration." *Wikipedia, The Free Encyclopedia*. Wikipedia, The Free Encyclopedia, 25 Sep. 2017. Web. 25 Sep. 2017.

In this sense, we can perhaps say that Israel was, indeed, Weizmann's reward for scientific discovery.

Shortly after the Balfour Declaration, there occurred two significant episodes in Weizmann's life. One of these was contact with Emir Faisal[332] in Trans-Jordan.[333] Weizmann wanted to ascertain the attitude of this leading spokesman of the Arab world to the Balfour Declaration. He found him, oddly enough, to be most sympathetic, and Faisal eventually entered into an agreement with Weizmann that Jewish emigration into Palestine was to be encouraged and stimulated, and all necessary measures taken to achieve it quickly.[334] Furthermore, in a letter to Felix Frankfurter, Feisal referred to the fact that Jews and Arabs were cousins in race and were working together for a reformed and revived Near East.[335] How unfortunate it has been that political scheming later deprived Faisal of his importance in the Arab world and broke down the original Arab-Jewish goodwill that existed immediately after World War I.

The second significant event was the ground breaking for the Hebrew University.[336] This took place even before the war was over, when it was not yet certain that the Allies would retain control over Palestine. General Allenby, who was in control of Palestine, could not understand why under the prevailing conditions Jews would be thinking of beginning to build a university in

---

332 "Faisal I bin Hussein bin Ali al-Hashimi (1885–1933) was king of the Arab Kingdom of Syria or Greater Syria in 1920, and was king of Iraq from 1921 to 1933... He fostered unity between Sunni and Shiite Muslims to encourage common loyalty and promote pan-Arabism in the goal of creating an Arab state that would include Iraq, Syria, and the rest of the Fertile Crescent. While in power, Faisal tried to diversify his administration by including different ethnic and religious groups in offices." Wikipedia contributors. "Faisal I of Iraq." *Wikipedia, The Free Encyclopedia*. Wikipedia, The Free Encyclopedia, 24 Sep. 2017. Web. 25 Sep. 2017.

333 "Transjordan, the East Bank, or the Transjordanian Highlands, is the part of the Southern Levant east of the Jordan River, mostly contained in present-day Jordan. The region was controlled by numerous powers throughout history... In 1946, the Emirate achieved independence from the British, and in 1952, the country changed its name to the "Hashemite Kingdom of Jordan." Wikipedia contributors. "Transjordan (region)." *Wikipedia, The Free Encyclopedia*. Wikipedia, The Free Encyclopedia, 17 Sep. 2017. Web. 25 Sep. 2017.

334 "The Faisal–Weizmann Agreement was signed on January 3, 1919, by Emir Faisal... and Chaim Weizmann... as part of the Paris Peace Conference, settling disputes stemming from World War I. It was a short-lived agreement for Arab–Jewish cooperation on the development of a Jewish homeland in Palestine and an Arab nation in a large part of the Middle East." tinyurl.com/FaisalWeizmannAgreement. Accessed 25 Sep. 2017.

335 Felix Frankfurter (1882–1965) was an Associate Justice of the United States Supreme Court from 1939 to 1962, the third Jew to serve on the high court, after Louis Brandeis and Benjamin Cardozzo.

336 The Hebrew University of Jerusalem is Israel's second oldest university, established in 1918, 30 years before the State of Israel. The first Board of Governors included Albert Einstein, Sigmund Freud, Martin Buber, and Chaim Weizmann.

Jerusalem.[337] But Weizmann told him, "This will be a great act of faith—faith in the victory which is bound to come and faith in the future of Palestine."

Weizmann's association with still another school in Palestine, the Weizmann Institute of Science, was perhaps of even greater importance.[338] The practical side of Weizmann felt deeply that if Palestine were to be developed, it must make a close ally of science. There was a time when Britain decided to permit Jews to enter Palestine only to the extent that they could be absorbed comfortably by the economy of the country. During those days, someone asked Weizmann what he was doing in his laboratory. He replied, "Creating absorptive capacity." The Institute has, indeed, served to carry on the research necessary to find ways and means of making a desert flourish so that more and more Jewish immigrants might be taken in. It has been one of the most influential forces in the scientific conquest of the land and in keeping Israel among the leaders in the field of modern science.

Weizmann had a long, significant career in the Zionist movement that culminated finally in the proclamation of the Jewish state. His story is told in his fascinating autobiography entitled *Trial and Error*. He was not always listened to nor always in top favor within the organization. He was always one of the leaders and a man to be reckoned with, but he was, nevertheless, sometimes repudiated. Through the years, he was much more patient with the British than many others wanted him to be. He was an early supporter of the partition idea, and this, too, caused opposition.[339] Despite moments

---

337 "Field Marshal Edmund Henry Hynman Allenby, 1st Viscount Allenby (1861–1936), was an English soldier and British Imperial Governor. He fought in the Second Boer War and also in the First World War, in which he led the British Empire's Egyptian Expeditionary Force against the Ottoman Empire in the conquest of Palestine... His forces occupied the Jordan Valley during the summer of 1918, and he continued to serve in the region as High Commissioner for Egypt and Sudan from 1919 until 1925." Wikipedia contributors. "Edmund Allenby, 1st Viscount Allenby." *Wikipedia, The Free Encyclopedia*. Wikipedia, The Free Encyclopedia, 23 Sep. 2017. Web. 25 Sep. 2017.

338 "The Weizmann Institute of Science is a public research university in Rehovot, Israel, south of Tel Aviv. It was established in 1934, fourteen years before the State of Israel. It differs from other Israeli universities in that it offers only graduate and postgraduate degrees in the natural and exact sciences." Wikipedia contributors. "Weizmann Institute of Science." *Wikipedia, The Free Encyclopedia*. Wikipedia, The Free Encyclopedia, 18 Sep. 2017. Web. 25 Sep. 2017.

339 The United Nations Partition Plan for Palestine was adopted on November 29, 1947. "The proposal recommended a partition of Mandatory Palestine at the end of the British Mandate... [creating] independent Arab and Jewish States and a Special International Regime for the city of Jerusalem... The Plan sought to address the conflicting objectives and claims of two competing movements, Palestinian nationalism and Jewish nationalism, or Zionism. The Plan also called for Economic Union between the proposed states, and for the protection of religious and minority rights. Despite its perceived limitations, the Plan was accepted by the Jewish Agency for Palestine. Arab leaders and governments rejected it and indicated an unwillingness to accept any form of territorial division, arguing that it violated the UN Charter's principles of national self-determination, which granted people the right to decide their own destiny. Immediately after adoption of the Resolution by the General Assembly, a civil war broke out and

of rejection, however, Weizmann did not take personal offense and did not withdraw from Zionist activity. And when the state was finally established, he was easily Zionism's leading figure. He was the leader in presenting Palestine's case before the UN, and his friendship with Truman was helpful in gaining immediate recognition for Israel in May 1948.[340]

Chaim Weizmann was a fortunate man. He fought for many years for an ideal which seemed impossible to fulfill, but he lived to witness its fulfillment. Moses did not see the Promised Land. Herzl died long before the coming of the Jewish State. But Weizmann not only witnessed its achievement, he enjoyed the honors heaped upon him as a result. His loss was felt all over the world, and when he died it was written of him editorially,

> *Not only was he the leading citizen of one of the world's nations. In many ways, he epitomized the civilized man, moved equally by profound religious faith and the belief in the betterment of man through science... To all who admire faith and courage Chaim Weizmann's name will remain an everlasting inspiration, his memory a blessing. That is why all people with hope and dreams in their hearts may say: "Know ye not that there is a prince and a great man fallen this day in Israel?"*[341]

---

the plan was not implemented." Wikipedia contributors. "United Nations Partition Plan for Palestine." *Wikipedia, The Free Encyclopedia*. Wikipedia, The Free Encyclopedia, 23 Sep. 2017. Web. 25 Sep. 2017.

340 "Harry S. Truman (1884–1972) was an American politician who served as the 33rd President of the United States (1945–53), assuming the office upon the death of Franklin D. Roosevelt during the waning months of World War II." Wikipedia contributors. "Harry S. Truman." *Wikipedia, The Free Encyclopedia*. Wikipedia, The Free Encyclopedia, 25 Sep. 2017. Web. 25 Sep. 2017.

341 2 Samuel 3:38.

36. Chaim Weizmann—1974

Dad—

The final words of the final sermon that you delivered were, "That is why all people with hopes and dreams in their hearts may say: 'Know ye not that there is a prince and a great man fallen this day in Israel?'" Three days later, you were gone, and your friends, family, colleagues, congregants, and many admirers had a similar thought.

Studying your sermons over the last six years, holding you and your ideas, your hopes, and your dreams close to me, has rekindled my awareness of the "prince and great man" that you were. I hope that I have been successful in passing on to your descendants a similar appreciation of their ancestor, Sidney Ballon, and the gift of this precious heritage.

Blessings.
Yesh

Western Wall, Jerusalem. c. 1972

Sidney Ballon's seven grandchildren, not all of whom he lived to see. Left to right: Sara Faith Ballon, Jacob Seth Ballon, Adam Nathan Steinharter, Shira Rachel Ballon, Joshua Simon Steinharter, Daniel Marc Ballon, Rebecca Joy Ballon.

The photo was taken on St. Simon's Island, Georgia in December 2001. Their grandmother, Jean H. Ballon, had died on September 9, 2001 in Riverside, California. Two days later the "911" terrorist attacks in Boston, New York, and Washington, D.C., and the subsequent closure of airports, made a conventional funeral impossible. Thus, the family gathered later in the year for a memorial service at Temple Beth Tifilloh in Brunswick among the many friends Jean had made during the decades she resided in the area after her husband's death.

BALLON/SHAPIRO WEDDING, Sonoma, California. June 13, 2010. Left to right: Daniel Ballon, Sara Ballon, Ann Lois Abramowitz Ballon, Jeffrey Ballon, Meghan O'Connor Steinharter, Joshua Steinharter, Martha (Muff) Ballon Steinharter, Adam Steinharter, Shira Ballon, Annette Maher Steinharter, Joshua Shapiro, Alan Steinharter, Rebecca Ballon Shapiro, Yeshaya Ballon, Deborah Halpren Ballon, Alana Kadden Ballon, Jacob Ballon.

A Precious Heritage

Afterword

Yeshaya Douglas Ballon

As I approach the end of a six-year dance with yellowing pages inscribed with my father's thoughts and beliefs, I have to ask myself what effect this has had on me. Even if I hadn't asked this question, others have asked it of me anyway.

First, let me put my response into context. Reading and editing these sermons did not happen in a vacuum. In parallel, over these years, I have engaged in the most significant period of religious and spiritual study of my life. Dad's words have been a cherished companion on this journey of Jewish study primarily with ALEPH: Alliance for Jewish Renewal.

Particularly relevant were the courses on spiritual eldering, in which the concept of leaving a legacy plays a significant role. This study stimulated my thirst to perpetuate my father's legacy and pass it on in my family as part of my own.

Also of great significance was the three-year certification program to become a spiritual director. This has helped develop the theological lens through which I view my life and, in particular, my father's statements on God. It also introduced me to a specific approach to reading and responding to sacred text that gave rise to the "Dear Dad" notes.

Yes, I have drunk deeply from the well of my father's words these past six years, *and* I have also been engaged in other transformational experiences. We cannot know what one experience would have looked like without the other.

This fits in nicely with the theological piece. Knowing and appreciating our "not knowing" is part of accepting and standing in awe of the sweet mystery of the universe, or, as my father might say, the "melody of faith." That melody has much richer harmonies for me now, as I increasingly engage in activities and conversations only to be reminded of something Dad once said in a sermon. His voice has always been with me. It is much stronger now, and I am so much more ready, eager, and open to listening to it.

On November 4, 1974, exactly a week before he died, Dad wrote me a letter. I was then a student at the Yale University School of Architecture. Apparently, we had just had a conversation in which I was contemplating bailing on this academic challenge, or at least taking some time off. After thinking about our conversation, he was moved to write to me—not a common occurrence. In the letter, he gently and effectively encouraged me "to see the whole course of schooling through instead of breaking it up as [I] did with undergraduate work" (five colleges in seven years). I remember being struck at the time by the strange phenomenon of actually receiving and agreeing with advice from my father! He used words, as I reread them now, that demonstrate, despite any emotional distance that I held between us throughout my protracted adolescence, that he was a rock of understanding, support, and love. He understood me better than I understood myself. What's more, he took the time to share this with me even as he was preparing to travel for the surgery that would fail to keep his heart beating. Maybe he sensed that he needed to offer this advice while he could.

Putting this collection together has provided me the opportunity to answer that letter—albeit forty-three years later. This work allows me to say to him: *Not only did I heed your advice, not only did I graduate and become an architect, but I have also listened closely to much of what you said to the thousands of people you loved and cared for over a lifetime of devoted service to your community.*

It brings to mind of one of our favorite phrases from Torah—*Na'aseh v'nishma*. When the Hebrew nation received the torah at Sinai, we said, "We will do and we will hearken," implying that the understanding comes *after* the doing, not the other way around. I have nearly seventy years of life experience now. I've had the gift of many years of *doing*. I have been blessed to learn something about *being* as well. Between the doing and the being, I may finally be "hearkening" a bit—hearing the messages that my father offered for so long, that fell more often on deaf ears than on receptive ones. I feel so blessed to have had the time to sit with and savor his words.

What difference has it made in my life? *All* the difference.

It's normal for a sweet child to become an obnoxious adolescent, and then mature over time into having a meaningful adult relationship with his parents. Dad and I had barely begun that adult conversation when he died.

I will share a key moment in that regard. It was June 16, 1974. Dad was being honored at a gala dinner at Nassau Community Temple as he was about to leave West Hempstead after twenty-three years as their rabbi. Debbie and I attended the dinner, but had no role assigned. We listened to various speeches and presentations. It just so happened that a few days before, we had attended her brother's wedding. This was significant because I was so impressed by the meaningful toasts that were made at the rehearsal dinner. I had never seen anything quite like it. It served as a beautiful model of people speaking from their hearts in praise of loved ones.

As we sat at my father's banquet, I felt inspired to say something on his behalf akin to the toasts I had just witnessed. I asked the emcee if I could take the microphone and he consented. I spoke for a minute or two at most—just long enough to express my gratitude and appreciation for the congregation and for my father in words that probably stunned most people in the room.

Three months later, my father was gone. The fact that I had even briefly acknowledged him in public during his lifetime was transformative. The memory of that moment has been a lasting treasure, an unexpected gift to myself ever since. How much more so this volume that represents six years of focused appreciation. Creating this book, admittedly, is self-indulgent. At the same time, it is a genuine tribute to a humble, eloquent, and devoted rabbi, a true *mensch*, and, above all, my loving father. With God's help, may it come to pass that like Abraham and Isaac, he and I walk together to fulfill his vision of passing on this precious heritage.

Priestly Benediction

People who remember Sidney Ballon in the pulpit often recall with a feeling of warmth and affection how he would raise his arms, cloaked in a black flowing robe with a white silk prayer shawl, and confer the priestly benediction to the congregation at the end of a service. Occasionally, he would lower those hands and gently cradle the head of a single individual at a bar mitzvah or confirmation service. Under this holy canopy, a person would have a very special feeling. Rabbi Ballon's blessing, the resonant sound of the Hebrew followed by the English translation flowing from his lips, was deeply received. One felt part of something timeless and boundless, and one felt his genuine love. To all readers of this book, I offer you that image and that love, and invite you to deeply receive this priestly blessing from the hands and the heart of Sidney Ballon.

Y'var-ekh'cha A-do-nai v'yeesh'm'recha.
May the Lord bless you and keep you.

Ya-eir A-do-nai pa-nav ei-ley-cha vee-chu-nei-cha.
May the Lord cause His face to shine upon you
and be gracious unto you,

Yee-sa A-do-nai pa-nav ei-lay-cha v'ya-sem l'cha sha-lom.
May the Lord lift up His countenance upon you and give you peace.

Amen

About the Editor

Yesh Ballon is Co-Director of the Yedidya Center for Jewish Spiritual Direction and the Morei Derekh Jewish Spiritual Direction Training Program. He is a *Mashpia Ruchani* (Spiritual Director) and *Vatik* (Sage-ing® Mentor), certified by ALEPH: Alliance for Jewish Renewal. In this work, he offers guidance and support for those seeking to deepen their personal connection with spirit, however they choose to define it.

Yesh is a teacher, artist, writer, and retired architect. He spent over thirty years working in corporate real estate departments in Silicon Valley and around the world as a trainer, a meeting facilitator, and an award-winning design and construction project manager.

He lives in Palo Alto, California with his wife, Debbie, delighted to be in close proximity to a growing number of Sidney Ballon's descendants.

The spiritual peak of his year comes and goes by very quickly on the first day (Rosh Hashanah) when he is humbled and blessed to sound shofar for his congregation as he has done virtually every year since his bar mitzvah.

He also bakes a pretty decent challah.

Links to more of Sidney Ballon's sermons, as well as Yesh's art, writings, and challah recipe, may be found on his website: www.yeshindeed.com.

www.ingramcontent.com/pod-product-compliance
Lightning Source LLC
Chambersburg PA
CBHW020608300426
44113CB00007B/553